Getting a Job in CG:
Real Advice from Reel People

Getting a Job in CG:
Real Advice from Reel People

SEAN WAGSTAFF WITH DARIUSH DERAKHSHANI

SAN FRANCISCO | LONDON

Maya PRESS™   SYBEX®

Associate Publisher: Dan Brodnitz
Alias Global Packages Services Product Manager: Danielle Lamothe
Acquisitions Editor: Mariann Barsolo
Developmental Editor: Willem Knibbe
Alias Acquisitions Editor: Erica Fyvie
Production Editor: Dennis Fitzgerald
Technical Editor: Keith Reicher
Copyeditor: Sally Engelfried
Compositor: Maureen Forys, Happenstance Type-O-Rama
CD Coordinator: Dan Mummert
CD Technician: Kevin Ly
Proofreaders: Laurie O'Connell, Nancy Riddiough
Indexer: Ted Laux
Book Designer: Caryl Gorska
Cover Designer: Leon Vymenets
Alias Global Packaged Services Product Development Manager: Carla Sharkey

LIBRARY OF CONGRESS CARD NUMBER: 2003106716

ISBN: 0-7821-4257-5

Acknowledgments

A special thanks the industry professionals who took the time out of their busy schedules to be interviewed for this book: Amy Bendotti, Nintendo; Carla Block, Sammy Studios; Kevin Cureton, Electronic Arts; Tina Dickey, ArtSource; Brian Freisinger, ESC; Douglas Hare, The Collective; Tim Johnson, Black Ops Entertainment; Craig Lyn, FrameStore; Marc Marrujo, Microsoft; Ken Maruyama, Industrial Light and Magic; Sean Miller, Sammy Studios; Randy Nelson, Pixar; Jo Ann Pacho, ArtSource; Sangeeta Pashar, Pixar; Andrew Pearce, ESC; Evan Pontoriero, Industrial Light and Magic; Emmanuel Shiu, The Orphanage; Mike Slisko, freelance 2D and 3D artist; Mitch Suskin, Paramount Pictures; and Matt White, Lucas Arts.

We'd also like to thank all those who have helped us throughout our careers.

About the Authors

Sean Wagstaff is currently a visual effects artist and technical director at The Orphanage, in San Francisco. Sean wrote the first books on Macintosh 3D graphics and animation on the Web, and has authored hundreds of computer graphics articles for print and online publications, including *Macworld*, *Game Developer*, *Computer Graphics World*, and CreativePro.com. He has worked in both the games and film industries.

Dariush Derakhshani is an award-winning animator currently working at Sight Effects in Venice, California. He has won the Bronze Plaque from the Columbus Film Festival and shares accolades from the London International Advertising Festival and the AICP. Dariush has a master's degree in animation from USC Film School and has worked on national TV commercials, music videos, as well as the TV show *South Park*. He also teaches animation classes at The Art Institute of California, Los Angeles. Dariush holds a bachelor's degree in Architecture and Theatre from Lehigh University in Pennsylvania.

Foreword

Welcome to the job hunt! Looking for the perfect job can be a rewarding and exciting experience. Unfortunately, even with strong credentials and the best of intentions, the truth is that few of us land in our dream job a week after graduation. The reality most of us face is that getting a good job—the job we want—is hard work. Hard work that can ultimately lead to a big pay off—the job you crave, the hours you can live with, an environment you look forward to returning to every day. Your dream job.

You probably already have a number of books on your bookshelves that have helped you improve the various skills you'll need in that job. You've got books on art, on technique, on software, on the industry. So why buy this book? Because the truth is, getting a job takes more than skill.

Getting a Job in CG will help you answer the questions your other books don't even begin to ask. What's the difference between a good demo reel and a bad demo reel? What's the best way to approach an interview? What do recruiters look for in a new hire? How can you get experience, when most jobs want you to have it already?

This book begins to answer all of these questions and more. *Getting a Job in CG* provides real strategies for getting, and keeping, your dream job. The information you'll find here is collected from numerous interviews with industry professionals, recruiters, artists, and technicians already working in your chosen field. Learn from their mistakes and their successes. You'll get to understand the strategies that have worked for others so that you can find ways of tailoring those strategies to suit your own personality.

Getting a Job in CG will help you better understand the industry you've chosen and avoid the mistakes that can cost you that job and save yourself time, money, aggravation, and disappointment. Armed with the substantial advice found between these pages, you will establish solid footing to begin the exciting (and sometimes intimidating) job hunt. Good luck!

—Danielle Lamothe
    Product Manager
    Global Packages Services
    Alias

CONTENTS AT A GLANCE

Contents

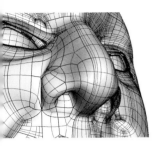

Introduction

In the Summer of 2002, I embarked on the task of finding a new job in the 3D industry. I had worked as a lead 3D artist, a book illustrator, and multimedia animator, and had held assorted other jobs in the entertainment and dot-com industries as a manager and a creative director. My skills were sharp: I could model a sea plane or craft a character in NURBS, polys, or sub-ds; texture and shade it; and make it look pretty with atmospheric lighting, dynamics, and rendering. I could rig a character, write a MEL script, and pretty much make Maya, Photoshop, After Effects, and sundry other tools of the trade dance to whatever tune the band was playing, or so I thought.

But that was just the stuff on my resume (which was tailored for every company I sent it to). I also burned demo reels on VHS and DVD, burned bank accounts feeding ink to my Epson printer, polished my website, crafted my cover letters, and single-handedly raised the bottom line of FedEx. I never stopped working the phones: I took informational interviews, networked with friends in the business, and crashed company barbeques with friends of friends. I avidly eavesdropped and even passed out business cards in cafes. Pretty soon, visitor name badges from ILM, PDI, Sony Entertainment, and other top-flight companies laminated the binding of my portfolio like stamps in a travel-writer's passport. I was landing interviews! I was bonding with interviewers!! Things were looking great!!! Sort of.

Six months later, I still had no job. Oh, I did some freelance work animating corporate product videos, volunteered on an amateur film for a few weeks, and took a contract job at a game startup for almost no pay and stock options with an improbable upside. (I worked there for 120 hours in a single week to finish environments for a demo the company was preparing for the Game Developers Conference.) I even took a character animation class at a local college, where I was routinely mistaken by the fresh-faced students as one of the faculty.

But, apart from an invitation from the aforementioned game company to continue working for little or no pay, I still had no legitimate offers to do the kind of work I knew I could thrive at.

Like any artist, my ego gets wrapped up in other people's affirmation of my work, and eight months in, my joblessness had me feeling about as big as an aphid in *A Bug's Life*. Was it my skill? I doubted it: I've been teaching people how to do 3D animation since

1993. Was it my artistic talent? Maybe, but why would I be getting called in for interviews by so many companies if they didn't like what they saw in the stills I sent? Was it my resume? I wasn't sure. None of us can honestly change where we've already been, but we can all do better at accentuating the positives.

Even though I was getting interviews, the versatility that had always seemed my greatest asset suddenly seemed to be a liability. ("It says here you've done a lot of writing. Wouldn't you rather be writing than doing design work? Do you plan to continue writing while you're working for us?") Were diverse skills and adaptability really a liability? Or had this industry become so obsessed with assembly-line specialization and budget control that what was really wanted was robots rather than artists? An even worse possibility occurred to me: maybe I was giving the impression that I had dabbled in lots of things without really mastering any of them.

Was it my demo reel? Could be. Few people had seen or critiqued it before I started sending it out, and I had watched it 5,000 times while putting it together. Watching it now only made me uncomfortable, and I could no longer see its flaws objectively. There were some pretty model turntables, even an interesting choice of music, but what was its point? Did it really show my potential? I knew it was too long, but if I cut some things, was I cutting out the part that would get me the job?

The panic-inducing questions flowed freely, but the answers were nowhere to be found.

Still, whatever flaws there were in my presentation, my friends who were working all assured me I was employable and that my skills were good enough to pass the muster in their own studios. Potential employers, even as they were escorting me out of the building, would tell me how much they liked what I had done.

There was a definite undertow in the current of conversations I had with friends in the business and potential employers alike. The 3D industry has achieved a remarkable level of maturity, if you can call it that, in the 10 years since I first fell into it. Having talent and skill is no longer a surefire ticket to finding work. Part of this is due to the economy, which, as I write, is (I hope) improving after being at its worst in 30 years. Companies are swamped with resumes from eager potential employees, many of whom have relevant skills and some of whom have no experience but are nevertheless firing out resumes like shells from a Gatling gun. Budgets are shrinking everywhere, not just in films and games, but in the U.S. economy as a whole. The number of projects getting made is on the decline, as studios are pressed to concentrate their time and cash on surefire hits, especially sequels and shameless clones. (Sequels are a calamity for artists because studios capitalize on the opportunity to reuse art assets, such as models and scenery, and cut costs by downsizing crews.) The problem is especially rampant in the video games business, resulting in a glut of skilled 3D and effects artists being thrown on the street. Finally, schools are turning out artists by the busload. Resumes and demo reels are literally heaped onto hiring managers' desks.

The studios are getting pickier and picker about hiring and cutting their risks, and in some cases, they want to turn rock stars into pigeons who will fit precisely into pre-arranged pigeonholes. I see it over and over in ads for 3D and effects talent:

> **Wanted** 3D artist with 3 to 5 years experience working on a series of hit [*fill in the blank*], must have a masters degree in fine art, know C++, Perl, MEL scripting and Linux network management, 3D modeling, character animation, lighting, color theory and motion capture, and must be certified in putting our highly specific proprietary widget Y into highly specific receptacle Z. Salary DOE.

I may be exaggerating the absurdity of hiring expectations, but the turning point in my crisis of confidence came the day I was given an impromptu interview by a hiring manager at a large, well-known studio best known for its lovable green ogres. (I was introduced as a *modeler* while he was having a smoke in front of the studio, and he rushed me into his office for a spur-of-the-moment grilling.) After I helped him reassemble one of the several two-foot-tall heaps of resumes and demo reels that he accidentally elbowed off his desk, he assured me that the company was searching for modelers, but that it didn't need any "character or hard surface people" because the characters and props for *Hit Movie II* were already in the bank. What the studio did need was someone who could model the organic props and scenery for an animated feature that took place in a tropical jungle. ("Oh, and by the way, we have a very tight budget for this position," he admonished me.) With only a hint of mirth, he asked me if I had any "cabbages, rotting logs, or dilapidated buildings" on my reel, which, to my immense regret, I did not.

Despite this gaping hole in my artistic background, he nevertheless arranged an interview for me on the spot with the modeling director. It turns out that this was the man responsible for the cabbage zinger (a zinger is a question designed to short circuit the sanity of the interviewee). In our interview, he first praised the detailing in my modeling, and then took great pains to explain to me that it scarcely mattered how beautifully I could model a sea plane or a human head. If I didn't have an extensive history of modeling cabbages—or something like them—I probably didn't have what it took to work on his movie.

Cabbages! Would you like those with corned beef? I wondered.

In some ways my interview was a disappointment. It would have been a fairytale ending if my lunch with a friend of a friend had metamorphosed into a production animation job on a blockbuster feature. On the other hand, the interview changed my perception of what I was facing. If I didn't have cabbages on my reel, there was a good chance nobody else did, either. The problem wasn't necessarily my skills in 3D, or what I had to offer as an artist. The problem was the director's expectation that he could find the perfect fit for his next project, coupled with my failure to convince him that I was the man for the job. He knew he could find someone in those towering stacks of resumes on the HR guy's desk who had already solved the specific problem he was facing. My job was to tell him—and more importantly, show him—that he already had. My problem was that even though I was certain I could model any vegetable or crumbling edifice the art director threw at me, I hadn't done the research beforehand to know what project the studio had coming up, and I hadn't put in the day or two of work I would have needed to show him I could take that project and run with it.

What could I or should I have done differently before and during that interview? How can anyone, newly graduated art student or CG veteran, possibly penetrate such resistance to an unknown candidate? How can you prepare for the art director who will only hire you if you've already done what you are being hired to do? What is the magic formula that directors and HR managers are looking for? How can you make your resume and reel float to the top of the heap and stick to the desk when the others are flying willy-nilly onto the floor? The answers to these questions are the topic of the next 250 pages.

It took months of revising my strategy, rewriting my resume, overhauling my reel, and building a strong personal network. Finally, in December 2003, I landed a bonafide job as a technical director working on a pair of big Hollywood movies. If I can overcome my cabbages and land a CG dream job, so can you. Happy hunting!

—Sean Wagstaff

I lead a charmed and lucky professional life in CG (knock on wood) that has helped sustain me the past eight or so years in Los Angeles. Having attended USC Film School's animation program after a number of years in architecture, I was hired to be an intern by an alumnus of my animation program. After graduation, my contacts lead me to another fellow alumnus who gave me "my first big break" in effects when he hired me to animate on a three-month freelance job that really bolstered my reel and gave me professional experience and credibility.

From there, I went with a school friend's recommendation and took a job as a technical director (and a subsequent promotion to supervising technical director) on the hit show *South Park* for a year. Though it took me away from animating 3D effects, it was an absolutely brilliant job and a fantastic experience I would never trade for the world (thanks, guys!).

Riding high and feeling strong, I re-entered effects work and began a freelance job creating 3D effects for network promo ads and season premieres. But then, as everyone in this industry will feel at one time or another, everything dried up, and finding work became an arduous and frustrating experience.

For six months I scratched out a living with some flying logos and web design work, but then out of the blue the ball began to roll again, and I became an effects compositor on a trilogy of independent films that freshened up my reel enough to land big feature work as a compositor for a little while.

As my compositing job was nearing completion, a fortuitous phone call to an old friend brought me all the way back to 3D effects work again, this time for national commercials in a position I still hold today, as a Maya CG animator on national television spots and music videos, a job I truly relish (thanks, Andrew!).

I've been lucky to have the friends I do, to have worked with the people I have, and to really enjoy what I do. And if there's anything I've learned and tried to share with you in the following pages, it's that staying with this business is all about loving what you do. Having that passion, and being able to show and share it with your friends, will bring you fortune and days full of work, if not a few late nights and the occasional migraine.

—*Dariush Derakhshani*

How This Book Is Organized

You may wish to read this book from front to back or drop in here and there along the way, depending on where you are in your job search. No matter where you may be in your search—at the beginning of your career, or midway through and in need of a change—there is something in this book for you.

Chapter 1: What 3D Job Is Right For You? Finding out what you want to do in CG is an important step in finding work. Without focus and a goal in sight, you will hinder your search and, more often than not, confuse the issue. Chapter 1 will show you what kind of work is out there and the types of jobs available, primarily in entertainment.

Chapter 2: Technical 3D Jobs and Other Industries Picking up from Chapter 1, this chapter is an exploration of the purely technical jobs people do in the CG fields. We also take a look at nonentertainment industries that make use of CG artists and technicians.

Chapter 3: What to Learn If you want to be somewhere, you need to know something. It may not be fortune cookie–elegant, but it's true. You have to have a solid education to gain experience and get ahead. Chapter 3 breaks down the essentials you'll need to enjoy success in CG.

Chapter 4: How and Where to Learn So now you know *what* to know, but *where* do you get that knowledge? Chapter 4 explores different ways to get educated for a career in CG. From schools to teaching yourself, there's an answer out there for everyone who wants to learn.

Chapter 5: The Demo Reel, Portfolio, and Resume There's only one thing that ultimately will get you work: your reel or portfolio. Without a shining showcase of your most brilliant work, how else will an employer know your stunning star qualities? Chapter 5 helps you put it together.

Chapter 6: Finding Jobs You're all set. You're educated, you have a reel bright enough to melt the sun, and your portfolio will knock over mighty oak trees. Where do you go with it all? See how others go about finding jobs in Chapter 6.

Chapter 7: The Real Goods: Who You Know Almost as important as what you know is *who* you know. Without a friend in the business to help your name along, it's a tough fight to get into a good company. Fortunately, there are about a million things you can do to make contacts that count, and Chapter 7 tells you what they are.

Chapter 8: Working with Recruiters Recruiters are adept at filling positions and finding the right person to fill them. Knowing how to approach and deal with recruiters will increase your job hunt's success rate. Chapter 8 tells you how.

Chapter 9: Interviewing for the Job Do you shake hands firmly? Do you wait till you're spoken to? Making an indelible impression in an interview is key to taking the step into a job. Chapter 9 shares insights from many viewpoints on how best to make a solid impression with employers.

Chapter 10: Frequently Asked Questions—Insights from Reel People This book is a compendium of advice from industry professionals who have been where you are now. From keen perspectives comes keen advice. Chapter 10 distills and organizes the most frequently talked about topics and gives it to you straight from all the professionals' mouths.

Appendix: Real Reels It's one thing to talk about a reel, and quite another to share it with everyone. These brave souls want to show you their reels to give you a good idea of what to expect and what to shoot for if you're just starting your journey into CG.

About the CD

There really is only one way to improve your demo reel, and that is to see as many reels as you can. For that reason, we are very thankful that Daniel Gutierrez, Roberto Jauregui, Juan Gutierrez, and Daniel Militonian have volunteered their reels for your viewing. Watching these reels is a strong step in creating your own winning demo reel. Please see Appendix "Real Reels" for more information on the CD material.

Staying Connected

Please see www.3djobs.net for more information and updates on the industry. Please also visit the book's web page at www.sybex.com.

CHAPTER 1

What 3D Job is Right For You?

To find the right job, you're going to have to dig deep into your skills, interests, and expectations about what kinds of work you want to do and what kinds of work environments make you happy.

One of the biggest decisions you'll have to make is whether film and television, video games, or one of the more unusual 3D jobs is a better choice for your job search. Films require highly specialized skills, an intense dedication to detail, and a willingness to work in the hard-knocks industry that hires and fires low- and mid-level employees as film projects come and go. The games industry, on the other hand, offers more opportunities, relatively good job stability, and the chance to do lots of different types of work on any given day. But to work in games, you'll have to live with a faster pace and you'll have to make major compromises in the quality of the artwork you produce. This chapter explores the different fields and takes a close look at the skills and tasks of specific jobs themselves. In Chapter two, we describe the more technical jobs in these industries, as well as 3D graphics opportunities in other fields:

- **Specializing for film and television industry jobs**
- **Getting into the video game industry**
- **Film jobs**
- **Television jobs**
- **Game jobs**
- **Job Descriptions**

Finding Your Niche in Film and Television

Only a decade ago, 3D and effects were considered part and parcel of the same discipline. In film work, "effects" referred to any part of a shot that required the effort of pyrotechnic technicians, stunt men, model makers, animatronics experts, or even computer graphics artists. The range of things you could do in 3D was limited: character animation, for example, was rudimentary. Huge, realistically detailed models, natural-looking lighting, and complex 3D environments could bring rendering systems quickly to their knees. Filmmakers thought of the computer as a tool for doing useful things like wire removal and compositing, but generally not as an alternative to other kinds of effects work. At the time, a skilled 3D artist could master the skills of modeling, texturing, lighting, and the basic animation that systems were capable of, and it wasn't uncommon for film studio pioneers to do an entire shot, more or less single-handed. When Craig Lyn, who won an Emmy for his work on *Dinotopia* at London's FrameStore, got his start in the multimedia and games businesses, and then at George Lucas' Industrial Light and Magic working on the *Star Wars* sequels, he did the whole spectrum of 3D work:

At ILM, I was a hard surface modeler to start with, then went into the Rebel Unit as a technical director. The technical director job in the Rebel was modeling, painting, compositing, animating, and lighting—more of a boutique style of working. From there, I went into the digital matte department, doing traditional matte paintings and 3D digital environments, and from there, went into the CG-TD department, which is basically ILM's big monstrosity pipeline thing, and from there, came over to London as a senior technical director on Dinotopia*, and then as a senior technical director on* Harry Potter—*which was one of their larger film shows—and now I'm CG supe on* Thunderbirds.

—*CRAIG LYN, FRAMESTORE*

Those kinds of opportunities to work on diverse aspects of a project are now exceedingly rare. The technology that has evolved over the last 10 years has become so specialized, and the associated artistry so highly refined, that if you're going to work in film, you're going to have to find a niche in which to hone and market your skills.

Take character animation, for example. Lifelike 3D character animation has only been technically possible for six years or so. (Pixar's Oscar-winning short *Geri's Game*, which it completed in 1997, proved to the world that it was possible.) It's astounding to see how far the genre has come. Watching characters in *Shrek*, Sully in *Monsters Inc.*, or Gollum in *The Lord of the Rings: The Two Towers*, it's easy to forget that you're watching a completely artificial animated creation. Body movement and expressions are utterly convincing and natural, and you can't help but feel you're looking into the eyes of real, living creatures. In part, this qualitative leap in animation has been made possible by the advance in tools used to create them. If you look at Maya's character tools, for example, there are now so many deep-level controls for rigging, constraining, animating, and deforming a character that it's hard to imagine something a living character could do that you couldn't convincingly animate with the tools at hand.

I get so many e-mails from people saying, "I want a job in the industry." And the first thing I have to do is say, "OK, what do you want to do? Do you want to be a TD, do you want to be a compositor, do you want to be a modeler, do you want to paint texture maps, do you want to paint matte paintings?" They say, "I'd like to do all of them." Well, unless you're very good, no one's going to hire you to do all of those. Your reel has to be so focused on saying, "I'm going to be a modeler," because when you run a modeling reel, you want to see a wireframe, you want to see a rendering of it, but I really don't care about your texture mapping skills, because that's not why I'm hiring you. For the games company, or the games industry, absolutely, you're going to have to do all of those things. But here, it's so focused and so stratified that they really have to tie one thing down.

—CRAIG LYN

For every quantum leap in capabilities in the software, there has been an equivalent leap in the skills of the artists using them. Ten years ago, there were no tools that could animate the subtle expressions of a human face in 3D. Being a computer *animator* meant you were someone who modeled and textured spacecraft or other inanimate objects and flew them across the screen, or you rendered pyrotechnic explosions or maybe lumbering robots that could be composited with live-action footage. Now, the word "animator" has repossessed the old Disney meaning: someone who brings inanimate objects to life. And once again, the term now specifically refers to a *character animator*. In some studios, *animator* refers to anyone working on animation, even if they don't make anything move:

Where I work, everyone is called an animator. The character animators are now called motion animators to include more than just animating characters. Basically, any object or character you see on the screen that moves, and is not an FX such as wind, smoke, fire, etc., is done by the motion animators.

—KEITH REICHER, PDI/DREAMWORKS

A 3D character animator today knows how to animate the subtle expressions of the face, the delicate gestures of hands and body, and the natural deformations of muscle and skin when a body moves. It's no longer enough to be considered an animator if you know how to move a solid object from point A to point B or to make natural-looking smoke. With so much to learn, how can an animator be expected to even think about the complexities of modeling with subdivision surfaces, mastering the infinite possibilities of dynamic simulations, or manipulating advanced shading networks for creating the multilayered textures of a human skin? Like almost all 3D artists in the film business, the character animator has become a supreme specialist.

In today's film studios, modelers are modelers, texture painters paint, effects animators wrangle particle effects and dynamics, and compositors work exclusively in the realm of 2D layers. Even the specialized jobs are becoming stratified: there are modelers who model only hard surfaces, other modelers who model only characters, and others who specialize in architectural environments. (As we pointed out in the introduction, there are even modelers who model only cabbages, or at least cabbage-like plant life.)

Of course, there are exceptions. There are great modelers who have earned the right to do their own texture mapping, typically by taking their work home nights and proving they can do it. And you'll find studios where artists both rig *and* animate their characters. But for the most part, if you want to get hired in Hollywood, you have to master a specialty. And if your specialty is texture painting, your demo reel better show nothing but great paintings and beautifully textured models. It's no advantage to show that you're a texture painter who dabbles in character animation or particle effects.

Mastering a specialty is especially necessary for film work, where specialists are sought for an existing studio's pipeline. In a growing trend in Hollywood, however, *generalists* are also being sought out, mostly for television work, where studios have not established such rigid pipelines and artists are freer to work on their shots to completion. Commonly, shots for television tend to go through stages of production, from modeling to animation to rendering and compositing. More and more studios are turning to generalists who have proficiency in all aspects of CG (3D as well as compositing, in many cases). These generalists are called upon to create the models; texture, animate, light, and render them; and in a growing number of cases, even composite them into the live-action footage for final delivery.

Although there is frequent crossover between film and television work, it is pretty much established that film workers engage in focused specialties for the film in question, while television workers tend to cover more ground. As a matter of fact, one film CG supervisor said that one way to get a great exposure to CG and a varied demo reel was to get television work, especially in commercials. The irony is, of course, to get these jobs, your reel should already be great and varied!

Whether the reel you wish to submit is for a film or television work, however, it is necessary to focus the work you include on the reel. Even generalists should show off their strongest proficiencies rather than including areas they are merely competent in.

The *demo reel* is the 3D artist's strongest form of self promotion and is a requirement if you want to land almost any job involving animation, effects, or compositing. (It's generally not required for concept art or engineering positions.) Even texture artists and modelers need a *reel* to show that their work holds up in motion. The reel is normally delivered on standard VHS or DVD and may run anywhere from 1 to 3 minutes. We discuss the making of a job-winning demo reel in Chapter 5.

Studios and Boutiques

While most generalists are used in television work, the big studios are becoming more stratified, as the number of small effects companies grows. With the drop in cost of hardware and software needed to produce professional-level CG effects and the constant flux of talent in and out of the big studios, there has been a growth in the number of lean, mean boutiques—many started by ex-big-studio employees—that can produce high-quality effects for less money than the big studios. These small shops don't usually hire artists to fit into such tiny niches as found in big studio film productions, and they place a premium on individuals who can do more than one thing well, whether for film or television projects. Many small boutiques work regularly in both film and television, in many cases requiring that their artists know how to work in both.

Even if you're only interested in working for larger studios, the fact that they are mostly interested in hiring specialists doesn't mean you shouldn't master multiple skills. On the contrary: If you can produce a credible demo reel as a texture artist and a *second* credible reel as an effects animator, then you can hire yourself out as one or the other, depending on which skill is in demand at the moment.

While it's crucial that your reel shows a strong specialization, it's also important that your resume reflects that you understand related skills. For example, modelers need to understand how a model is texture mapped so they can build models that will work with the requirements of the texture artists. When building models with non-uniform rational B-splines (NURBs), for instance, it's important that models have evenly spaced isoparms, so textures won't pinch or stretch across surfaces. Of course, in games, the modeler must double as a texture artist, since modeling and texturing are so tightly intertwined.

The point is that if you see that a studio is hiring modelers, present yourself as a modeler. If it's hiring character animators, present yourself as a character animator. (And if at first you don't succeed as a modeler, try, try again as a character animator!) Just don't try calling yourself a modeler/character animator hoping that that's going to impress anyone more than showing you're an expert at one or the other will. The odds are that's not how the studio is going to evaluate you, and it's an approach that probably won't get you hired.

If you are applying yourself to work in a boutique house, your reel should still be very focused on your strengths as an artist, rather than a hodge-podge menagerie of samples from all the different disciplines of CG. Boutiques look for a strong eye toward detail and a strength in lighting, as well as one other facet of CG such as animation, modeling, or dynamics. They know they have other staff who tend to lean in one direction or another, and they look to augment their in-house skill set. But because project deadlines and the demands of shorter-term television work is sometimes ambiguous and always hard to predict, whomever they hire must be able to produce a shot from beginning to finish at some point in their tenure.

The short of it is that you should target your reel toward the company or companies you want to work for. Be prepared to make minor revisions based on the studio, whether it's a huge film studio or a small boutique. The following applies to presenting yourself specifically for the industry and environment you're targeting:

Several years ago, I had applied for a job with a well known company in the video game industry. One of the comments made about my reel was that it was too "Hollywood." Rather than showing that I had experience and the desire to make video games, the demo reel portrayed me as wanting to work in the film industry. I didn't get the job.

—*KEITH REICHER, PDI/DREAMWORKS*

The Film and Television Businesses

Film effects studios typically set the standard for what's possible with 3D and special effects. In an outfit like Industrial Light and Magic (San Rafael, Calif.), ESC Entertainment (Alameda, Calif.), Digital Domain (Venice, Calif.), or Weta (Wellington, New Zealand), production budgets can be huge, and the time and resources devoted to a single tour-de-force effects sequence can dwarf an entire video game or television production. Some of these studios also have divisions that take on TV effects, particularly to serve the demand for high-budget commercials, such as those featuring beer-drinking frogs, cola-guzzling polar bears, and especially new-model cars in all sorts of improbable driving scenarios.

Meanwhile, the small boutique studios do a similar caliber—in some cases better—of CG work. Most boutiques try to pick up film work for lower-budget productions, television series such as *CSI* or *Angel*, television commercials, gaming intros or cinematics, as well as *pick-up work* contracted from larger studios for high-end blockbuster films. Pick-ups are generally less involved or shorter-length effects sequences that large studios cannot find the time to generate themselves on deadline. Some boutiques can even earn contracts for various effects shots in a film from the film's producers directly, or take them over from other CG studios with whom the producers are unhappy.

In TV and video production, studios are expected to render good-quality effects with tight budgets and impossible deadlines. A generous amount of work in the video world is for commercials, where the pace is frantic and attention to detail paramount. Music videos, where the opportunities for experimentation are greater than in the product-focused world of TV commercials, usually require some amount of effects work (usually compositing, though 3D is frequently needed to some extent). Television series, such as *Star Trek: Enterprise* and *Buffy the Vampire Slayer*, and long-format mini-series, like *Dinotopia*, are also big consumers of effects shots, and the emphasis is usually on producing effects that serve the shot within deadline, as opposed to pioneering the stunning CG effects seen in film work. Not only do television shows use a lot of 3D and CG effects, but motion graphics, such as title sequences and logos for commercials and corporate videos, are in constant demand, usually from *design boutiques* that specialize in motion graphics and typography. Studios (a.k.a. post-houses) also find work in corporate videos, which are essentially long-running infomercials, and TV interstitial (short promotional spots in between shows or right after credits of shows on TV), bumpers, and promos. These are the short TV ads you see advertising new shows or premiere times of TV movies and the like.

Even though the demand for CG effects in film and television is increasing steadily, the film business in particular has regular ups and downs that seem to strike randomly, and *job security* is an oxymoron because the employers must ride these waves as well (see sidebar on contractors). While television work can be more constant throughout the year, it is still a field mostly filled with freelancers, as is film, where contract workers can sometimes be brought on a per-day or per-week basis. Staff jobs in television and film are few and far between and usually very difficult to come by, especially because most boutiques and large studios prefer to keep their overhead to a minimum.

Another sobering fact is that the number of new artists entering the field is growing much faster than the industry itself. Consider for a moment that in the year after its introduction in early 2002, some 370,000 users downloaded the free Personal Learning Edition of Alias' Maya. In the same time frame, the number of Maya's educational site licenses had tripled. That's an awful lot of home-schooled artists and art-school students working on the skills needed to enter the field, and it's certain that those numbers dwarf the number of unfilled effects jobs in the television and film industry. So if all those people are going to be hunting for 3D jobs in a year or two, where will they go? More than likely, they'll go to games.

Get in the Game

If you've got the skills to do 3D for film, you've also got at least some of the essential skills to work in computer and video games. Modeling requires the ability to visualize 3D space and to translate forms into wireframe objects; texture mapping requires an eye for surface detail and color and good painting skills; and character animation requires a keen sense of timing and weight—the ability to breath life into something. What's different in games is the requirement to do more with less. Models have to be built with sparing geometric detail because every polygon counts; textures are tiny by comparison and are forced to do

CONTRACTORS: HOLLYWOOD'S GLORIFIED TEMPS

It's a cold, hard, nearly fast rule in film effects studios that there is no such thing as a new employee. There are jobs, to be sure, and new ones are filled every day. But most artists today are hired on a Project Length Contract basis, not as a permanent employee. In short, when the film is done, so are you, at least at that studio.

That's not to say that being an employee is any guarantee of job security, but you can be sure that staff employees have earned that status through experience or tenure, and contractors will always be the first to get the axe.

The causes of this lamentable circumstance are clear. Film budgets get tighter, costs go higher, and effects studios are working on ever-slimming margins of profit, even as the size of crews needed to complete a film balloons. When you're hired at a film studio, it's typically because of one specific skill, be it hard surfaces modeling, character animation, lighting, or dynamic effects. When a film ends, unless there's another project close on its heels with similar needs, you'll find yourself working "on overhead," meaning you've got nothing to do, and as far as the bookkeepers are concerned, your continued presence is all red ink.

Companies don't like to subsist on contract labor because they bear the cost of constantly finding and training new talent to fill positions when new work does roll in. But you're going to like it even less. As a contractor, you'll usually get paid a pretty good weekly or hourly rate (usually with some overtime pay as well), but chances are you won't get any benefits such as paid vacation or sick time, daycare, health, dental and vision care, or 401K retirement tax breaks (never mind matching contributions from your employer). You may also be excluded from bonuses if the film does well. In some studios, bonuses can account for 10 percent of a staff employee's income, or more in a good year. Companies typically calculate the value of benefits at around 15 to 25 percent of salary, so someone making $60,000 per year as a contractor is actually getting $9,000 less compensation than an employee with the same paycheck, and that's not including bonuses. Even though as a contractor you'll do work that's every bit as vital to the film as what's being done by the permanent staff, you're working for the company as something of a tourist, without all the rights of citizenship. On the other hand, successful freelancers who have proven themselves can demand a fantastic rate that can more than make up for the lack of benefits of a staff job, and still have the opportunity to move from project to project with as much time off in between as they can stand.

But what's the worst thing about being a contractor? Taxes. When you're an employee, you're paid what the IRS calls "W-2 wages." As a contractor, you're on the "1099-miscellaneous income" program. With W-2 income, your employer pays your taxes through withholding, including Social Security, Medicare, and unemployment insurance. But with 1099 income, it's all up to you. You may or may not get some money back when you file your returns. As a contractor, you have to pay your own taxes, typically in quarterly installments, and unless you're aggressive about accounting for and deducting your expenses when you file returns (a major, agonizing pain), you're going to pay far more tax than you legally have to. Because of this, it's imperative to have a good tax accountant and to save every single applicable receipt, including those from taking potential clients out for dinner.

In fact, as far as film studios are concerned, the IRS is actually the prime motivator for letting you go as soon as a film is finished. If the studio keeps you on after the project you were signed for finishes, you cross the line of what's considered a project-length contractor and become what the IRS considers an employee. If the studio keeps you without changing your status to a W-2 employee and paying the appropriate employee taxes, it will eventually get in big trouble with the tax man. Take heart: in the best case scenario you'll get fired on Tuesday and have a new contract with the same studio on Wednesday. Stick at it long enough, and the company will probably throw in the towel and hire you on as an employee.

Is being a contractor all bad? If you like fast-paced work occasionally punctuated by long unpaid vacations of indefinite length and don't mind switching from one crew to another, it can be an exciting life full of new and interesting challenges. It's also a great way to work if you want to travel and experience new places, since you could be working in L.A. one month, London the next, and three months later land a gig in Sydney. There are tax advantages if you have the fortitude to track and deduct your expenses. And if you're not particularly concerned with stability and job security, then occasional down time may give you the chance to develop your own artwork and skills, write a screenplay, or take a leisurely surfing safari.

On the other hand, if you do need consistency, or at least a steady paycheck, plan on putting your base somewhere near lots of different studios (Los Angeles County, San Francisco, or the Orlando area are good choices) or working on games, or other freelance or fill-in-the-blank jobs, when the film work runs dry. If money and stability are your two prime motivators, then you're far better off working in games and paying 9 bucks (plus another 12 for a tiny bag of popcorn and stale candy) to see your movies at the cineplex like everyone else.

multiple duty in endless creative ways; lighting is subject to strict controls; and animation is pared down to its essential repetitive motions. Even artists are required to do a wider spectrum of work. The rule in game art is economy, and in games you'll learn to understand that budgets can apply to art as easily as to your household finances. In games work, you'll learn to cringe when someone tells you that a coveted effect or prize-winning model is too *expensive* to make it into the game, meaning it will cost too many processor cycles. Here's what Sean Miller, Lead Artist at Sammy Studios, in Carlsbad, Calif., says about the transition between film and games:

> *I think that a lot of the people who come over to games from feature film and broadcast have a very different idea of what they're getting into, because the rules are different.*
>
> *It's interesting because it's the same medium. OK, I'm working in Maya, I'm building my models, so I'm using polygons, not NURBs, I'm still making models. But what you're worried about is a lot different. And I think a lot of people who come over from the games industry don't realize that we are still low resolution. For the game industry, it's, "Wow, we've got 5,000 polys—I can put a 512 texture on that." Whereas a guy coming from Hollywood is used to using a 3,000-by-3,000 pixel texture for the inside of the dragon's eyelid. And understanding what you're getting into is important.*
>
> *…It's something that I always encourage people making that transition to do. Don't say, "Oh, yeah, I can do that." The reality of it is, do you want to? I'm sure you can, but do you want to, are you going to be happy doing it? Or is it going to be like pulling teeth? We all want higher resolution stuff, but there's as much of a learning curve going down as there is going up. I mean going down specifically in terms of the budgets that you get.*
>
> —*SEAN MILLER, SAMMY STUDIOS*

Whereas film studios hire specialists who are the very best at the specific thing they do, game studios are far more likely to hire artists with a range of skills. The teams in game development tend to be relatively small compared to film work—typically 20 to 30 people—and game companies generally hire artists as permanent employees. That means once you're done building models for a game, you'll be expected to move on to texture mapping, lighting, or some other segment of the production pipeline or another game. Because the range of effects possible in games is severely limited compared to what's possible in film work, it's easier to master what's required in each of the areas but, as I'll describe in later chapters, there are lots of game-specific skills you'll need to learn to succeed in the industry.

Should you still have a specialty if you're going to work in games? Yes. As a rule, game companies will take an interest in all the things you can do, but they will also evaluate your candidacy based on the strength of one core area of talent, whether it's the role of a 3D artist, technical art director, or character animator. 3D artists are modelers that are also expected to texture map their models; level builders are expected to model, map, and light their environments, plus populate them with props. Animators may animate characters with key framing or by manipulating and managing motion capture data, and they're often expected to rig the characters they're animating. As in film, your demo reel and portfolio should emphasize your depth in only one of these core disciplines (the one they're hiring for!), but make sure it covers all of the bases in that discipline.

The Games Business

In many ways, game art departments are like those of film studios, but the specific demands of real-time artwork are different from those in the film business. For example, where a film studio may spend weeks to build and texture a single important 3D model of a car to exacting detail, a game artist will use the same amount of time to build a dozen different cars, each of which is limited to a few hundred polygons and a tiny handful of low-resolution texture maps. Although the jobs have similar titles and job descriptions, the film artist might be modeling in nonuniform rational b-splines (NURBs), while the game artist works in polygons. Game companies are constantly dreaming up new games, but most of those that are of interest to the 3D and effects specialists are a couple familiar types.

Real-time 3D games feature virtual worlds and 3D characters that are rendered by the game engine and 3D graphics hardware as the game is being played. Examples of this type of game abound, but good ones to look at include Unreal Tournament, Halo, and the Grand Theft Auto series. Many other 3D games use prerendered artwork, which can benefit from higher-resolution models and textures, and characters that are rendered as 3D sprites. Classic examples of this type include Diablo and SimCity, but there are many others.

Now that you have a sense of what to expect from game and film and television companies, the following section introduces the jobs in these industries and the relevant skills you'll need for each position. You'll also see what real-world companies look for in some of the positions. In the next chapter, we describe some of the jobs outside of the film and games industry, including entirely new areas where 3D skills are being put to work. Later chapters, and the book's website (www.3djobs.net) list some great 3D job resources where you can find even more job descriptions.

3D Job Descriptions

While every company and job has unique requirements, the following generalizations will help you see what professions are most suited to your skills and interests. We'll discuss each job and then show a representative job posting. The following jobs are loosely presented in the order of those that have fewer technical requirements to those that have more, although this is arguable in the case of the visual effects directors and art directors. These lead roles don't typically require hands-on technical work, though most used to be artists themselves. And since they deal with very technical issues and have to communicate with technicians as well as artists, people in these positions tend to be more successful the more technically savvy they are. Starting with the concept artist position, which really requires only traditional art training, we end our list with technical directors, who are a strange hybrid of artist and engineer. (Chapter 2 discusses actual engineers, as well as jobs in other industries.)

Visual Effects Director; Film and Television

A visual effects director is a position unique to the film business. The in-house director in an effects studio and the person directly reporting to the director on any shot, the visual effects director coordinates the artistic efforts of the entire effects department. In big studios, the director may have captains in the role of animation director, CG supervisor, and practical effects supervisor. In smaller studios with fewer separate departments, or studios that solely work with digital effects, the visual effects director may serve as chief of the technical directors, making the ultimate decisions on how any effect should get done. Like an art director, a visual effects director has to divide time between directing creative work and performing other management tasks. While the visual effects director is ubiquitous in film effects studios, most game studios have no comparable supervisory position, unless there is a creative director to which the group leads report

Art Director; Film, Television, and Games

At the head of the art department is the art director. This person provides the artistic vision to guide the other artists on the team and needs a wide array of fine art skills, along with a capacity for project and team management. The art director is concerned not only with the ultimate appearance of artwork, but is endlessly occupied with mentoring, schedules, and providing the artistic vision to drive the work of the other artists.

In the film business, the art director is solely concerned with the look of the film's artwork. It requires lots of film design experience but almost no technical understanding of how 3D effects are created.

The games art director, on the other hand, will probably have worked their way up to that position by doing lots of game art and is likely to have more technical experience than most of the artists on his team.

INDUSTRIAL LIGHT AND MAGIC (SAN RAFAEL, CALIF.): VISUAL EFFECTS ART DIRECTOR

Summary Responsible for design, development, and presentation of concept art, storyboard, environments, creatures, vehicles, hardware, etc. for both commercials and feature films. Involved in guiding design work through model/miniature and stage processes. Supervises/mentors others where necessary in the creation of artwork and other presentation materials.

Education, Experience, and Skills Required Prior experience in visual effects art direction a must. Prior miniature and stage experience a must. Bachelor's degree in art, industrial design, theatrical design, or painting. Three-plus years storyboard and conceptual artwork experience. Knowledge of production design, computer graphics, animation and filmmaking. Excellent presentation skills. Strong interpersonal and communication skills. Proven ability to lead and mentor artistic talent. Demo reel and portfolio required.

The following ad for an art director was posted by Electronic Arts, one of the world's most successful gaming companies:

ELECTRONIC ARTS (WALNUT CREEK, CALIF.): ART DIRECTOR

Summary The ever-popular and best-selling SimCity team is looking for an experienced Art Director. The successful candidate will be the heart and soul of the Art team and is someone who is a hands-on director willing to get directly involved with some of the day to day art tasks. A person who leads by doing not just directing through others. And a person that is really interested in the environment and design of a game rather than the characters.

Skills/Experience Needed Previous experience in console games. Knowledge of 3D Max and Maya. Background or education in Architecture, 3D Design, UI Design or related environmental design experience. Technically inclined and can or has worked with Software Engineers. Keeps up technology advances in the world of graphics. Has interest, knowledge, and focus on the environment, not the characters of a game. Familiar with previous versions of SimCity and/or other Maxis games!

Requirements Skills: 3D, 3D Studio Max, Maya, MEL Scripting. 6–10 years experience. Expertise: Artist-2D/Front End/Texturing, Artist-3D/Worlds/InGame Modeling, Artist-Art Director. Education: Associate or equivalent work experience.

Production Assistant; Film and Games

A *production assistant* is the 3D studio's equivalent of a *gopher* or a *runner*. 3D studios use PAs to organize collections of images; scan artwork; clean up sketches; process frames of video into animation for rotoscoping; perform simple compositing, cleanup, and rotoscoping tasks; research reference material; and perform a thousand other thankless but essential jobs such as running tapes around town and making dubs (duplicating tapes). Before you scoff at a production assistant job, consider the opportunity to work beside and learn from other artists in a studio that might otherwise not even consider hiring you. Many an artist has found their way into a career in graphics through one of these positions, and the connections and friendships you can make are probably more valuable than any paycheck you might earn. This is one of the jobs that you're likely to be offered as an internship at a 3D studio.

A PA should have a world of patience and an untiring spirit that allows them to stay later than everyone else and learn new things from the artists around them. Most new entrants into film and television CG come in as PAs if they don't have either substantial CG experience from school or a mind-blowing reel. But a good studio will appreciate the efforts of their PAs and slowly move them into more creative roles. It can take some time, but it can be a good way into a good studio, especially for those straight out of school lacking professional experience.

Because production assistants do so many kinds of work, there is no specific set of requirements for landing a PA job, although a strong student portfolio with an emphasis in at least one relevant area of 3D production is a good place to start.

> Another similar entry-level job is *render wrangler* or *render support*, which is described in the next chapter.

INDUSTRIAL LIGHT AND MAGIC (SAN RAFAEL, CALIF.): PRODUCTION ASSISTANT
This entry-level position provides administrative and backup support to the production team while providing an opportunity to learn about the production environment and process at ILM. They can be temporary positions but may evolve into longer term project positions (from as short as two weeks to as long as one year).

Principal Duties and Responsibilities: Provides administrative and backup support to the production team including typing memos, documents, and schedules and photocopying and filing tasks.

Inputs storyboard information into the computer including shot description and element breakdown. Prepares, maintains, and distributes storyboards to the appropriate personnel.

Assists with day-to-day activities, including the distribution of various reports, entering Daily Report notes, and organizing dailies.

Assists with the preparation of live action stage and location shooting as needed including craft service, running errands, and catering setup.

Completes special projects as needed or requested.

Education, Experience and Skills Required: Bachelor's degree in film production or equivalent preferred.

Minimum two years of related experience.

Computer literacy; word processing and spreadsheet experience helpful. 50 wpm typing.

2D/Concept Artist; Film and Games

Film projects employ a great many traditional artists and designers. These range from set and prop designers to the character and costume artists for animated features. Art department artists need traditional training in drawing, illustration, painting, clay sculpture, character design, fashion, architecture, and industrial design. Many concept artists are engaged in storyboarding, creating the visual comic-book version of the project's script. Others are traditional illustrators with an emphasis in design and color. In general, art department artists have little or no need for 3D software, and their computer work may never call for more than basic Photoshop skills.

The concept artist's job in games is similar to the role of the 2D artist in film studios. The concept artist sketches and draws characters, environments, and props. However, concept art for games rarely demands the level of detail seen in film-studio art, since the finished product has a comparably low level of detail. While practical models and 3D scans of clay sculptures, or *maquettes,* are often employed in films, the relatively low resolutions and coarse modeling details in the current world of games mean these techniques have little application except where relatively hi-res game characters need to resemble their celebrity inspiration.

Once a game's characters and sets are designed, a concept artist may move on to painting textures and backgrounds, or to creating artwork for promotions, packaging, and props.

INDUSTRIAL LIGHT AND MAGIC (SAN RAFAEL, CALIF.): STORYBOARD/CONCEPT ARTIST

Summary: Create characters, vehicles, environments, and/or storyboards for film and television under the supervision of the Visual Effects Art Director.

Education, Experience, and Skills Required: Strong creature/concept drawing and storyboarding skills a must. Proficiency in Photoshop required. Demo reel and/or portfolio required.

Previsualization or Layout Artist; Film and Television

Very fast and versatile, *previz* artists are the virtual cinematographers who take art department concepts and screen direction from a script and turn them into low-resolution 3D animations—*animatics*—designed to let directors and cameramen visualize and work out the problems in technical shots before they happen. The ideal previz artist is a film school or animation graduate with an eye for staging, timing, and camera work, and with enough training in 3D animation software to extend those principles into animatics.

A previz artist needs a demo reel that includes animatics showing interesting camera angles and moves that are possible and likely with a real camera, continuity in shot sequences, an eye for action and timing, and character animation that gives a sense of lifelike weight and motion. Film-quality rendering and high-resolution artwork are not an important consideration for this position, but it won't hurt as long as your animations adhere to the other requirements. A *flat portfolio*, or a book of physical artwork, is also sometimes required to show your layout and design skills.

TIPPETT STUDIO (BERKELEY, CALIF.): LAYOUT ARTIST

Qualifications Experience with SoftImage, Maya, or similar 3D animation software is essential. Proven knowledge of cinematographic techniques and principles is essential. Experience working with CG cameras, including lenses and editing animation curves, is necessary. Experience with CG model building and basic rendering skills desired. Knowledge of Unix operating system and general scripting literacy desired. Experience with traditional camera operating is a plus. Proven ability to be detail oriented and to work efficiently within a production environment.

Responsibilities Create and edit camera moves within CG environments to match storyboards and shot descriptions. Set dressing: creating and moving set pieces and models to match storyboards. Place and animate stand-in models for all characters and effects in a shot. Organize and track revisions of all sets and model pieces used in a shot. Render shots with basic lighting to check composition and timing. Follow up on directorial notes and instructions for composition and timing of shots.

3D Modeler; Film, Television, and Games

3D modelers build wireframe models in NURBs, subdivision surfaces, and sometimes in polygons, to bring the art department's 2D designs and sculptures into the third dimension. Modelers, like technical directors, tend to bridge the gap between visual artist and technical problem solver. Modelers are sometimes stratified into the specialties of environment modeling, the creation of architectural and exterior sets; hard surfaces modeling, the construction of vehicles and props. Character modeling, the creation of lifelike 3D people and creatures, is often treated as a separate job.

Modelers need to have an intuitive understanding of how objects are put together and the details that make shapes look real. Film modelers require a near-obsessive attention to detail, and minutia as small as nuts and bolts and small chinks and dents are often modeled into important objects.

For games, the requirements are very different. All games models are ultimately converted to polygons before they're inserted into a game, so even if you're modeling in subdivision surfaces or NURBs, you'll ultimately have to convert your objects to seamless polygon meshes. This requires a thorough understanding of polygon management and the ability to retain the integrity of a shape while adhering to strict resolution budgets. You'll also have to master UV mapping techniques for assigning textures to various regions of a model. There are few studios that draw clear distinctions between character modelers, hard surface modelers, and environment modelers, so you're better off if you can do all of them well.

One particular mistake recruiters see artists make on modeler demo reels is that they feel compelled to texture and animate their models. As you'll read throughout the book, a modeling reel should show models mostly in turn-table animations (where the model is turned 360 degrees in front of a camera) or with the animation of a bona-fide animator (who should be credited with the animation, of course). If your textures and animation are subpar to your models, don't go through the extra steps. Light your models well, and leave it at that. A flat book of printed model sheets is not a bad idea, either. Remember to send out copies, and always keep your originals.

TIPPETT STUDIO (BERKELEY, CALIF.): CG MODELERS

Summary Modelers will use technical expertise, artistic ability, and knowledge of animation to create models that meet the needs of production.

Qualifications 2-3 years of experience with Maya and Paraform. Basic knowledge of Unix operating system. Ideal candidate would also possess knowledge of construction techniques, and traditional 3D art skills such as sculpting. Proven ability to be detail oriented and to work efficiently within a production environment.

Responsibilities Responsible for building three-dimensional computer graphic models of characters and props to be painted and animated for visual effects shots. The modelers work within a team and are supervised by senior members of the Art Department.

FILM MODELER MEETS GAME MODELER

Modeling is one of the beachheads where the technical differences of film and game work come face to face. In film, the final look of the rendered image has the last word, and that means detail is everything. The rule is, if there's a detail you can see, model it. That means features like bevels on edges, dents in metal surfaces, holes in smooth skins, wires and screens, moldings around windows, and sticks and stones are often modeled in detail and then texture mapped with even more painstaking care. Film models are often modeled in NURBs or subdivision surfaces because these surfaces are perfectly smooth and resolution independent—no matter how close the camera gets to the model, you can't see the faceted edges the geometry. This is particularly true of characters, whose muscular and facial expressions and gestures demand smooth, seamless surfaces. If you're building architectural or mechanical objects, you might use polygons, but forget about lazy modeling that leaves razor sharp edges on the corners of a building. In film, the lack of a highlight on an edge is a dead giveaway that a model is a fake. That edge needs a bevel to throw a specular highlight, and depending on the age of the building, it might also need cracks, chips, and a bunch of rusting metal brackets bolted on to hold the corner together. Anyone who has done much modeling for film will tell you that putting the edge on the edge of the box is a lot more work than building the box in the first place.

In games, modeling is a constant trade-off in detail versus economy. Models have to adhere to strict performance guidelines, specifically, polygon counts. For a particular model, a car for example, you may have a budget of no more than 1,000 polygonal triangles, which is roughly like saying you have to build a life-sized Porsche out of 500 8.5-by-11-inch sheets of unbendable aluminum that can be cut and welded only across their diagonals. Sounds like plenty, until you realize that to model a single tire and wheel that looks more or less round, you'll need 32 polygons (16 more if the wheel needs a hubcap). There goes 192 polygons, just for the wheels! Really want a nice specular highlight on the top edge of the car's bumper? That beveled edge is going to cost you 20 polys. Need an air duct in the car's fender? You could model it for 32 additional polys (per side), or here's a budget-minded solution: just paint it into the 128-by-128-pixel texture map! For game artists, a new challenge has recently begun to develop—the need to build models at both high and low resolutions. Many games now feature elaborate prerendered cinematic animations, with visual qualities approaching those of film, and the game engines themselves are undergoing exponential increases in rendering power. As the trend continues, game modelers will be working with methods and at resolutions that more and more closely mimic their film counterparts while still having to sample models down to in game resolution budgets. For example, it's now possible to render normal maps based on high-resolution geometry, and to apply these to low-res surfaces to make them appear like high-resolution models. This technique requires both high-and-low-resolution models. In the future, having command of detail at low polygon counts will have to complement an eye for detail.

Character Modeler; Film and Games

Character modelers have to be intimately familiar with physiology—the way bone, muscle, and skin hang together to form a body and a face. If you're going to model characters, you have to be sensitive to the subtleties of expression and the intangible qualities of character appeal. It's relatively easy to model something like a human head, especially with the latest generation of subdivision surface modeling tools, but it's not so easy to master proportions or the details, such as how lines and wrinkles crease a brow, or how the muscles under the skin of the face push and pull on eyebrows, eyes, cheeks, and lips.

In film, character modelers must be able to model realistic human and animal bodies and faces, in correct proportion, with a firm understanding of skeletons, muscles, and skins. In the past, film character modelers have worked primarily in NURBs, and some studios still require NURBs-based character modeling, but that technology is quickly being supplanted by subdivision surface modeling, which can be faster and easier to use for this type of organic surface creation.

Character modelers in real-time games usually work with very low-resolution models where the challenge is to preserve a character's proportions and details while paring polygon counts down to a minimum.

In this ad from Industrial Light & Magic, applicants are warned about heavy use of the keyboard. You know you're in trouble when the job description requires a disclaimer.

INDUSTRIAL LIGHT AND MAGIC (SAN RAFAEL, CALIF.): CREATURE MODELER

Summary With an emphasis on anatomy and form, the creature modeler will create three-dimensional CG characters to be painted, enveloped [rigged], and animated by the creature development team.

Primary Responsibilities Creates three-dimensional creatures for the Animator and Technical Director. Employs specific software tools to build the geometric structure of the object and ensures that the model will satisfy the requirements of the production. In building creatures, the modeler must incorporate technical expertise, artistic ability, and a basic understanding of animation. Works with production team (Sr. Modeler, Technical Directors and Animators) to determine the "look" for an object. Builds the geometry of computer graphic models, with an understanding of how the geometry will be used in the production process. Performs other tasks related to the creation of computer-generated animation.

Education, Experience, and Skills Bachelor's degree in Fine Arts or equivalent with a thorough understanding of anatomy, character design, and animation. Portfolio demonstrating traditional artistic skills including illustration and sculptural abilities a plus. Proven experience creating digital creatures or characters in a feature film or production environment. Requires familiarity with film and video post -production techniques and with computer graphic techniques. 2-3 years Alias, SoftImage, Maya, or XSI experience and/or a demonstrated desire to develop computer skills. Knowledge of Unix is a necessity to navigate through ILM's production pipeline.

Physical Requirements Uses computer keyboard 95 percent of the time.

Environment Artist; Film and Games

In many game companies, modelers are also responsible for texturing and lighting their models and are referred to as *environment artists.* These are the architects and stage designers of the game world. The environment artist builds the sets in which the game's characters live and move. This might include both interior and exterior architectural models and props, as well as the background scenery, textures, lighting, and atmospheres that make the environment interesting to look at.

Some film companies have a position that's analogous to the games environment artist, called a *3D environments artist,* or *digital environments artist,* but this is a highly specialized job that's often combined with the role of matte painter. These artists create digital scenery and populate it with 3D models, often of architecture or natural features, such as trees, mountains, or waterfalls. They must have both the eye of a painter and lighting artist and the technical director's ability to render the scenery with realistic effects and animated props.

ELECTRONIC ARTS (WALNUT CREEK, CALIF.): ENVIRONMENT MODELER/TEXTURE ARTIST

The ever-popular and best-selling SimCity team is looking for an experienced Environmental Modeler. The successful candidate will be a critical part of this incredible team! And a person that is really interested in the environment and design of a game rather than the characters. (Please note this position is located at the Maxis studio located in beautiful Walnut Creek, CA, about 25 miles east of San Francisco.)

Skills/Experience Needed Previous experience in console games. Knowledge of 3D Max and Maya. Background or education in Architecture, 3D Design and/or related environmental modeling experience. Keeps up with technology advances in the world of graphics. Has interest, knowledge, and focus on the environment not the characters of a game. Familiar with previous versions of SimCity and/or other Maxis games!

Requirements Maya. 3–5 years experience. Expertise: Artist-3D/Worlds/InGame Modeling. Education: Associate or equivalent work experience.

Texture Artist

Texture or *surfacing* artists paint and shade the 3D objects created by 3D modelers. Texture artists need a thorough understanding of what makes surfaces look the way they do in life—the effects of wear and tear and the accumulation and layering of dirt and grime are important concepts. Technical underpinnings of surface qualities, such as specularity, luminosity, reflectivity, and displacement, are part of the texture artist's daily vocabulary. Texture artists often combine understandings of photography and painting with a command of the complex tools, shaders, and techniques used to translate real-world and imaginary surfaces into 3D-rendered textures.

In years past, texture art in games has been severely hampered by the limitations of games' rendering engines and hardware, and many artists working in the games industry have only limited comprehension of effects like bump mapping, environment mapping, and specular mapping. As game hardware makes quantum leaps in performance and capabilities, game textures are requiring more and more of these film-style effects. For example, nVidia's hardware used in the Xbox and many desktop PCs allows for the use of *normal maps*, which can be used to influence the apparent bumpiness, specularity, and environmental reflections on a surface.

The game texture artist is a Zen master, making do with almost nothing to create an interesting and immersive world. For example, a game artist has to be able to reuse a single texture map in many different ways, and to tile small textures seamlessly across large areas of geometry.

TIPPETT STUDIO (BERKELEY, CALIF.): CG PAINTER

Creates the textures, colors, and organic surface qualities needed in the completion of creatures and/or objects used in production.

Qualifications Background in Art with strong composition skills required. Strong technical knowledge of Command files as relating to Renderman. One year experience as a CG Painter in a film production environment. Familiarity with film post-production techniques and with computer graphics techniques preferred. Knowledge of Photoshop, Painter, Studio Paint, and Maya. Experience with Unix and Renderman. Must be able to work as a team, with strong communication skills and attention to detail in a fast-paced environment. 2D drawing and sculpture knowledge a plus.

Responsibilities Works with production team to execute the desired look of an object. Participates as a team member in determining various design solutions. Creates and maintains texture maps and command files.

FILM TEXTURE PAINTER VS. GAME TEXTURE PAINTER

By now it's no news to you that film and game art differs in its technical demands and limitations. Here's another one: texture painting and mapping. In games, texture memory is one of the most tightly constrained budget items. The Sony PlayStation 4 offers 2MB of texture RAM. To put this in perspective, that's the equivalent of two 1,000-pixel-square images, or about two photographs (uncompressed) from a cheap 1 megapixel digital camera. Now imagine trying to represent all of the textures in an entire 3D world—walls, floors, ceilings, props, vehicles, and characters—within those two photos. Game texture artists are masters of making do with the resources at hand. The same texture map might be used to portray concrete on the ground, stucco on the walls, and the coarse, grainy leather of a car's upholstery. Texture maps are often forced into unnatural aspect ratios (usually powers of 2), so every texture image has to be either a square or a square cut in half: 64-by-64, 128-by-128, or 128-by-64, for example. Texture artists have to make a single texture work for entirely dissimilar objects. For example, one map may serve to texture the entire surface of a car, with fenders, windows, headlights, and other features, all painted on different portions of the single texture map. Current game engines are quite limited in the types of rendering effects they will support. Bump maps and specular maps have a dramatic impact on the quality of rendered surfaces, but they're supported in only the most sophisticated rendering systems. (Keep in mind that those effects maps also get subtracted from your texture memory budget.) But things are looking up for texture artists in games. As nVidia, ATI Technologies, and Sony (the major players in game rendering hardware) drive up the power of their chips, real-time procedural effects and advanced texture mapping are pushing game rendering to higher levels of realism. Game artists are rapidly getting more flexibility and creative freedom. Microsoft's Xbox, for example, has 64MB of texture RAM and uses advanced nVidia rendering hardware that supports more advanced texture effects than previously possible. And for computer games, 3D hardware with 128MB texture RAM and advanced programmable shaders is becoming standard in new systems.

In film, there are hardly any limits on what can be done in textures and procedural surfaces. There are shaders for realistic skin, hair, fire, water, and every type of surface imaginable. For these artists, the challenge is not how to do more with less, but how to achieve the utmost realism, regardless of the surface's complexity. A surface texture in film effects might include channels for color, bump, specularity, luminosity, reflectivity and glow, plus ramps to modify the attenuation of reflectivity based on the surface's angle to the camera, and the degree of glow based on the color of the underlying color map. All of this might be animated, so that the surface takes on a life of its own. Painting a surface in such a world requires not only an ability to paint a picture that looks realistic, but an ability to paint and manipulate the underlying surface qualities that make metal look metallic, corrosion look corrosive, and oil look oily, as these surfaces move in and react to their environments. Depending on the studio, film effects artists may also work extensively with procedural shaders, such as those used by Pixar's Renderman software. These shaders are pure computer code that may have only limited visual interface elements, and they are controlled by manipulating procedural values, rather than through painting of bitmapped textures. In this world, creating new materials is the work of programmers with a sophisticated understanding of rendering algorithms and complex math.

Matte Painter or Background Artist; Film and Games

Like art department artists, matte painters are primarily traditionally trained artists who specialize in painting background scenery in films and television productions. While it's important to be able to do realistic painting, the matte painter is usually more concerned with being able to paint scenery that fits the style of the film. Increasingly, matte painters incorporate 3D elements into their scenes and use traditional painting techniques to blend 3D and 2D elements into a coherent realism.

In smaller studios and games companies, this job is often combined with that of the texture artist, the theory being that if you have the painting skills to paint realistic scenery, you can also paint realistic textures and surfaces.

DIGITAL DOMAIN (VENICE, CALIF.): DIGITAL MATTE/TEXTURE PAINTERS

Digital Domain is looking for skilled Digital Matte/Texture Painters with 2–3 years experience in feature films/commercials and in their respective resolutions, i.e., NTSC, 2K, etc. Candidates should have a highly developed photorealistic painting style with knowledge and ability in perspective/motion and proficiency in matte painting and/or creating and applying textures. Knowledge of Deep Paint 3D, Amazon, and/or Photoshop is required. Familiarity with 3D modeling packages relative to texturing a plus.

Lighting Artists; Games and Film

Lighting artists set lights and fine-tune highlights and shadows within a scene. They may also manipulate light-related effects, such as glows and flares. Lighting artists are often former students of photography or stage lighting, and they have a keen sense of color and contrast and know how to use lights for dramatic and artistic effect.

Frequently in film work, the task of the lighting artist is to match the lighting in CG scenes to that in live footage, so that the CG elements blend seamlessly into the live plates. Current standards of lighting in film work call for the use of advanced lighting and rendering methods such as global illumination, radiosity, ambient occlusion, and high dynamic range image (HDRI) rendering.

In games, the lighting artist's job is much different. Games usually allow a few light sources at most to be rendered in real-time in any scene. Anyone with experience in lighting will vouch that "a few "lights is too few to produce effective or dramatic lighting. The solution in games is to bake lighting into a scene, so that it becomes embedded in the scene's texture maps or attached to vertices of the model being lit. This allows a game artist to use advanced lighting, and many lights, without impacting the game's performance.

What follows is ESC FX's ad for a lighting artist during its work on *The Matrix* sequels II and III:

ESC FX (ALAMEDA, CALIF.): COLOR AND LIGHTING TD

Duties include but are not limited to: Design and implementation of complex shading networks and lighting schemes for realistic object appearance as required by production's needs. Work with complex rendering pipeline, both at the application and scripting levels. Receiving many elements from other departments and assembling virtual scenes for shots often using scripting languages for automation.

Position Requirements Ideal candidate will have photography/visual arts or computer science degree or relevant experience. Minimum 3+ years experience in a production environment. Broad, practical knowledge of rendering theory. Both eye for lighting and technical skills are important. Should be familiar Maya scripting and Perl, and working in an environment where 3D and compositing work closely together. Experience especially with Mental Ray renderer but also Renderman and scripting languages (e.g., Python, Tk) very useful. Good interpersonal/communication skills necessary.

2D/3D Artist; Games

The term *3D Artist*, or *CG artist*, is sometimes used as a catch-all name for an artist who may do all kinds of 3D work in a game studio, and that job is even sometimes combined with the job of the 2D concept artist and painter. This position may require any or all of the following: storyboarding, sketching, painting, modeling, texturing, lighting, character modeling, animation, and technical direction.

For us here at Sammy Studios, we're very interested in artists. Artists first, more than technical people, although we do have some technical artists. It's very important to us that they have really strong art skills. We are very interested in artists who have a traditional background, if not professionally, at least traditional skills that they can demonstrate on their reel or their portfolio. Most come from art schools: we have people from Savannah College of Art and Design, from Art Center of Pasadena, from the Academy of Art in San Francisco. We put a high premium on artistic skills and artistic talent, because if you know good art, you're going to be able to create good art, regardless of what tool you use.

I'm more willing to train someone to use the tool than to train them in art. It's much more difficult to train someone to be a good artist.

There are exceptions to the rule, where you have guys who didn't need to go to art school who are phenomenal artists, but in general it's certainly helpful.

—*SEAN MILLER, SAMMY STUDIOS*

These days, there's almost no equivalent position in large effects studio based films (as opposed to boutiques), unless you consider technical directors, who sometimes have their hands in every aspect of 3D, or previsualization artists, who do some of everything at game resolutions.

MICROSOFT XBOX (SEATTLE, WASH.): 2D/3D ARTIST

It takes an unusual creative talent to know how to build an inscrutable alien race of characters. It takes an even more unusual talent to know what happens when they atomize their enemy with an arsenal of bad-ass alien explosives. If you think you are unusually creative and talented enough to address this difficult task, we have a job for you. Inscrutable alien references are a plus, but not required.

Major Responsibilities Concept, build, and texture characters and character permutations. Concept and paint 2D and 3D effects. Requirements: Be an excellent artist. Be able to work with a team. Have experience with 3D Max and Photoshop. Have two years or more of professional experience. Possess the ability to work well under pressure and deadlines. Must be willing to take art direction well.

Character Animator; Film and Games

Character animators breathe life into inanimate objects. A character animator's job is to extend a character from the realm of *action* into the world of *acting*. As animated 3D characters are becoming the stars of films, character animators are being asked to infuse their characters with the emotional expressiveness equal to that of a human actor.

In some ways, character animators in film are animation's equivalent of concept artists. At least in theory, they aren't required to be highly technical in their skill set, but they are required to have a mastery of the principles of animation (as defined so clearly by Frank Thomas and Ollie Johnson in their classic book *The Illusion of Life: Disney Animation*). This means understanding the subtleties of weight and timing, anticipation, slow-in and slow-out, moving in arcs, and the other principles that are the focus of any first-time animation class. But the reality is that the setup and rigging for character animation has its own world of technical requirements and issues, and a character animator equipped to troubleshoot, or at least explain the nature of problems in a character's rig, is going to be far more useful in production than one who has to report every problem to a TD and wait for assistance.

In many studios the job of rigging is given to a TD and the animator does nothing but animate. Still, getting to know the technical aspects and rigging of character animation is a huge plus. If you want to learn character animation, and the rigging behind it, you'll have to study bone and joint setup, inverse kinematics (IK) and forward kinematics (FK), as well as skin weighting and deformation systems. You may also need to familiarize yourself with motion blending and motion capture tools and techniques.

In real-time 3D games, the majority of hard-surface animation is generated by in-game physics simulations, so animators in games are primarily character animators. This may involve key frame animation, where animated moves such as a karate kick are saved as individual clips that can be replayed when the player pushes a particular button sequence, or it may mean directing motion capture performers and manipulating motion capture data to blend performances into 3D action sequences.

In games, character rigging is simpler than in film work, since most game engines won't handle sophisticated deformations in real time. In many game companies, character animators also do their own rigging.

ESC FX: CHARACTER ANIMATOR

The Character Development Animator is directly responsible to the Animation Supervisor and is instrumental in developing the behavior and personality of the computer generated characters.

Duties include but are not limited to Review the previz with the Animation Supervisor to understand meaning, emotion, action, continuity, and plot as they relate to character development and storytelling in the assigned sequences or for assigned characters. Work with Animation Supervisor to define personality, create fluid motion and organic movement of character(s). Work with modelers/riggers to ensure that characters are equipped with the necessary range of motion for their performance. Maintain awareness of the characters' behavior and motion throughout the assigned sequences to ensure consistency of performance. Prepare tests of proposed animation to show to the Animation Supervisor and the CG Supervisor for approval. Confer regularly with the Animation Supervisor to apprise him/her of progress.

Position Requirements Minimum 2 years experience with character animation for feature films required. Experience with traditional character animation techniques such as stop motion desirable. Experience with character set-up required. Experience with Maya and Mental Ray required. Knowledge of Windows NT and Unix required. Ideal candidate should have strong artistic sensibilities in the areas of character movement, storytelling, modeling, and lighting.

Cinematic Artist, Games

In games, the cinematics artist does pretty much exactly what a character animator does in film work, only they'll generally have to do it faster, with less attention to detail. Cinematics are the story-based movies that give meaning to the game play that is the meat of any video game. Often cinematics are rendered in real-time (by the game's engine), but it's also common to see prerendered cinematics that play out as a movie while the game loads, or in between levels. Depending on the game, the cinematic artist will need character animation skills, as well as the ability to do screen direction and camera work.

Summary

As you've seen in this chapter, the skills and techniques used in film, television, and games work are closely related, and most art jobs have analogous positions in all three industries. However, the need to specialize is pronounced in film work and much less so in television work. In games, you need to acquire a breadth of skills specific to the games market. The specific jobs described in this chapter can all be considered more or less visual arts positions. For the most part, none of them require extensive programming or scripting, although they may require extensive knowledge of technical subject matter, such as advanced shading and rendering systems, or hard-to-master modeling skills. The next chapter introduces truly technical jobs, many of which require at least some knowledge of programming, or a mastery of the very technical aspects of the 3D production process. Chapter 2 also describes some of the 3D jobs outside of the film and video game industries.

CHAPTER 2

Technical 3D Jobs and Other Industries

While the jobs in the 3D and effects industry discussed in Chapter 1 require plenty of education and training, they are primarily visual art jobs. In this chapter, we introduce the jobs that require at least one foot in the nefarious world of scripting, coding, and engineering. That's not to say these jobs are all about writing software, since the end product is still pretty pictures and animation or pretty pictures and fun games. For many of these jobs, such as character rigging, technical direction, and effects animation, you'll have to straddle the line more or less evenly between art and science and between the visual and technical aspects of 3D effects. However, there are a few jobs in 3D and effects that require a degree in electrical engineering, or at least professional experience in software coding.

As in Chapter 1, we've organized these jobs roughly by those that have fewer technical demands to those that have more, with character rigging and effects animation occupying the artsy end of the spectrum, and full-blown engineering and software development redlining the geek gauge.

Later in the chapter, we discuss a couple of jobs that are integral to CG, though they may not be as hands-on in CG creation itself: the *coordinator* and the *producer*. Also, there are jobs in the games business—*game designer* and *game producer*—which are neither art nor engineering, but a mix of script writing, system architecture, marketing, and project management.

Finally, we introduce other industries that have embraced 3D and require many of the same skills you need for entertainment-related jobs but are far removed from the glitz and glamour of the Hollywood-centered games and film businesses.

You'll find the following in this chapter:

- **Technical art jobs in games and film**
- **Engineering jobs in games and film**
- **Game designers and producers**
- **Other 3D jobs**

Technical Art Jobs

The following jobs are all technical in nature, but that doesn't mean they don't require a good eye for art, too. After all, the end product is the final frames of film or the finished game you'll help to create. Here's how the spectrum of jobs in 3D stacks up from least technical to most technical (some of these jobs have different titles or may be combined in various ways in different companies):

Render wrangler or render support	3D artist
Director	Character rigger
Visual effects director	Motion capture artist
Concept artist	Compositor
Animator	Effects animator
Previsualization artist	Technical director
Texture artist	Animation supervisor
Lighting artist	CG supervisor
Modeler	Shader and tools engineer
	Pipeline engineer

Render Wrangler or Render Support; Film

We launch this section with the render wrangler because it is probably the best place to get your foot in the door on the way to a position in technical direction and other 3D jobs, whether technical or not. As a matter of fact, render wranglers sometimes move into CG jobs within their company by using the company's resources to expand their own reels and learn more about CG.

Today, with machine costs so low, most 3D effects studios employ a render farm on some scale, whether it's a rack of machines dedicated to rendering or several workstation-by-day/render-by-night machines. Large studios however have a large network of Windows, Linux, or Unix computers wired together that render 24/7 and are in need of supervision. Anyone who has ever rendered a high-quality image knows that it can take many minutes or hours to render a single frame of animation on a single computer. In film work, a single frame of film can take six hours or more to render. At that rate, a studio could render only a minute or so of animation in a year. The only way such studios can possibly function is to throw hundreds computers at the problem, with each computer ganging up to render single animations. When 3D artists get to the stage of a project when they need visual feedback about what they've accomplished, often at the end of each day, they send rendering jobs to the render farm's queue, where they're rendered in turn, much like the workers in a business office queue up jobs to a network printer.

The render wrangler is the guy who baby-sits this network, usually at night, after everyone else has gone home to watch *The Sopranos*. It's an unglamorous job, involving debugging files when they cause servers to crash, restarting servers after the file is debugged, making sure nobody runs out of disk space, and ensuring that all the rendered frames end up intact where they're supposed to.

Character Rigger; Film and Games

Like other technical direction jobs, character rigging requires a command of the technical underpinnings of animated 3D characters, including skeletons, skinning, inverse and forward kinematics, constraints, deformations, and blend shapes. Riggers not only create the animation skeletons and deformers that are used by animators to control a character and make it move in realistic ways, but they also have to create the control structures and interface elements that make it easy for a character animator to manipulate their subject. This requires extensive use of scripting combined with expressions, driven keys, and an arsenal of tricks for making characters behave as expected.

To rig characters in a way that works for animators, character riggers need extensive knowledge of character animation, since they'll be working with animators on a daily basis to rig and re-rig characters to meet the needs of particular shots.

As a result, character riggers are commonly referred to as character technical directors. (Additionally, character TDs are sometimes required to direct motion capture and to work with motion capture data.)

Character rigging in games uses the same tool set as in as films, but due to limitations in performance, it's not usually possible to rig characters with the same level of complexity and detail. However, the need to create interfaces and controls for characters is the same, so in terms of scripting, the job is just as technical in games as it is in film. Additionally, the level of detail in games animation has been changing rapidly as rendering engines and hardware advance the possibilities, so it's a safe bet that, for the future generations of consoles, games will feature characters with realistic motion requiring far more sophisticated rigs.

Tippett Studio (Berkeley, Calif.): Character Setup TD

Creates animation controls and surface deformations simulating an organic surface quality which is influenced by an underlying skeletal and muscular system. Creates "puppets" that are accurate, detailed and easily controlled by the Animators.

Qualifications One-year experience in CG Animation Setup in a production environment preferred. Knowledge of Alias Maya preferred. Thorough understanding of CG skeletal tools and principles. Thorough understanding of anatomy and physiology. MEL scripting or programming experiences a plus. Strong problem solving skills. Must be able to work in a team, with strong communication skills and attention to detail, and able to take direction in a fluid, fast-paced production environment.

Responsibilities Works with the production team to create the desired animation controls and deformation qualities for an object or character. Actively participates in making design and animation control solutions. Monitors effectiveness of animation controls and deformations; makes adjustments as necessary throughout the production. Takes direction from team and show lead.

Effects Animator; Film and Games

Effects animators are technical artists who specialize in the creation of physics-based motion and dynamic phenomenon, such as wind, explosions, and fire. Some effects artists work only in certain areas of dynamic effects, such as cloth and hair animation, or in the pyrotechnics of action movies. Effects animation often requires advanced scripting or programming skills to customize out-of-the-box dynamic effects and shaders, and it also requires a keen eye for color, timing, and the nature of real-world phenomenon. Effects animators also need a working knowledge of 2D compositing systems, since 3D rendered effects have to blend seamlessly with other plates and often require motion blur, filtering, and other post-processing to complete the effect.

Hard-surface animation is often considered part of effects animation and includes making inanimate objects fly, drive, or roll around on screen. In some studios, this type of animation is handled by the character department, since this type of rigging is similar to the work done by character riggers or technical directors.

Effects animation is used in both film and games, although in games most hard-surface animation is handled by the game's AI (artificial intelligence), and effects such as pyrotechnics are generally quite simplistic compared to what's done in film and television. These effects are often produced and rendered by technical artists who then move on to other responsibilities.

ESC FX (ALAMEDA, CALIF.): TECHNICAL EFFECTS ARTIST

A Technical Effects Artist is responsible for a variety of technology-intensive effects. This may include: natural phenomena (fire, smoke, explosions, debris, water, rain); procedural modeling, deformation and/or animation; interactive lighting; and pipeline issues. The work may involve scripting or light programming, package integration, running test shots, and possibly lighting and/or compositing duties where appropriate.

Duties include but are not limited to Reviewing concept art, storyboards, and animatics to plan the type of effects required. Brainstorming design solutions with the R and D staff.

Creative eye to develop the look of an effect from concept. Providing estimates of time and materials required for implementation of effects solutions. Testing proposed effects techniques. Coordinating with other digital effects staff on pipeline integration and optimization. Integration of effects into shots. Providing continuing updates to the Digital Supervisor as to progress, obstacles, and requirements.

Position Requirements 2–3 years experience with effects animation for feature film required. BS/BA or equivalent experience required. Proven ability to interface with both creative and technical types. Thorough knowledge of both 3D and 2D graphics techniques required. Intimate knowledge of Alias Maya required. Prior knowledge of procedural shading required; mental ray experience a big plus. Prior knowledge of Shake a plus.

Motion Capture Artist; Film and Games

Motion capture (*mocap*) is increasingly used to bring huge amounts of complex character motion into CG film and game projects. For example, Gollum, the pathetic, schizophrenic anti-hero of *Lord of the Rings: The Two Towers*, was almost entirely animated with motion capture that had been tweaked and augmented by character animators. In mocap, human actors, athletes, and dancers are called upon to perform the movement of everything from super-heroics to the acrobatics of soccer stars. Mocap artists rig 3D characters to work with motion capture data, they operate the actual motion capture hardware and software, and they manipulate the dense data gathered by motion capture systems to make it work smoothly in the context of their project. (Working with motion capture is often a part of a character animator's job description, especially in games.)

The motion capture artist works hand-in-hand with the animation director and sometimes serves as the animation director during motion capture sessions. In this role, the mocap artist must direct the actor to perform in a way that achieves the goals of the scene, whether it's a realistic depiction of an athletic maneuver or an exaggerated rendition of a kung-fu expert's attack (see Figure 2.1).

Motion capture artists are technicians with a deep understanding of character animation tools and techniques, as well as a keen sense of character animation. Although most motion capture artists are hired as character animators, this job will increasingly be awarded to animators who specialize in motion capture and its idiosyncrasies.

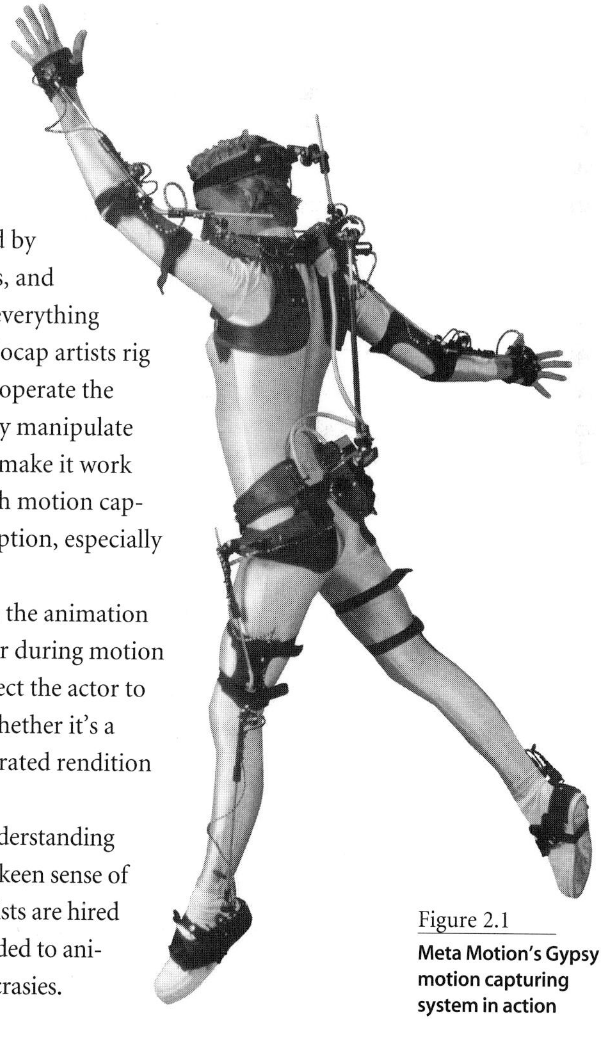

Figure 2.1

Meta Motion's Gypsy motion capturing system in action

Here's what Sean Miller, lead artist at Sammy Studios, says about the importance of acting experience in a motion capture artist:

> *It comes in handy in a number of senses. When you want to create some reference motion, you could get in there and direct the motion capture shoot—that's where having the motion capture facility in house is helpful—or you could even get in the suit and act the motion out yourself. Whether that becomes the final motion that's used in the game, it's a terrific tool for you to be able to realize it in your final art. If you have an animator that can't move that doesn't know how to move his body, when he does the animation, a lot of times he's going to be basing it on how he thinks the body moves. So, if they're stiff, their animations will very often be stiff. Even in terms of motion capture, if you can't recognize good motion and clean poses, you're not going to be able to direct a motion capture shoot to get the kind of data that's going to be useful to you.*
>
> —*SEAN MILLER*

Technical Director; Film and Games

TDs, as technical directors are commonly called, bridge the chasm between the engineers and the artists, and their job is one of the few left in 3D that requires strong abilities across the board. In fact, TDs need to be a little bit of both artist and engineer, and on any given day a TD may have to model a character, rig it, animate the cloth of the character's dress, fine-tune the rendering of her hair, find a way to work around tearing seams in her NURBs skin, and solve a problem in compositing the finished renderings with a live-action plate. TDs need a good eye for lighting and color and a keen sense of what looks real.

As the TD's job becomes more and more complex, studios are subdividing the roles of the TD. For example, some studios have technical directors who do only hair and cloth, others who exclusively rig characters, and still others who manipulate motion capture data, match the motion of a 3D camera to the camera used in the filming of a live-action plate, or ensure the smooth transfer of data through the production pipeline.

There is no single job description for a TD, and you'll see the same company advertising for TDs with different skill sets, depending on the hole the studio is trying to fill. Some jobs emphasize art direction, modeling lighting, rigging and shading; while others demand more technical troubleshooting and building tools with MEL, C, and other programming languages.

Technical directors in games—sometimes called technical art directors to distinguish them from the programmers who populate the other end of the hall in game studios— have a similar set of job requirements. Games TDs today need an art background and a good eye for colors, surfaces, and lighting. They need modeling and rigging skills, and they need to know MEL and at least one scripting language, such as Perl. Also having a grasp of a compiled programming language like C++ can't hurt.

HOW MUCH YOU'LL EARN

Pay rates in the games industry are pretty good. In the San Francisco Bay Area, an entry-level 3D artist will earn at least $50,000 per year in any established studio (which is just enough for a young, single person to get by in that high-rent region), but salaries escalate quickly from there. An "Artist III" at Electronic Arts (the company does not give functional titles, such as *art director*, to its employees) with art direction responsibilities and five years or more experience, can enjoy a salary near $100,000, plus bonuses and royalties that may add 20% to the annual income. Bonuses and royalties are tied to the performance of the titles the artist has worked on, as well meeting milestones on time. EA also offers a generous benefits package, including 401K benefits with matching contributions, full health coverage, and 3 weeks or more per year of paid vacation and sick days.

Compare this to the film industry, where the same entry-level artist might come in at $40,000. A senior-level, experienced artist in film and television work can expect between $60,000 and $90,000, but a highly qualified and extremely experienced senior artist might expect a salary cap at just over $100,000, although this is rare, especially as budgets decrease with time. In addition, film companies generally hire artists as contract labor for the duration of a project, so most pay should be seen as weekly rates. As a freelancer, you rarely make money throughout the entire year, so your annual total will be lower than multiplying your weekly rate by 52. And, while some of these companies pay similar benefits to both employees and contract help, most contractors don't enjoy company benefits or time off, so those costs should be factored in as well. As a freelancer, "vacation" time is compensated only by a check from the unemployment office!

Truly qualified technical directors and engineers with real-world 3D graphics experience are hard to find, so naturally they can expect salaries significantly higher than those of less technically skilled 3D artists.

Note of caution: Many small game studios, particularly startups, lure inexperienced artists and engineers with stock options in lieu of pay. Since the failure rate of such small shops is astronomically high (about one in ten game startups will survive to publish a second game), you should weigh the value of these options carefully against the possibility of earning a real salary. If you get "options," you're going to have to pay something to exercise them—typically 10 to 50 cents per share if a startup is in its early stages. But that can add up to real money if your options are for, say, 10,000 shares. Consider what happens if you take those 10,000 options, at 10 cents per share exercise price, in lieu of $5,000 in pay. If the company produces a hit game, or gets bought by another bigger company, your *upside* could be tens of thousands of dollars. But if the company bombs (which is statistically ten times as likely), your shares will be worthless, and you'll be out $5,000 in never-to-be-paid salary, plus $1,000 in out-of-pocket cash. Looking on the bright side, this might be an opportunity to earn *something* for on-the-job training that you would have to pay for if you were going to school instead.

Just to add to the difficulty of qualifying for this role, TDs also need to be able to manage and direct other artists. Here's one ad from Tippet, a film studio, and another from Electronic Arts, so you can see how widely the requirements vary:

TIPPETT STUDIO: TECHNICAL DIRECTOR

Position involves lighting and rendering of animated 3-D creatures and props and for integration into live-action background plates.

Qualifications Background in Art with strong visual skills. Proficiency with Maya, Renderman, and Python. Some experience in computer programming preferred (C shell: C or C++ a plus). Familiarity with film post-production techniques and with computer graphics techniques. One year experience as a Technical Director with highly proficient skills in either lighting or technical problem solving in a production environment preferred. Must be able to work on a team, possess strong communication skills and attention to detail in a fast-paced environment.

Responsibilities Responsible for all aspects of lighting and rendering of the computer generated elements and scenes. Participates as a team member in determining various design solutions.

Compositor/2D Technical Director; Film

Composite artists specialize in seamlessly blending together the layers of a shot, including live-action footage and multiple layers of 3D-rendered imagery. Frequently, composite artists incorporate 2D effects, such as special effects filters, rotoscoping, or motion blur, to achieve the perfect final frames. Compositors spend most of their time using 2D software tools like After Effects, Combustion, Shake, Commotion, Flint, Inferno, and Flame, rather than 3D animation software. And they're as likely to be painting wires out of live-action plates as they are to be animating smoke and fire in rendered sequences.

Here's how Andrew Pearce, pipeline supervisor at ESC FX, describes the role of the compositor where he works:

There are a lot of effects that can be done through nonprogrammatic means. Compositors can do some amazing things given the elements that they have. They can do effects that surprise me. Things I thought you could only do in 3D. They say, "Oh no, I just did that in 2D." Wow.

Compositing is math. You have to understand the order of operations. You have to have a good eye for artistic elements, as well. You have to make things look like what you're trying to achieve. How do I tweak the color of that, and how do I make sure that each element I'm bringing in is color corrected so it looks like they're all in the same environment? That's the artistic part of it. They have to have some animation skills, as well. They're going to be compositing some moving elements, like clouds or a plate moving in the background so it looks like someone's on a train. They have to be able to say, "Yes, that's moving correctly."

[Compositing is] a very important component. It's almost the most important component. You can have all these beautiful 3D elements and all these beautiful photographic scenes, but if someone is sort of slapping them together in a comp that doesn't look convincing, that doesn't put things in the same color space, that doesn't integrate the edges properly, it's going to look like someone's standing in front of a green screen in a different place. It's going to look like the weatherman. It's not going to sell it.

—ANDREW PEARCE

DIGITAL DOMAIN (VENICE, CALIF.): 2D TECHNICAL DIRECTOR

Digital Domain is looking for a 2D Technical Director. The ideal candidate will have a technical background and understand compositing in a high-end visual effects studio environment. Experience as a Digital Artist is not necessary, however, we are looking for someone who has enough knowledge of the process to be able to recognize 2D problems (i.e., matte edges, clamped values, etc.).

The following skills and experience are preferred Node-based compositing system experience, experience working with a range of image formats including Cineon, an understanding of core compositing operators, and the ability to diagnose where scripts need to be optimized and come up with solutions to do so.

Scripting experience (preferably TCL [Tool Command Language]) is desired, and strong communication skills are a must (should be able to communicate problems to software engineers and solutions to artists).

Engineering Jobs

3D graphics has always required the support of software engineers. These are the technicians who write the tools that do everything from modeling to shading and network data management. While the other types of technical 3D jobs require an understanding of the artistic end of 3D and animation, the following engineering roles require much more technical knowledge about the underlying mathematics and physics, as well as mastery of programming languages.

Software Developer/Engineer

Modern big-budget film effects studios all employ an army of in-house software developers. Programmers write workflow tools that help data move through the production process, commonly known as the *pipeline*. They write custom programming shaders, which control the appearance of surfaces. And in some studios, such as Pixar and PDI, programmers write modeling and animation software from scratch. While it's possible to do 3D and effects with out-of-the-box software, and most studios use at least some commercially made tools, the cutting edge of 3D is almost always led by studios writing proprietary software and plug-ins to create never-before-seen effects. This is also true in games, where quantum leaps in games hardware require a similar expansion of the software universe.

Software developers in 3D studios are familiar with object-oriented programming languages and techniques (C++, etc.), as well as scripting in languages such as MEL, Perl, and COBRA. Particularly in game development, engineers need familiarity with operating system components such as OpenGL and Direct 3D. The underlying concepts of 3D, including shading and rendering, are also typical requirements.

…The pipeline department is a generalist, because if there's a problem at all, the first one they're going to turn to is you. It may be a problem with the model. It may be a problem with the Perl script; it may be a problem with some of the software components we're using (it could be a bug in that). They don't know, so you've got to be a generalist and good enough at problem solving that you can narrow down where the problem's occurring, isolate it, and either find them a workaround—not if, definitely, find them a workaround to get them going again—and then report the bug, or fix the bug, or do what's necessary to make sure the problem doesn't come up again.

—ANDREW PEARCE

Even more than in film, programming is an integral part of the game development process. Every piece of artwork in a game is controlled by logic generated by the programming team. Game programmers write the AI (artificial intelligence) that makes characters in a game behave a certain way, and they also often write rendering tools and code that incorporates the elements of art and animation. There are a number of specialized programming positions in the game world, as there are in films. Some of the areas in which programmers specialize include the game AI, user interface, the rendering and graphics system, asset and data management, and the audio systems.

ELECTRONIC ARTS (REDWOOD CITY, CALIF.): ANIMATION SOFTWARE ENGINEER

You will be involved with all of the animations aspects of the project. Position responsibilities include: Designing, creating, and optimizing core animation components and related tools for console and PC platforms; working closely with animators and AI software engineers to ensure extremely high-quality animation.

Required Skills Proficiency with C++ (Visual C++ or Visual .NET recommended). Experience in object-oriented design and implementation. Demonstrated knowledge of good software engineering practices. Bachelor's degree or higher in Computer Science. Good communication and writing skills. Be an avid gamer with a passion for creating A+ sports titles. Two or more years of experience working in video games or a CG-related field. Experience in current animation techniques including knowledge of multidimensional blending, character skeletons, character models/weighting, basic linear algebra, and good knowledge of quaternions. Excellent problem solving skills. Able to support customers within a large team environment in quick and professional manner.

And of course, we want self-starters who can work with others in a team-oriented environment as well as independently.

Assets Prior experience shipping a console product (PS2, GameCube, or Xbox). Strong math skills. Experience with memory management and code optimizations. Leadership experience and skills.

Requirements Skills: C++. Expertise: Software Engineer-Animation. Education: Bachelors or equivalent work experience.

Management Jobs

With any group of workers, you will certainly need management. This isn't the top-level management who make the decisions on how to run the company, but the managers who deal with the artists directly. Film, television, and the game industries all use them and they have similar functions in each.

Producers and Coordinators

Film and television studios and boutiques all have a need for people who interact with their clients, directors, executives, and the artists. While it is true their work is not hands-on as far as creating CG, without the talents of these people, nothing would ever get done.

Coordinators schedule artists and freelancers to keep the production running smoothly and on time. They frequently create and update shot lists, as well as keep track of the work completed and the work that still needs to be done. They do this by sustaining a running dialogue with all the artists in their scope of work. They often report to the producers and are usually hired from the ranks of eager production assistants.

Producers, who usually have had years of coordinating experience, are used in film, television, and games. The title of producer is used loosely in Hollywood, but it essentially refers to people who make things get done and appropriate the resources to do so. Producers interact with the clients: TV commercial directors or ad agency execs, the CG supervisor of a big film, the publisher of a game title, and so on. Producers make sure a production has what it needs to deliver quality on time and under budget.

Within the gaming industry specifically, there are two jobs that often catch the attention of game fanatics: game designer and game producer. However, these jobs are not what many novices in the industry would assume. While a game designer is the architect of a game and its logic and game-play and may contribute to the decisions about how the game should look, a game designer is rarely directly involved with the *graphic design* of the game. This is the province of the art director and other artists. The game producer is a manager whose job it is to get a game made on budget and on schedule and is also the marketing manager and point person for communications with the publisher and other players who hold the purse strings.

Game Designer

The game designer is analogous to the script writer and director in a movie. The game designer's direction determines how the game will be played out, the puzzles the players will have to solve, and the other essential elements of the game. The game designer may be involved in deciding the look and feel of the game and is also likely to be involved in the logic behind the game's AI. The game designer needs a keen understanding of game-play and must know what competing games are out there. Game designers must also have a sense of story scripting and game logic. They often have an engineering background, since they manage the entire creative team, beginning with the engineers whose AI system is at the heart of the game-play.

Primarily, however, game designers need to be fanatically devoted to games, have a long history playing and studying games, and be able to effectively conceptualize and manage a game to completion.

Here's a job description for a game designer for Sammy Studios, a game company near the beach north of San Diego:

SAMMY STUDIOS (CARLSBAD, CALIF.): LEAD GAME DESIGNER
Established in 2002 and headquartered in coastal Carlsbad, California, Sammy Studios is a new publisher of video games for PS2, GameCube, and Xbox video game systems. A subsidiary of Tokyo-based amusement giant Sammy Corporation, Sammy Studios is undertaking a major recruitment drive for its new 47,000-square-foot facility.

Description Responsible for implementing the vision of a next-generation game title for PS2, GameCube, and Xbox.

Required Experience: Minimum 5 years game industry experience with a proven track record of a successful published first person shooter or action/adventure games in a Lead

Designer capacity. Experience in designing and developing games for console systems in a collaborative environment. Experience in managing teams.

Required Skills Proven ability to create and direct game production at the interface, features, story content, and engineering level. Ability to establish design schedules, create working design documents and ensure that prototypes are developed. Proven success in defining the creative vision and fun factor of a game while executing design and working through design revisions. Strong game literacy in console games.

Bonus Skills Fluency with 3D modeling software, Maya experience preferred. Development familiarity with Renderware. Familiarity with scripting and debugging tools. Experience creating new intellectual property, including characters, storylines, and game-play mechanics. Literacy in PC games, board games, and other game forms a plus. Film, TV, or animation experience a plus. Art or architecture experience a plus. Programming experience a plus.

Game Producer

The producer of a game is the game's project manager. The producer coordinates the efforts of the game designer and the art and engineering teams. Occasionally, multiple producers are involved in the same game, with the art producer managing the art team, the technical producer managing the engineers, and the senior producer managing everybody.

Typically, a producer is a person with technical expertise. A technical producer needs many years experience as an engineer, and an art producer needs years in the trenches making art. All producers need managerial know-how (project management, budgeting, and team leadership skills are all part of this job). The producer is the team's point man in marketing decisions and represents the team to the publisher, upper management, investors, and the press. Producers will spend as much time in meetings, Microsoft Project, and Bugzilla as they will looking at the actual game in progress.

CRYTEK (COBURG, GERMANY): TECHNICAL PRODUCER

Crytek is an interactive entertainment development company located in Coburg, Germany. With our cutting-edge 3D-Game Technologies such as the CryENGINE and Polybump, we're dedicated in creating exceptionally high-quality video games for all the major platforms! We are currently working with Ubisoft in the upcoming hit title Far Cry!

The Technical Producer has the responsibility for taking a Development team through all phases of development, including project scheduling, defining and communicating vision, motivation, and team-development. He works close together with other Producers and other Management to ensure AAA Game-Projects.

Requirements 5+ years experience in Video Game Industry as a Lead Programmer. Successful track record in the development of 3+ high profile entertainment software products. Exceptional writing and oral team-communication skills. Strong leadership, people/staff development skills. Excellent understanding of C++ and other multiple programming languages. A high sense of creativity and practicality. The ability to work under tight deadlines. Knowledge of all areas of game-development from inception to gold. Enthusiastic, positive, team oriented, and organized with a hunger for success. Bachelor's degree in Computer Science or equivalent thereof.

Responsibilities Creating project plans for short and long term development projects. Preparing accurate and reasonable project budgets. Responsible for documentation, quality and testing procedures. Coordinate and Manage aspects of game-development cycles.

Writing marketing and promotional documentation. Liaising with international publishers as well as outside vendors. Update team-departments about plans and development schedules to ensure deadlines are met. Daily interaction with artists, programmers, and designers.

Other 3D Jobs

Film, television, and game jobs might have the most glamorous image in the 3D and effects world, but they're by no means the only source of jobs. As more artists are being trained to work in 3D, more traditional consumers of graphics are turning to 3D for its unique advantages in animation, illustration, and visualization. This section features a number of jobs you might not have considered: courtroom animation, information graphics, print illustration, presentation, architectural visualization, and industrial design product visualization. Even gambling and amusement park entertainment are areas that are only beginning to tap into the creative possibilities of 3D and effects. An artist with entrepreneurial and adventurous spirit might find that these job markets hold untapped veins of opportunity for employment.

Courtroom (Forensic) Animation

Forensic animators provide animations for courtroom presentations. The emphasis in forensic animation is on realism—not in terms of rendering, which is often rudimentary, but in terms of accuracy of simulation with a given set of facts. Courtroom animators frequently animate subjects such as automobile and airplane accidents, medical procedures, and other liability-related subjects.

If a lawyer is going to prove to a jury that an accident was caused by driver A crashing into driver B, then the lawyer needs to be able to say that the simulated accident the jury is watching on the screen was created by mathematical measurements and an accurate physical model of the events that transpired.

The forensic animator needs the essential skills of a previz artist: the ability to model and animate characters and vehicles with realistic timing and good camera work. It's also very helpful to have command of dynamics, soft- and hard-body collisions, expressions for animating objects based on mathematical formulas, and tools such as Motional Realms' ReelMotion that are specifically designed for creating simulation animation.

One of the authors had a potential client ask him if he could model an airplane with plus or minus an inch of accuracy if the client would provide point-cloud scan data from an actual aircraft. The client had a legal firm and needed to show that a propeller could have impacted the airplane's fuselage when the wing deformed for a pending case. However, the strength of the client's legal argument would depend on whether he could show that the 3D simulation was physically accurate, based on the actual dimensions of an existing airplane. Unfortunately the resolution of the point-cloud data was too low for the model to be that accurate for the client.

Architectural Visualization

While architecture firms now do much of their work in software that works in both 2D and 3D, the architectural design process is primarily focused on producing working drawings and management data that is used in project management and construction. To architects focused on creating working drawings, the creation of photo-realistic images is often an afterthought.

But many architectural firms now employ 3D and effects specialists in house or as contractors to produce realistic 3D renderings that help the firms sell their designs.

Having experience in architecture is immensely helpful in this field since you're likely to understand construction and materials, as well as lighting, landscaping, and other issues that go into making high-quality architectural renderings. Such experience also means you'll be able to interpret drawings and architectural symbols. Technically, you'll need to be good at architectural and prop modeling, texture mapping, lighting, and rendering—in particular rendering with radiosity and HDRI (High Dynamic Range Images). Many architecture firms prefer hand-painted renderings to the hard-edged, CG look so often produced by 3D artists with poor artistic skills, so if you want to sell your services in this field, learn to produce really great looking 3D renderings that are either truly photorealistic, or manipulated with tools like Photoshop and Painter to have a more natural, hand-rendered look.

This is one field where the ability to produce fine-quality large-format prints of renderings will really pay off, since this is the format architects will use to present and display their work.

BALLENA TECH. (SEATTLE, WASH.): 3D ARCHITECTURAL MODELER

Ballena Tech. is the leader in visualizations of architectural facilities via the Internet. We are looking for future 3D modelers, which possess the ability to create 3D architectural models from video and still photographs.

Hiring Criteria All work is in-house (Seattle, Washington, U.S.A.). Ability to model from video and still photographs while keeping scale and perspective. Self motivated. Proficient in 3DSMax 4+. Proficient in Photoshop 5+. Contract positions only. Wage depends on experience and performance.

Please send resumes and sample images. Make sample images less than 1MB! We don't need your whole demo reel!

Industrial Design

Unlike effects artists, industrial designers are concerned with designing things that will actually be made into products, and as such, they need a special set of skills. An industrial designer is part inventor, part stylist, and part engineer. Not only does the designer create objects in a way that solves a particular need, but the designs must be attractive and incorporate the engineering that makes the product feasible to manufacture. Surprisingly, the modeling and rendering tools used by industrial designers are often similar to, and sometimes the same as, those used by 3D and effects artists.

Tools like Studio Tools, Proform, and Rhinoceros are used to model designs, which are then rendered for presentation and exported into CAD systems for producing working drawings or into computer-aided manufacturing (CAM) systems for producing actual molds and prototypes for the working designs.

Here's an industrial design job working for my favorite boat manufacturer.

BRUNSWICK BOAT, BOSTON WHALER (EDGEWATER, FLORIDA): INDUSTRIAL DESIGNER

Summary Boston Whaler, Inc., a manufacturer of high-quality boats, located in East Central Florida, has an immediate opening for an Industrial Designer. Minimum of 2 years experience in the marine industry. Degree required, BS in Industrial Design preferred.

Responsibilities Candidate would be responsible for developing new products, designing and styling ergonomics in the form of two and three-dimensional drawings, and maintaining styling through 3D modeling. Would interact with all areas of product development to ensure marketability, manufacturing ability, and product image. Coordinate with Marketing and Sales input into design objectives, Upholstery styling, graphic layouts, and development of console to include layouts and styling as well as the development of hardtops and T-tops and all rails.

Military/Aerospace Simulation

The military and aerospace industry is a huge consumer of 3D animation and simulation. The branches of the military use real-time 3D game systems, not unlike your favorite first-person shooter (see Figure 2.2), to train personnel in the use of military equipment and to handle tactical situations.

3D modeling and illustration is often used to document the endless array of equipment used by the armed forces, and the military industry's PR machine churns out illustrations and diagrams for ready consumption by the popular media. Most of the money in military is in the private sector—the countless makers of electronics, aircraft, vehicles, and weaponry—and all of these companies love to produce sexy 3D illustrations and animations of their products in action.

The following ad was posted by Raython, a major military manufacturer. Note that all military-related jobs specify the level of security clearance required. Sorry, but chances are slim that you'll get to put "Top Secret" on your ID badge.

RAYTHEON (LOS ANGELES, CALIF.): 3D MODELING AND ANIMATION

Responsibilities For this part-time position, we are seeking a graphics professional who is highly proficient in realistic 3D modeling and animation to produce stunning conceptual realizations of technical projects. This individual will create broadcast-quality videos displaying the kind of animation talent seen in big-budget productions.

Will specifically use advanced forms of technical modeling, landscape modeling, texturing, composition and lighting, timeline- and physics-based animation, atmospheric particle effects, pyrotechnic effects, dynamics modeling, coding of custom shaders, and other custom scripting.

Position Part-Time

Security Clearance Required None

Positions at Raytheon may require U.S. citizenship for purposes of obtaining clearances. Additional clearances may also be required from the DoD.

Required Skills Broadcast-quality video portfolio displaying the kind of animation talent seen in big-budget productions. LightWave and/or Maya (and advanced plug-in packages), Photoshop. After Effects (or equivalent). FinalCut Pro and/or Avid.

Desired Skills/Experience Portfolio work representing other artistic ability (such as static illustration and/or design) would also be helpful.

Print Illustration and Graphic Design

As 3D becomes more mainstream, consumers of print media, primarily companies with products to sell, are looking for print designers with 3D skills. 3D is an ideal tool for illustration and information graphics, and it's popping up in all sorts of unusual places, such as advertisements for electric toothbrushes and info-graphics for annual reports.

Not only is there demand for 3D in advertising and brochures, but the demand for 3D in the popular media has also mushroomed. For example, CNN.com posted real-time 3D models of aircraft and weaponry during America's recent assault on Iraq, and it's impossible to open an issue of *Newsweek* or *Time* without being assaulted by 3D illustrations of the technical headline du jour. One of the authors recently created roughly 40 3D illustrations of shipping containers for a book publisher that sells its books exclusively to customers in the international shipping industry.

Here's an ad from one of the business-oriented clients.

AQUENT (AN EMPLOYMENT AGENCY): CENTRAL-PRINT/3D GRAPHIC DESIGNER

Our client, a prestigious pharmaceutical company in the Princeton area, is seeking a Print Graphic Designer with 3D skills for an ongoing, full-time, contract position.

We are looking for an experienced, talented Print Graphic Designer who also has good 3D design and production skills. A minimum of 3 years experience is expected.

The position is 80 percent Print design, with 3D projects arising intermittently, so any candidate MUST possess a strong print portfolio. Any candidate should have samples of brochures, direct mail, sales slicks, marketing kits, and related collateral in their portfolio, along with samples of 3D work. Please, no relocation or 3rd-party requests. This is a great growth opportunity for the right person.

Required Qualifications: 3D design and production skills, particularly with LightWave. Candidates should also have proven skills in QuarkXPress, and a minimum of 3 years experience is expected.

Summary

3D is not all about art. You can be an engineer, or a very technically oriented person with a good eye, or you can be an adept manager with a gift for games or money matters, and still play a vital role in the 3D and effects production process. 3D is not all about film and games, either. As the tools become better and more accessible to more people, 3D is becoming a mainstream tool for illustration, visualization, presentation, and marketing, across a huge segment of the business and media world.

The next chapter will explain the details of many of the skills you'll need to pursue these jobs, as well as tell you where and how you can acquire the knowledge you need.

CHAPTER 3

What To Learn

Knowing the job descriptions in 3D and effects described in the first two chapters can help you find the kind of job that fits your skills and interests. Perusing the descriptions and sample listings, you might have realized that there are skills you lack.

This chapter explains the skills involved in 3D and effects and gives you direction on how to acquire them. We first discuss the groundwork of an arts education, then move on to highly technical, engineering-type skills, and then describe specific 3D skills—in particular, using Maya—that you'll need for any of the jobs where 3D is the major focus of your work.

- **Core art and technical skills**
- **3D-specific skills**
- **Other skills**

Fundamental Skills

The first thing you must accept about 3D design, graphics, and effects is that it's an art form. The ultimate product of your work will be images, film, or interactive media, made to inform, entertain, or move the emotions of an audience of hundreds, thousands, or millions of viewers. The second thing you must accept about 3D is that it involves many highly technical skills and aptitudes tied to the bane and benefactor of the modern commercial artist's existence: the computer. It is these fundamental characteristics of 3D that attract and hold a special kind of person: the tinkerer with a good eye, the visual storyteller with a gift for spatial complexity, the inventor with a keen sense of line and color. 3D design appeals to the same people who might have been cathedral architects or bridge builders in another time, and some of these people are Leonardo da Vincis of the twenty-first century.

Does that mean everyone doing 3D is a Renaissance genius? Alas, *hardly*. But, to be truly good at 3D, you have to see with your right brain while still moving fluidly in the left-brained world of the digital medium. Some people are better at this than others.

Can't tell your left brain from your right brain? According to Dr. Betty Edwards, author of perennial bestseller *The New Drawing on the Right Side of the Brain*, the mind is split down the middle functionally, as well as literally. The right side is the part that's good at seeing and communicating visually. The left brain, which often dominates, is all business and is preoccupied with processing the verbal and symbolic information that's so prevalent in the use of computers. Because our left brains dominate our daily life, they also tend to control how we draw, resulting in symbolic rather than realistic representations of what we see. Edwards' fascinating, practical book provides exercises to help you learn to switch from left-brain mode to right-brain mode, more or less on demand. It's a great book for 3D artists who have to make this switch all day long.

Undoubtedly, the best way to learn to see with your right brain and still function with your left is to spend a considerable amount of time doing both. For students, that means getting a thorough education in visual arts, with a liberal dose of computer skills thrown into the mix. Listen to Brian Freisinger, lead 3D modeler at ESC Entertainment, who built many of the digital humans, props, and sets for *The Matrix* movies:

I hear people bitch when they go to art school, "I'm not going to take drawing classes; I'm going to be on the computer." But it's those core fundamentals, basic design skills—you know what, the software changes, the pipeline changes; everything changes, but your core skills, that's what you build off of. If you built your career on being an expert in this one software package, and all its ins and outs, what happens if that software company goes out of business next year, and the next thing you know, you've got to start again. But not if you have this core of understanding things, you spread yourself out a little bit.

You don't have to be a programmer, but take a Perl class, or read a book. Take a drawing class, or read a book. Be broad-based in the fundamentals. When you understand the principle concepts of how something works—like on the core level, how design works and composition works and how things are put together—for modeling, that's the basis of it. And for software, if you just understand the basics of how the software works, you don't have to understand everything, not how to program it, just the basics, you can pick the other stuff up very quick because you know what you're looking for.

—*BRIAN FREISINGER*

Brian is one of many artists interviewed who repeatedly emphasized that the most important part of preparing for a job in 3D is to master the fundamentals of art.

Art Fundamentals

A basic education in fine art includes courses in art history, film history, drawing, painting, sculpture, architecture, and photography. More specialized areas of instruction include graphic design, storyboarding, character design, character animation, and cinematography. Although all of these studies are valuable and teach skills that will stay with you throughout an art career, many artists get only a fraction of this scope in their education. What they all get, if they're going to have a prayer of success, is an understanding of the fundamental aspects of art: line, color, composition, form, and proportion.

Drawing

Drawing is a fundamental skill for many 3D artists, especially at the concept art stage. Concept artists in games and film draw characters, props, and environments for nearly every element that makes it into production. Environment artists produce working drawings of their levels before they start working on 3D models. Character artists produce drawings of characters in multiple poses, with many different expressions, before modelers take on the task of molding the character into 3D. Many managers cite a preference for hiring professional illustrators who are not only good at communicating design internally, but who can produce the fine-looking artwork that sells a project or concept to clients. The theory goes that if an artist can conceptualize and then actualize in drawings, they will take to CG much easier than those not experienced with drawing.

Figure 3.1

Storyboards sets the tone and plan for a production and are important to the overall production as well as to the creative process.

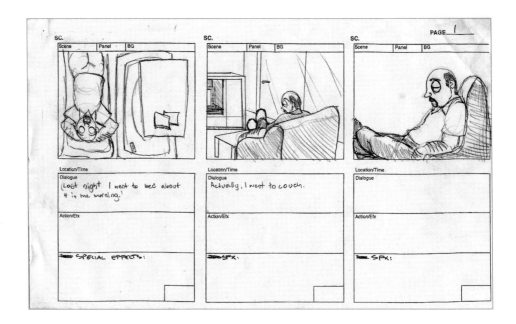

Figure 3.1

Storyboards sets the tone and plan for a production and are important to the overall production as well as to the creative process.

Storyboarding

Storyboard artists produce comic book-style drawings to plot out the elements of a shot or a scene. Storyboards can range from very simplistic barely-better-than-stick-figure drawings that simply block out action, elements, and camera moves in a sequence to highly stylized artwork that gives a strong impression of key emotional changes and poses that a character will go through (see Figure 3.1). Storyboards are a dead giveaway that you're in a real-live animation studio.

Painting

Painting is even a more common requirement than drawing in 3D art departments. Concept artists paint characters and scenery to develop color schemes and set the tone for visual environments. In games, the job description for 3D artist includes painting textures, which are used on nearly every surface. Texture painting involves manipulation of photographic images such as car wheels, stone walls, or concrete, as well as painting realistic surfaces from scratch. In film work, texture painting is usually relegated to a separate department, and texture painters sometimes overlap with matte painters, who are artists skilled in painting the believable but not necessarily realistic stylized backgrounds used in many film shots. 3D painters need a good sense of color and texture and an intuitive understanding of how light interacts with surfaces (see Figure 3.2). Emmanuel Shiu, a matte artist at The Orphanage, a fast-growing effects studio in San Francisco started by former Industrial Light and Magic employees, talks about one niche for painters.

Matte painters are very much of a niche market, and to do that, you basically have to have strong painting skills, you need to be able to make a shot look like it could be in the film. The reason I don't say "realistic," is because realism is probably not exactly what they're looking for. There is no such thing as realism. Realism could be the most boring thing you ever see. So they're not looking for that. They're looking for something that could fit in a film. You could take a concept, bring that into a 3D-generated world, or a painted matte—they want to see that you can make that transition, to take a piece of concept art and make that alive.

—*EMMANUEL SHIU*

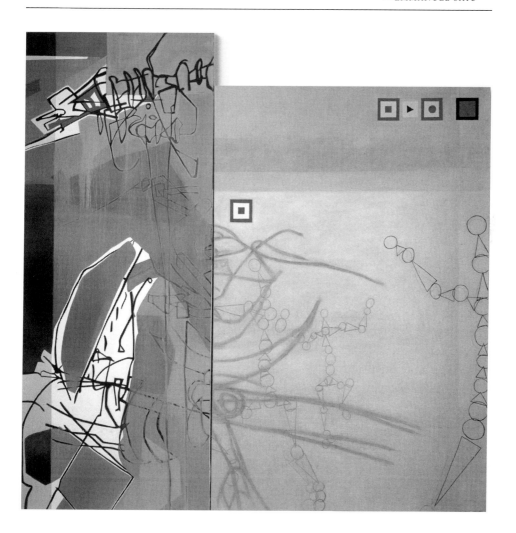

Figure 3.2

Traditional painting helps develop the artistic eye. This is a fine art painting by Kim A. Dail, 3D animator.

Sculpture

Sculpture is the closest analog in the physical world to 3D modeling and in fact, clay models, or *maquettes*, are often used as the basis for creating highly detailed CG models (Figure 3.3). Even if you exclusively produce artwork in the digital medium, modeling in clay can help you work out the problems in a 3D design.

Art departments in film effects studios in particular rely on clay sculptors to create life-like models of everything from human characters to dragons. These are then scanned using laser, optical, or mechanical 3D scanners, and the resulting meshes are converted into NURBS (nonuniform rational b-splines) or some other geometry suitable for 3D animation. Related to sculpture, practical modeling—the building of architectural, industrial, or prop models—often accompanies the creation of CG versions of the same forms.

Figure 3.3

Sculpting abilities will help you understand modeling in CG. This is a maquette sculpture of a proposed CG character by Juan Gutierrez, graduate of Art Institute of California, Los Angeles.

Fashion Design

Character artists are often challenged to invent wardrobes for their virtual characters, and nothing serves this end better than an understanding of fashion design through the ages. If you can confidently reproduce a realistic Victorian dressing gown, the chances are you can probably come up with a convincing cape and collar for the Prince of Zorg. On the other hand, if your knowledge of wardrobe is limited to hip-huggers and T-shirts, your ability to concoct interesting wardrobes will be limited. Animators and effects artists will also benefit from learning how fabric moves and behaves on a human form.

Cinematography and Photography

The art of film is an essential component of most 3D production environments. In film work, an understanding of camera angles, screen direction, camera moves, lens selection, and effects is essential. If a sequence supervisor asks for a dolly or a tracking shot, a medium shot or a close-up, you'll be expected to know what the difference is and how to do them. If a shot calls for more depth of field, you'll have to know how to achieve that. Similarly, if you're working in a studio that produces effects for many different clients who may work in different formats, you'll have to understand aspect ratios, frame rates, and other essential aspects of each medium. Previsualization artists work as virtual directors, and their work is directly comparable to that of a director who works behind a camera. But even 3D animators working on real-time cinematics for games need to be able to direct and cut a sequence in much the same way as a director and editor. Evan Pontoriero discusses how cinematography applies to his job of "layout" or "previsualization" at Pixar:

A lot of it is understanding composition, which you're taught in design school or art school. Some of it's just being someone who enjoys film. If you studied film and you understand good cinematography and film, just by watching you can get a grasp for it because a lot of directors just cut up pieces of other films together to come up with their films: they buy their cinematography from other films. So no, you don't need to go to film school necessarily, although I think it would help...There's a lot of stuff that can be learned on the job.

—EVAN PONTORIERO

Photography also teaches you a great deal about lighting and how to see form, space, and shadow (Figure 3.4). Having a basic grasp of how light functions in addition to composition, as Evan Pontoriero mentions, is an invaluable asset to a 3D artist.

Figure 3.4

Photography is a great way to hone composition and lighting skills. This fine art photography is by Stephen M. McClure, 3D animator.

Character Animation

Character animation is an art form unto itself, and the classic reference is *The Illusion of Life: Disney Animation* by legendary Walt Disney animators Frank Thomas and Ollie Johnston. These artists, along with a handful of others at the Disney studio, invented not only the art form of animation as it is known today, but the language to describe what they had made. The 12 fundamental principles that these animators described have become the golden rules for all character animators:

1. Squash and stretch

2. Anticipation

3. Staging

4. Straight-ahead action and pose-to-pose

5. Follow through and overlapping action

6. Slow in and slow out

7. Arcs

8. Secondary action

9. Timing

10. Exaggeration

11. Solid drawing

12. Appeal

Much has been written to add to these basic principles and the descriptions that Thomas and Johnston provided, but these new rules are really just amendments and nuances that contribute to an understanding of their original work. While character animators will work with the principles of animation every day, learning the fundamentals will help all 3D artists better appreciate and understand the art form they work in. Concept artists, modelers, character technical directors, and effects artists all dip into this well of understanding whenever they work with characters. If you're planning to be part of an art team—and you will be, unless you're uniquely equipped to produce film and games in total isolation—knowing the rules of animation will make you far more useful when it's your turn to constructively criticize what you see in dailies.

Dailies are a ritual in almost every animation environment. Most film effects studios have a theater where artists gather on a daily basis to view and critique their peers' work in progress. While your work is going to have to survive their scrutiny, the real key to surviving dailies is to learn to form and express a constructive opinion about everything you see because sooner or later you're going to be asked what you like about a shot and why.

YOU NEED CHARACTER

A mistake that students and inexperienced animators often make is they plan their animations around the physical actions of a character without thinking of the character's motivation: *why* would it move? They focus more on what the character does and what looks cool, such as a bullet-time fight scene (which is getting cliché), or a John Woo "shooting two pistols while flying over a table in slow motion" move. But this sort of thinking overlooks a very big part of character animation: *character*. Simply making your character move around is not enough; you need to have motivation and emotion to drive the character's motions. Without that, you'll do your animation a great disservice. As many character animation studios will agree, recruiters look for emotion in character work, not just body movement. Plan your animations to scratch deeper than the surface. Have a clear motivation for your movements, and you'll find your animation much the better for it.

Dance and Theater

Understanding how a human body moves and communicates a character's thoughts, and understanding the difference between action and acting are essential to creating interesting character animation. The ability to act, and to move in interesting ways, can even play an important role in how an artist works with motion capture, as discussed by Sean Miller of Sammy Studios:

It comes in handy in a number of senses. When you want to create some reference motion, you could get in there and direct the motion capture shoot—that's where having the motion capture facility in-house is helpful—or you could even get in the suit and act the motion out yourself. Whether that becomes the final motion that's used in the game, it's a terrific tool for you to be able to realize it in your final art. If you have an animator that can't move that doesn't know how to move his body, when he does the animation a lot times he's going to be basing it on how he thinks the body moves. So, if they're stiff, their animations will very often be stiff. Even in terms of motion capture, if you can't recognize good motion and clean poses, you're not going to be able to direct a motion capture shoot to get the kind of data that's going to be useful to you.

—SEAN MILLER

Technical Fundamentals

3D and effects are part art and part science. The science part is mostly math: algebra, trigonometry, geometry, and physics. But the discipline also requires an understanding of a variety of technologies and tools that help achieve the ends of the 3D process: scripting and programming, computer networking and management, and a variety of tools for specialized work such as motion capture and match moving.

You don't have to be a mathematician to do some kinds of 3D work, but you do if you want to really master the form. 3D modelers use math to create accurate forms and to build mechanical objects whose proportions are correct for animation; texture painters use mathematical relationships to control the appearance of surfaces; animators use math to calculate the timing of motion; and effects artists and technical directors use math for everything from scripting to rigging to driving animation with physics-based expressions.

Math

Algebra, trigonometry, and geometry are fundamental math in 3D design and effects. For example,

```
You are modeling an airplane's n-bladed propeller by creating a single
blade, then duplicating it around the x-axis n-1 times. How many degrees of
rotation (a) do you need for each of the copies?
```

> The answer is that the angle (a) is equal to 360 divided by the number of copies: (*a=360/n*).

The following is a basic expression in Maya that causes a vehicle's wheels to rotate at the proper speed, no matter how fast the car travels across the ground. (Without this expression, it would be very difficult to animate the car without the wheels sliding unnaturally across the ground's surface, especially as the speed of the car changes.) To write this expression, you have to know that:

- The circumference of the wheel is equal to 2πR, where R is the radius of the wheel.
- The number of rotations of the wheel is equal to the distance traveled by the car divided the wheel's circumference, and
- The angle of rotation is the number of rotations times 360 degrees.

The resulting Maya expression looks like this:

```
WheelRadius=1.5;
$Pi=3.14159;
Wheel.rotateX=360*CarBody.translateZ/(2*($Pi)*WheelRadius);
```

The good news is that such an expression is easy to set up once you know the math. The bad news is that this equation barely scratches the surface of what's possible with expressions. For example, you might create an expression to generate wind-blown particles from the crest of a wave when the wave's height (generated by a randomized sine function in another expression) exceeds a certain value. A second expression could control the speed of particles and the rate of the particle emission, based on the speed of the wind. Once these expressions are in place, you have only to tell the system how big to make the waves and how hard the wind should blow, and voilà, you have foamy, wind-swept waves that change with the weather.

Never mind how long it takes for a plane to fly from London to Paris in a head wind, scripting dynamics and effects is one place where you'll really need that math class you may be tempted to sleep through.

Physics

Physics are also part of the art of animation: the timing and weight of characters, the inertia of follow-through, and slow-in, slow-out are all expressions of physical laws. Effects animators use physics to define the action of objects as they react to world forces and the interaction of particles as they move through space. Physics are also a necessary component of game-play in most 3D games, and whether they are applied through a game physics API, such as Havok, or through custom programming, game engineers must have a basic understanding of how physical rules apply.

Among all of the laws of physics, few are more fundamental to the art of animation and effects than those discovered by Sir Isaac Newton, paraphrased here:

1. A particle remains at rest or continues to move in a straight line at constant speed as long as there is no opposing force.

2. The acceleration of an object is proportional to the force acting on it and is in the direction of this force.

3. For every action, there is an equal reaction in the opposite direction.

In 3D, physics are used in particle systems, cloth and other soft and hard-body dynamics, collision effects, and even "ragdoll" effects in the animation of characters. Of course, with dynamic effects such as particle systems and fluids in motion, the physics become increasingly complex, and simple laws are insufficient to handle the orderly chaos of events such as tornados and storms at sea.

Let's Get Physics-al

Having a sense of physics and how objects move in relation to each other and the world can help you make the transition into animating not just effects, but objects and even character motion. We all have an inate sense of the world of motion around us. As an audience member, you can see mistakes or inconsistencies in animated motion very easily because you've been an observer of natural movement your entire life.

However, creating that motion as an animator is much more difficult. Getting a good understanding of the basic tenants of physics will really help your animation, and therefore your chances of landing work. If you can distance yourself from your animation and watch it as an objective member of an audience (as opposed to subjectively watching your own work), you'll see areas you can improve upon immediately. Hey, we're not ragging on your work, but it's true. If you have even a base understanding of physics, you'll be much better equipped to translate problems you see into tenable, quantitative solutions.

Computer Science and Engineering

If you want to be a game programmer, pipeline engineer, or even a shader writer (those who write the mathematical code controlling the way exotic surfaces, such as oil on water, molten glass, or shimmering fish skin, are rendered) you'll need a degree in computer science or equivalent experience. This prepares you for the logic of programming and gives you the essential technical skills, such as programming in C and C++, Perl, Python, and so on.

Here Andrew Pearce talks about how a programmer can use his or her skills to create tools for CG creation, and how knowing how that kind of programming works can help you as an artist understand the world of CG:

> *To write a basic renderer is not that hard. To write a raytracer is not that hard. Writing a fast one, writing one that does all the things it needs to do, like motion blur, depth of field, that's harder. But write a basic ray tracer—people have written a basic ray tracer on a business card, not a great one, not a fast one, but a ray tracer—just to understand the problems that are encountered in rendering. Because if you're going into 3D that's the end result…It's going to make you understand the hierarchy of the scene, how to decompose that, how to put objects in the right place, it's going to teach you world space versus object space versus camera space, how textures are applied and filtered, how pixels are filtered, and how antialiasing is done, and all that stuff is going to be very, very important.*
>
> *—ANDREW PEARCE*

Project and Team Management

If you're an undergraduate art student, the odds are slim that you're going to need a great deal of management skills in your first job. Any project management you do need to perform, as with a heavy school load, will primarily be an exercise in time management. But if you're switching jobs and hoping to land a position with more responsibility (and perhaps a bigger paycheck) there's a good chance you'll be asked to take on a more formal management role. In this case, it will serve you well to have some training in, or at least to study, basic management. This will include issues such as directing employees, managing schedules, and preparing budgets. Much of management is common sense applied to everyday problems, but sometimes solutions aren't so obvious. Basic training in management can help you understand what you need to accomplish in this role, as Andrew Pearce points out:

> *Take at least some course in how to manage people. Because as much as that's against our totally antisocial nature, being engineers, it is of paramount importance to understand that different individuals need to be treated differently and that your behavior—your natural behavior—is probably not good management style. That's probably one of the hardest things that I fight against, is know your own nature. Your job as a manager is not to control the people who are reporting to you. It's to guide and set priorities and to make sure that they are enabled to do their job, that you are removing obstacles for them.*
>
> *—ANDREW PEARCE*

DIFF'RENT STROKES FOR DIFF'RENT FOLKS

Management in this industry requires finely honed people skills, since you're apt to run into a wide variety of personalities in the profession. There is a bit of truth to the cliché that creative people in Hollywood and the games biz are a bit outside the mainstream. Being a highly creative person in one of the toughest industries on our blue and green little planet is not easy. It's a tough, demanding business, and requires a strong stomach and an unbendable will. To that end we say, it takes all kinds!

As a manager of artists and a conduit of information from supervisors, directors, and clients, you have the unenviable task of delegating and corralling a group of people who have strong personalities and stronger opinions. That takes stamina, perseverance, and an ability to politic. All those folks who rough it for a month on the CBS show *Survivor* would be the first ones voted out of the production studio.

3D Graphics Skills

Even though a fundamental education in art or engineering will take you further in this business than a mastery of any one 3D program, this *is* a book about 3D and effects, so let's discuss the actual 3D skills that are at the heart of 3D graphics jobs. There are hundreds of specific things you can learn, so we'll leave the details to other books, but the 3D basics include:

- Modeling
- Texturing and shading
- Lighting
- Animation
- Technical direction
- Rendering

Modeling

3D modeling is the creation of the wireframe representations of 3D objects. These can be as simple as a box representing a room or as complex as a human character with every detail, down to fingernails and eyelashes, faithfully represented. For every 3D software package, there are tens or even hundreds of modeling tools specialized for creating various types of shapes, but there are essentially three modeling technologies in widespread use today: polygonal, NURBS, and subdivision surfaces (Figure 3.5).

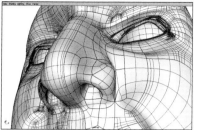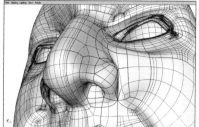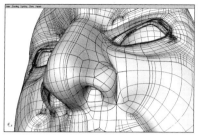

Figure 3.5

Three heads are better than one. The same head shown (left to right) in NURBS, subdivision (sub-D) surfaces, and polygons. Note that the NURBS model still needs a lot of rebuilding to get the mesh down to a manageable size; the sub-D surface is almost automatically clean and has dialable resolution; the polygon surface is lightweight but coarse.

Games use polygonal models exclusively. A polygon mesh, in its simplest form, is made of nothing but triangles. To add more resolution or detail to a model, you simply use smaller triangles. All 3D rendering hardware uses triangulated meshes as its ultimate data format, so this is the fastest and most efficient way to deliver geometry to a game. Although triangle meshes are very simple, working with them is not. For example, there's nothing particularly intuitive about defining the shape of a human with a bunch of triangles. This is especially true when you have to carefully limit the total number of polygons in a mesh, as you do in a real-time 3D game. Probably the most essential skill to building 3D models in polygons is learning to make the most of the available polygon budget and to optimize the appearance of low-poly surfaces to make the most of what you've got.

For many years, NURBS (nonuniform rational b-splines) were considered the standard modeling format for film—and in many studios, they still are. NURBS excel in their capability to accurately define curves and surfaces containing complex compound curves. NURBS are also very intuitive for texture mapping. The down side to NURBS is that they're a digital equivalent of rubber sheets. While you can stitch multiple sheets together to make surfaces that are too complicated to represent with a single sheet, it's sometimes impossible to hide these stitched edges, particularly if the surface goes through dramatic deformations. Although to some extent NURBS are resolution independent—meaning you can view them from any distance and still see a smooth, unfaceted skin—in practice, NURBS surfaces are displayed using *approximation*, which can break down, showing holes or seams when you get too close.

Subdivision (sub-D) surfaces are the latest development in modeling methods used in games, television, and films. They work by fitting a smooth NURBS-like surface to a coarse polygonal cage. This lets you model with polygons to generate realistic, seamless surfaces that avoid many of the pitfalls of NURBS, while keeping the ability to create organic shapes typical of NURBS. Studios have been relying on sub-Ds for some time, but using them to model real-world objects is a relatively novel technique. Increasingly, modelers use sub-Ds to create characters and other models for real-time games because the sub-Ds let them produce high-res models for prerendered artwork and generating normal maps, as well as low-res polygonal models for in-engine rendering. These sub-D models can also be easily converted back to polygon models for high or low poly count use.

Here's what Brian Friesinger of ESC Entertainment had to say when we asked him if subdivision surfaces modeling tool is the modeling tool of the future:

It depends on who you ask; if you ask me, yeah. For these films, everything is sub-D or poly. NURBS, while they have strengths, have a lot of limitations, and in my opinion, they're very dated. I prefer sub-Ds for everything. The argument against sub-Ds is, it's very hard to get a good UV map on them for texturing. We've got good techniques at ESC to do that. I've come up with a lot of techniques to do that, and they work really well. When you see the film [The Matrix Reloaded], hopefully you'll decide that, too. I would always prefer sub-Ds over NURBS. I started out as a NURBS modeler. As soon as I discovered sub-Ds, I said this is way cooler, way better…

If it's going to be sitting there and just looking pretty from a distance, just go with polys. The cool thing about sub-Ds is their dialable resolution. I use sub-Ds on architecture if we're going to wreck it, if I'm going to twist the metal, twist the hell out of it, sub-Ds hold up so good. You can just dial the resolution and really get that twisted metal look. You can do a lot of stuff on-the-fly. NURBS require a lot of planning, and sometimes it will lock you into a situation. Somebody comes by and says we need you to do this now. And you didn't build it to do that…. —BRIAN FRIESINGER

As a modeler in games, you'll need to know polygonal modeling techniques, and in many environments, you'll also need to know techniques for using NURBS or subdivision surfaces for creating high-resolution models. In addition, game modelers need a solid understanding of UV mapping techniques. In high-detail environments such as television or film, chances are you'll be using NURBS, subdivision surfaces and polygons almost interchangeably. The main objective is to create very realistic, believable surfaces.

HOW TO GET AHEAD IN MODELING

Modeling is often the first thing people get into when they start up with CG. Because so many people get into modeling it's a good idea to get really proficient in certain kinds of models, be they creatures, cars, humans, etc. Having a good sense of design also helps, as you're sometimes required to design parts of your own models, or even to come up with several versions of a single idea. Here having a good drawing skill will also be helpful to you.

Modelers are usually the first group of people hired for a film project, and quite a few get to stay on to texture or light if they have the proven skill for it. Being a successful modeler in film, television, or games means you have an eye for detail, a fundamental understanding of how to model with different surface types, and the ability to quickly actualize tests and designs.

Shading and Texturing

Modeling is only the first step of creating a 3D object. Shading and texturing are the steps that attach a color and surface qualities to the 3D skin. Textures are surface materials that have been painted, photographed, or otherwise pregenerated as images that are then projected or wrapped around the surface of a 3D object. Textures can be used not only for colors, but also to apply underlying surface qualities, such as specularity, transparency, bumpiness, and glow.

Shaders are the mathematical code (in Maya it also refers to the network of nodes used in texturing an object) that tells the renderer how to render a surface A shader may be as simple as a set of effects that modify the appearance of a texture—making it shiny or rough, for example—or as complicated as elaborate surface materials, such as scales, feathers, or fur, that completely replace painted textures (Figures 3.6 and 3.7).

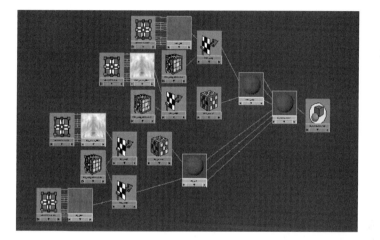

Figure 3.6

A shading network in Maya is used to create materials and textures to map to models.

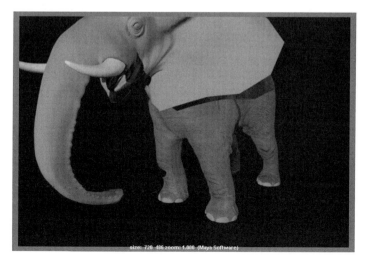

Figure 3.7

The shading network is applied to the legs and body of the elephant model.

Current games rely primarily on simple color maps, although advanced rendering engines in high-end gaming PCs and 3rd-generation consoles, like the Xbox, are allowing for the use of more sophisticated shaders and texturing effects. Already, it's common to see transparency, specularity, and bump maps in games, and future games will also feature normal maps, which simulate very detailed geometry while still using simple underlying polygonal meshes.

To work in games, you'll have to understand UV mapping (the assignment of sensible surface coordinates to a polygonal mesh that may bend and fold on itself in countless ways) and painting of textures and texture effects. You'll also have to learn how to work with lighting and to bake lighting into material textures. With the increasing prevalence of global illumination and radiosity rendering in 3D packages, it's also becoming more common to see radiosity solutions rendered and baked into texture maps.

In television and film, Mental Ray (supported by 3D packages such as Maya, SoftImage XSI, and 3ds max), and Pixar's RenderMan (also supported by Maya and SoftImage XSI), have been industry standard renderers for a number of years. Working with these renderers requires knowledge of the texture and shading techniques that work with them. For any film work, you'll need to understand how to create realistic-looking surfaces with color maps and a wide variety of effects maps on a very high resolution and detailed level. Television work tends to be somewhat more forgiving due to its lower frame resolution, though textures do need to look extremely detailed with photo-realistic flare.

You'll need to master UV mapping, projection mapping, and intrinsic NURBS mapping. And since you'll probably be dealing with different surface types, it'll be very beneficial to understand modeling techniques for polygons and subdivisions as well as NURBS.

Lighting

Lighting requires a keen eye for color and tone, as well as an understanding of the technicalities and limitations of 3D lighting systems and renderers. If you're aspiring to be a 3D lighting artist, you'll want to study photography, which is primarily a study of light and how it interacts with surfaces and film, and cinematography, which deals with lights in motion. Lighting is also an important component in the study of architecture.

KNOW YOUR TOOLS

A texture artist, more than any other CG artist, needs to know a handful of applications outside their primary 3D package. You need to know image editing techniques and programs like Fractal Painter, Photoshop, and plug-ins that allow you to paint directly on a 3D object like Deep Paint, and be good and damned fast at them too. You'll be switching back and forth between painting images and your 3D model all the time, so it's a good idea to get to know your image editing applications pretty well. The keyword here is *Photoshop*.

Lighting in 3D requires a mastery of the basic light types—directional, point, ambient, area, and spot lights—as well as an understanding of how lights interact with surfaces and the creation of shadows in 3D. Lighters should also have a firm grasp of how textures will be affected by their lights. Some lighting artists in some film studios are also asked to fix or create textures for their scenes or even to composite their shots into the live action backgrounds. Knowing color and how to get the right look for a frame is imperative to a lighting artist.

If you want to master lighting in 3D, start by turning off all ambient lights and relying on point, spot, and directional lights to illuminate your scene. It's almost impossible to create realistic or interesting lighting with any significant 3D ambient light in a scene because ambient light evenly increases the brightness of every diffuse surface, as if they were all glowing with subtle radioactivity. Once you've lit your scene with point and directional shadow casting lights, adjust the color and opacity of the shadows, and only then consider adding an ambient light to uniformly raise the values in the shadow areas, or leave out ambient lights entirely to better mimic real world light. There is no such thing as ambient light in reality.

CG AND LIGHTING

In film, lighting in CG is frequently regarded in photo-realism work as the most important part of the CG pipeline. It is lighting that will make or break a CG scene when it has to fit into a live-action background or plate. If the lighting is even slightly off from matching the real lighting of the plate, the shot is thrown because the CG is obvious. The job of a photo-real lighting artist is to make it look as if CG doesn't exist in that scene. In other words, the shot should look so realistic that you'll have a hard time convincing people that a CG worked on it at all.

In real-time 3D games, lighting effects are severely limited by game engine performance budgets, so lighting requires many creative workarounds to achieve artistically pleasing results. Lighting is often relegated to environment artists, who compensate for the limited number of live lights in any scene by prerendering scenery to bake lights and shadows into texture maps. As Emmanuel Shiu points out, knowing lighting is beneficial to games but critical to film work:

> So it's always best in the game demo, or game portfolio, to show that you're multifaceted. Maybe you're not the best at lighting, but it's good to show that you can do some lighting, so maybe they might be able to train you.

> But in film, that does not apply. They want only the best in that field. The sharpest knife. They don't care if you can do a little bit of lighting because they don't need a little bit of lighting, they need really good lighters.

> —Emmanuel Shiu

Because of the considerable complexities involved in lighting film projects, lighting is often the domain of technical directors with acute color sensibilities. When you're lighting a CG set or props, they often have to blend with live plates, and achieving lighting that matches the scene requires balancing not only the direction, color, and diffuse values of light, but the play of shadows and highlights on surfaces. Lighting is tightly intertwined with the complexities of rendering systems, and as these become more advanced, with capabilities like radiosity and global illumination, lighting also becomes more complex. For example, High Dynamic-Range Radiance Imaging (HDRI) rendering extracts incredibly realistic lighting information automatically from a scene's environment maps, but it requires painstaking preparation of an environment to achieve useful results.

Animation

Animation is the most crowded field in the whole of 3D computer graphics. It seems everyone wants to be an animator, which is understandable, given its capacity for expressive storytelling. The mechanics of animation are fundamentally not too difficult. You'll need to master the use of characters that are rigged with combinations of inverse kinematics and forward kinematics, constraints, motion graphs, and shape blending.

Few animators in film are expected to rig their own characters, so whether you can do this is wholly secondary, but if you're going to work in a smaller boutique, you may need to become proficient at setting up joint hierarchies and deformations as well. State-of-the-art characters include rigs that make their muscles and skins move and deform in realistic ways, so depending on your studio's expectations, you'll have to build such complex rigs, animate characters that use them, or both.

The real prerequisite for being an animator is an almost intuitive grasp of the fundamental principles of animation and the ability to tell a story and elicit an emotional response with animation. In short, your characters need to be first-rate actors. Some studios require a demonstrated knowledge of these skills in software such as Maya, but if you want to be an animator at Pixar, one of the premier animation studios, your technical skills and what you've done in 3D are almost an afterthought. Consider what Pixar's recruiting manager, Sangeeta Prashar, looks for in an animator's reel:

A comprehensive understanding of animation fundamentals—a good sense of weight, timing, movement, and acting ability should be reflected in the characters. Computer animation is helpful but not necessary. Your reel should also reflect a storytelling sense.

—SANGEETA PRASHAR

SO YOU WANNA BE AN ANIMATOR?

If you want to become a well-rounded animator who works on mostly physical animation (like cars, trees swaying, dancing pasta, talking cows, etc.), you should look toward the television or gaming industries first. These jobs require a well-versed ability to rig and animate your own objects (including some character work, but usually not much) and deal with some particle animation and environment effects typical of a generalist's calling.

If you want to specialize in character for film, however, you'll want to sharpen your traditional animation skills as well as CG character work. This is the hardest animation niche to get into as it's a very coveted position. Whether you're aiming for TV, games, or film, however, you will need a solid reel of nothing but character animations.

Technical Direction

Few schools teach technical direction as a course of study. The film studio technical director is typically a 3D technician with a command of both the art of 3D and the technical tools used to drive the process.

A TD needs a wide breadth and keen depth of knowledge of the entire 3D pipeline. In modeling, TDs are required to analyze and repair problem geometry, as well as to create expressions to generate geometry on-the-fly. For example, a TD might create a script to automatically generate dynamic air hoses that move in synch with an animated space creature, or to animate the displacement of surfaces to create the effect of a giant sand worm burrowing under the ground.

In texturing, a TD might be required to write a complex shader to make a metal surface appear to corrode under the influence of dripping acid or to solve a problem with tearing seams along the NURBS edges of an animated character. What it takes to be a great TD depends a lot on who you talk to and how a specific company structures the role, which makes it even more important to be an accomplished and well-rounded artist-technician. Craig Lyn, CG supervisor at London's Frame Store, wishes TDs had more artistic and technical balance.

The great failing of ILM is that they haven't been hiring enough people with an artistic background. They've been hiring a lot of people with a very technical computer sciences background. And it needs to be a balance between the two. Someone with a good eye, and also someone with a good technical background. We have TDs that are amazing artists who have someone sit there and run their shots for them. On the other hand, you have people who can write amazing programs and tools, but can't paint worth a damn. It's a hard balance between the two.

—CRAIG LYN

Andrew Pearce, Pipeline Supervisor at ESC, sees the TD as a more technical role:

It doesn't always necessarily involve scripting. We have some tools to make it more of a UI scripting. But they still have to understand what's going on in those scripts. And if they have the ability to script, it makes it easy for them because if they have something they have to do that's very specific to their shot, they can make that script. They don't have to rely on someone else to provide it for them. So the TD is really a technical position.

—*ANDREW PEARCE*

Most dynamic simulations are created by effects animators, who are essentially animation-specific TDs. Such animators create explosions, smoke, fire, and weather-system effects and are often responsible for the animation of hard surface objects, such as vehicles, which are more dependent on physics than on the 12 principles of character animation. This requires a command of expressions and MEL Scripting, as well as the dynamics toolbox.

TDs also use scripting extensively to build interface components and workflow tools and to move around the large amounts of data generated in any 3D environment. To streamline the flow of data in a production pipeline, TDs need a working understanding of the relevant operating systems, which might be a mix of Unix, IRIX, Linux, Windows, and the Mac OS.

Although there are TDs who deal primarily with the art end of the production process, others spend most of their time writing scripts and software. Scripting tools, including MEL in Maya, Perl, and other scripting languages, batch scripting, and even C or C++ are necessary components of the TD's toolbox.

In games, TDs, often called *technical art directors*, have similar roles, although they are engaged in getting data into games rather than into rendered images and must make sure the art and animation created for a game can work well within the game engine.

Character TDs are also an increasingly important position. They build the complex rigs that are used to control a character, whether the motion is generated through motion capture or by a keyframe animator. As character animation becomes a more vital part of games and film, the demand is soaring for character TDs with knowledge of muscle deformation systems and highly detailed facial animation controls. Character TDs also handle the rigging of objects such as vehicles and other props that may have to interact with characters or environments.

Rendering

Rendering is a technical director's domain. The goal of rendering is to take all of the elements of a 3D scene—geometry, textures, lights, animation, and backgrounds—and to render them into a single image or series of animated images that fulfill the vision of the director.

In modern film studios, rendering is usually done with advanced rendering systems that work in conjunction with the 3D animation software, typically Mental Image's Mental Ray, or Pixar's RenderMan, or SplutterFish's Brazil. These renderers support highly realistic lighting models and are designed to work seamlessly with mammoth render farms.

Rendering requires an understanding of 3D lighting, shaders, and textures, as well as the rendering tools and the almost endless minutia that are used to configure these systems. For example, film renderings are often done in many passes to generate layers that are ultimately composited in programs like After Effects, Shake, Inferno, or Combustion.

Rendering for television work is often part of the job of the TD or CG artist working the shot because many CG artists in TV take a shot from beginning to end, and some even composite the results themselves. Rendering in this case can be done through primary animation applications like Maya's Renderer or Mental Ray for Maya or through an external renderer like RenderMan. In television, however, rendering is less of the pipeline step it is in film work and more a general part of the CG artist's workflow. The renders are then composited or handed off to the compositing team for integration and finishing.

In games, rendering is often an intermediate step in the texture mapping process. Real-time 3D games don't use advanced rendering effects, such as radiosity or global illumination. Instead, all rendering in real-time 3D games is done in real-time by the 3D hardware, through the game engine. On the other hand, games like Maxis's SimCity 4 rely heavily on prerendered artwork that rivals the quality of film rendering.

Although rendering presents similar challenges in most 3D software, it's not really a fundamental skill, like drawing or composition. Rendering is a highly technical process that requires some in-depth knowledge of each renderer and how it works, combined with an eye for the ultimate finished result. One of the best ways to learn the art of rendering in depth is to find your way into a job as render wrangler (see Chapter 2), where you'll be required to manage the countless details of render jobs.

The first thing I'll look at is at the bottom of the resume. Software and skill set. I'll look for programs that we're using. You need to know Maya, RenderMan, MTOR [Maya to RenderMan]. That's what I'm looking at. A lot of other companies are looking for things such as XSI or Mental Ray, but for the stuff we're doing, a lot of people are heavily into RenderMan.

—*CRAIG LYN*

Other Skills

Like all industries, the 3D games, television and film world has many specialties. Some of the more common specialties are game design, Linux and Unix skills, and compositing, which each require a unique set of skills.

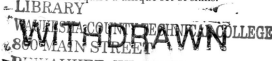

Game Design

Game design, contrary to what you might expect from the name, does not imply graphic design. Game designers are the unique individuals who create the game concept, puzzles, and game-play that make games fun and interesting. Often, hardcore gamers who fantasize about working in the games industry set their sights on being a game designer without actually understanding what the job entails.

To get a job as a game designer, your best hope is to establish yourself as a successful artist or engineer in the game industry. Because game development is exceedingly expensive, most game designers first hold some other well-respected position in the gaming industry before being trusted with this crucial job.

There are numerous things a game designer must know, but the exact combination of skills and aptitudes will depend both on the game company and the type of game being created. Here are some of the typical requirements:

Writing A game designer must be able to translate game concepts into clearly written documents that other members of the team can use to guide their work.

> Recommend reading: *Postmortems from Game Developer: Insights from the Developers of Unreal Tournament, Black and White, Age of Empires, and Other Top-Selling Games*, edited by Austin Grossman. It's an anthology of *Game Developer* magazine articles that have become an industry standard for learning game development best (and worst) practices. This book details what happened with the design, development, and release of many real-world games. It's fascinating reading, and there's nothing like learning from other people's mistakes.

Art and graphics You must be able to guide the visual design of the game to support the theme, or, as is often the case, to maintain consistency with the expectations established by the license the game is based on.

Puzzle and game-play design This is one of the most intangible qualities to specify in a game designer. The job requires an intuitive understanding of game logic and what makes a game fun and compelling to play. This ability to create a challenging, interesting, and addictively playable game comes from studying games, playing games, and contributing to the design of games.

Marketing While game designers are subordinate to the producer in the marketing role, they do need to know what other games are on the market, which ones do well, and what makes those games successful. You can't expect to make a good game if you don't know what's already out there. In addition, as a game designer, it will be your job to communicate the essence of the game to the media and, ultimately, to the consumer who may be tempted to buy it.

Management and leadership The game designer is ultimately the driving force behind creation of the game. In conjunction with the producer, the designer has to inspire the team with creative leadership and will be expected to direct the art and engineering teams to adhere to the requirements of the game design.

Programming knowledge While game designers don't necessarily have to be programmers, they do have to understand programming well enough to direct engineers in their software development. This might mean, for example, balancing the performance demands of audio effects with the requirements for game-play and rendering quality.

Linux and Unix Platform Skills

Most 3D artists get their start working on Windows or Macintosh desktop systems using off-the-shelf 3D software such as Maya, 3ds max, or LightWave. While many studios have also standardized off-the-shelf software for most of their work, the Linux operating system has become a new standard in 3D film studios and even some boutiques. There are several reasons for this: one, it's inexpensive, which is always a compelling argument for a business tool. Two, Linux, like all flavors of Unix, is a powerful network operating system that makes it easy to share the resources of multiple computers. This may not be so important to students, but in the film and television production environment, it's vital to have fast, transparent access to file servers and render farms. Three, Linux also supports powerful scripting systems such as Perl and Python, shell scripting, and command-line controls. Maya, and at least some professional-level hardware accelerators, have also been ported to the platform.

SHELL SCRIPTING

A *shell* in computer terms has to do with a text window or command prompt that gives you access to the OS. For example, a Windows shell is called the command prompt. These shell windows merely allow you to easily and quickly access operating system commands for file maintenance and the like.

Scripting is the task of writing strings of commands together to have a batch of processes execute from the shell. This makes for an efficient way to manage large groups of files typically seen in CG production.

Similarly, Mac OS X is based on a Unix kernel and has a usually invisible underpinning in Unix that can be used to great advantage in production environments. With the advent of the 64-bit G5, which appears to have exceptionally fast performance for 3D applications, this may become increasingly important as a 3D operating system.

Many studios require a basic knowledge of Unix and/or Linux, so it's a great idea to familiarize yourself with these operating systems before you start job hunting. For TDs, it's not just a good idea, it's essential. To learn the basics, simply install a copy of Linux or dig into the Unix terminal of OS X, and pick up a book to help you learn basic commands like cd (change directories), ls (list the files in a directory) and mkdir (make a directory).

Compositing

Compositing is the final stage in the 3D process that merges multiple layers of rendered animation and live plates into a single cohesive sequence of film or video. Compositors have to be experts at manipulating digital images of every kind. They must also be masters of color because color matching and color balancing are an important part of the composite artist's job.

Frequently, compositors are required to create 2D effects to complement 3D plates. For example, they might be required to animate background clouds, manipulate depth of field and motion blur, or add smoke or fire to a scene.

A number of compositing tools are used in high-end studios, such as Adobe After Effects; Discreet's Inferno, Flint, Flame, and Combustion; Houdini Halo, and Apple's Shake. Some studios such as Digital Domain and Rhythm and Hues rely on their own proprietary compositing programs.

Because compositors work closely with 3D artists, they'll also need to understand at least how 3D applications are used to render scene elements into multiple layers so they can communicate problems and needs to technical directors. A sense of lighting can also be helpful for compositors to be able to effectively communicate with CG artists to get the elements properly.

THE MERGING OF COMPOSITING AND CG

Some boutiques are beginning to require that their 3D artists know how to composite their own shots. For management, this removes an entire step from the pipeline, saving some time and cost. Some film studios are also realizing that lighting artists can control their shots more precisely if they also composite them. That way they have the final image and its color correction in mind as they light the preceding scenes.

Increasingly, compositing is becoming a tool all CG artists should be familiar with on some level, if not intimately. It's all about knowing how to put together the frame.

Summary

While there's no clear path to educating yourself for a job in 3D, there are some basic rules you can follow. Be a generalist when acquiring art and visual storytelling skills; the more you know, the better you'll do in any 3D career. Specialize in at least one core talent and devote yourself to perfecting that talent; all studios, whether game or television or film, are looking for people who do at least one thing exceedingly well, but have a core understanding, if not applicable skill in other areas of CG. Embrace the technology you'll need to make your art but do not become a slave to it. 3D is a technical field, but remember that the tools change constantly and without warning; expertise in one tool cannot match a core competency in creative arts.

CHAPTER 4

How and Where to Learn

There's a lot you'll need to learn before you take on a career in 3D. Whether you choose to acquire the necessary skills by going to school or by educating yourself, it's helpful to have a clear outline of your goals, your educational needs, your timeline, and your budget. If you're going to school, choose your school based on your objectives and a realistic assessment of what that school has to offer. The quality of 3D educational programs varies tremendously, and only you will be able to determine if any one program offers what you need. If you're going to train yourself, invest in good tools and enough training materials to master the basics and use what's left of your time and energy to find a mentor to guide you and help you learn. Once you decide what you need to learn, you'll be able to find the appropriate training opportunities and materials and tackle your new subjects one at a time.

In this chapter, we'll discuss these topics:

- Pros and cons of 3D school
- Choosing a school
- Teaching yourself
- Finding a mentor
- Books and training materials

Going to School vs. Teaching Yourself

While it may seem obvious that the way to learn 3D skills is to go to a school where 3D skills are the focus of study, many working 3D artists have found their way into the business in other ways. School is a long, slow, and often expensive road—most public colleges have relatively limited programs in this specialized field; comprehensive 3D graphics training is generally available at far more expensive private institutions. A middle ground of taking specialized courses offers some advantages at both ends of this spectrum, but raises its own disadvantages as well.

The Pros of Institutional Schooling

For many artists, an education and solid grounding in fine art and/or film will go much further than a degree specifically tailored to 3D graphics and effects. While 3D technical skills are important, many of them can be learned on the job—or in extreme conditions in preparation for the job hunt—while composition, painting, sculpture, lighting, and cinematography are the universal currency of any career in the arts. No matter what kind of education you get, however, your portfolio and demo reel will say more about you, your skills, and your artistic vision than anything else. In the end, no one but your parents care about your grades.

There are numerous advantages to spending your time in a school with a broad curriculum in the arts. First of all, a good school will completely immerse you in the subject matter you're trying to learn, a definite advantage to getting motivated and staying focused.

As Joseph Bowers, a student at the Art Institute of California at Los Angeles, puts it:

I'm sure all the things I learned at art school I could have taught myself, but it would have taken me 50 years. There are many things I was never aware of that were revealed to me—simple concepts, techniques. A lot of it is also motivation. When you are paying for school you are very motivated to do your best. If I were at home playing on my computer I would have nothing pushing me, there would be no competition, no standard set that would challenge me.

—JOSEPH BOWERS

A good general arts program will give you grounding in fine art, including sculpture and painting, composition, and color. And if 3D and animation is part of your curriculum, you'll also learn the practical aspects of modeling, texturing, animation, and effects in the context of specific software packages. School, however, is more than just a place to learn. It's one of the best environments to network with others in your field, including the faculty, who are often moonlighting artists from nearby studios.

Students who capitalize on their connections generally go much further, as fresh graduate of an art college Charlie Lac mentions:

My contacts made all the differences in my future leads. What I mean by that is anyone you meet can give you a contact to your next job, especially in such a small community. Also, the job I currently work in was introduced to me by a figure art model. I have made really close contact through figure drawing workshops, which is much better than reading a posting and trying to apply as a stranger.

—CHARLIE LAC

In addition to future connections, schools offer at least usable equipment, and the better programs have state-of-the-art production facilities, including motion capture systems, 3D digitizers, and network render farms. Having unfettered access to a fully outfitted facility is probably the greatest asset of going to a full immersion art school or college (see Figure 4.1).

Figure 4.1

Savannah College of Art and Design, like most art and animation schools, offers a guided tour and online galleries of student work on the Web.

Many schools have clubs that focus on specific areas of interest. Club members team up to produce working games or short films; this is a good opportunity to spend some time in the trenches with like-minded artists or developers. Several schools also offer contests or other opportunities to showcase your work, and this can be a good way to earn some recognition, particularly with those moonlighting studio staff.

Finally, being in school improves your chances of landing an internship, which may be the best way to prove yourself in a working studio and get much needed professional experience or demo reel work. Some schools even host recruiting events where studios come to meet and greet prospective hires, and many students have landed their first jobs this way. Sean Miller from Sammy Studios shares why studios may seek out those from art schools.

We are very interested in artists who have a traditional background, if not professionally, at least traditional skills that they can demonstrate on their reel or their portfolio. Most come from art schools: we have people from Savannah College of Art and Design, from Art Center of Pasadena, from the Academy of Art in San Francisco. We put a high premium on artistic skills and artistic talent, because if you know good art, you're going to be able to create good art, regardless of what tool you use…

If you don't have the art school, you should be able to demonstrate the art skills and the art background in your portfolio. The thing that's most important when we look at somebody's work is what we see. It's what we see on the reel, it's what we see in the portfolio.

And there are plenty of people who have tremendous amounts of art, and many who have a reel, that don't reflect the standard of work we're looking for. We do have a couple of people here who don't have art school in their background, but they are among the most talented.

The art school is sort of a means to an end. The ones who don't go to art school have a harder time developing those art skills. That's where you get your mentorship, and also to get used to doing iterations. It's also a lot of times your first exposure to real art direction. You have to please the teacher who plays the role of art director for the class.

—*SEAN MILLER*

Some of the hiring managers interviewed complained that too few students come out of school demonstrating the mastery of a single area that would meet their needs. These students are so busy getting *well rounded* that they never come close to becoming proficient in the area they may want to specialize in. If you spend your time focusing and exclusively working on becoming the best modeler, texture painter, animator—whatever you've set your sights on actually doing as a profession—you may be better prepared to enter the job market than a student who's spent four years studying and working on some of everything.

The Pros of Teaching Yourself

Not everyone in the 3D and effects business has gone to a traditional art program, or even a traditional form of higher education. Such long-term degree programs aren't right for everyone. Perhaps you already went to school for something else before you discovered that 3D is your true calling. Maybe you're working at a job that doesn't give you the time or flexibility to attend classes. Or maybe you're the type of person who learns better on your own, and for what you'll spend on a handful of classes in a private school, you can buy pretty much every 3D training DVD and book on the market with money to spare.

You will have to give yourself credible training in fine art and 3D technology, and you'll find the skills hard to master without a mentor or someone you can turn to for advice and constructive criticism, but on the other hand, there's no guarantee that two or four years of expensive education is going to send you off with a professional quality portfolio, either. The grades you get in your classes will mean nothing compared to the grade prospective employers give to your portfolio. If you're disciplined, study well on your own, and can find a mentor to critique and guide you, you may gain advantages in the real world that full-time art students have no idea they're missing. The truth is that many 3D artists manage without any sort of degree at all.

WHEN IN SCHOOL, DO AS THE ROMANS

Going to school is not enough. You have to keep your focus and apply yourself fully to your course of study. Merely enrolling in classes and relying on teachers to show you how to do stuff with the software will be a slow and expensive trip to nowhere. Far too many students while away the days and nights at school, refusing to commit all their time to its facility, doing barely enough to pass their classes. If you choose to go to a school, be committed to it and your studies fully; otherwise, save yourself the aggravation and expense and get the most out of your time with a few classes at night after your day job, or learn at home. The earlier students realize this sentiment, the easier and more productive their education will be. According to a now-employed recent art school graduate Daniel Gutierrez:

"You must be willing to work out of class, on your own time, doing work that pushes your personal limits. If you don't, you are dead in the water. You may become familiar with a technique or program, but so are thousands of other students." In the end, employers won't care what your grades were or if you got a certificate or degree, but they do want your student reel to be every bit as good as the pile of professional reels they just went through.

Take it from Craig Lyn, whose Emmy award and role as CG supervisor at the Frame-Store belies his education as an English major. Here's what he said when asked if he had fine art training:

Absolutely none. And I'm proud to say that. [Laughs]

I'd highly recommend it. I think it's absolutely important. There are things that catch me now. As you slowly move up, a Cinematics 101 course really helps, so you know when someone says camera track left, jib up, screen left, your basic aspect ratios, 1.33:1 and 2.35:1, and all that stuff, what it means. The difference between anamorphic and 35 mil, or what VistaVision really is, is really just picking up a book—that's really helpful—it's literally bedtime reading.

But the fine art side, absolutely, the more you know the better. At ILM, they offered things such as character drawing classes, sculpture classes, that really helped a lot.

—*CRAIG LYN*

You may find it much easier to get over the hurdle of teaching yourself a 3D program by taking an introductory or beginner-level class offered at a community college or specialized school or training facility in your area. You will find the initial difficulties are easier to overcome if you learn in a classroom environment without having to commit to school full time. You can then use that class as a stepping stone to work on your own projects at home until you feel you're ready for taking some advanced or specialized courses. This still leaves you in the driver's seat of your own education, but it gives you the advantage of structured learning and even mentorship when you need it most, in the beginning.

Choosing a School

While it may be a challenge to get a job in 3D, it won't be hard to find a school willing to teach you 3D skills. According to the website Animation World Network (www.awn.com), one of the best sources on the topic, there are approximately 578 schools in 42 countries with study programs in animation-related subjects. Of course, those programs are fairly loosely defined and may include character animation and 3D graphics as well as voice acting and fine arts training. In the United States, AWN lists 217 animation schools, including 75 in California alone.

Other useful resources for information on 3D schools and programs is Gamasutra.com (www.gamasutra.com), which lists private instructional programs as well as accredited colleges and universities, and this book's website, which offers its own list of schools and links to numerous online resources: (www.3djobs.net).

There are numerous ways to get an education in 3D, including correspondence courses taught over the Internet and do-it-yourself educational materials. For example, in the San Francisco Bay Area, there are over a dozen places to learn 3D skills: specialty schools such as Cogswell College and the Academy of Art; community colleges, including De Anza and Foothill; state colleges, including San Jose State University and San Francisco State University; and major universities, including University of California at Berkeley, University of California at Santa Cruz, and Stanford University.

Almost all of these schools offer courses that qualify them as having an "animation program," particularly if you include the software engineering that's used to write the software that drives 3D animation. However, only a few of them (Cogswell, the Academy of Art, and California College of Arts and Crafts) specialize in computer graphics and emphasize the field in their programs and marketing. The other schools offer 3D training of varying intensity but will demand that you pursue a broad, general course of study in addition to the subject you choose to major in.

Of course, just because California is the epicenter of the industry doesn't mean you have to live in the Golden State to find great 3D schools. In fact, some of the schools most often mentioned as standouts in the field are far removed from the West Coast:

- Full Sail (Winter Park, Florida)
- Ringling School of Art and Design (Sarasota, Florida)
- Savannah (Georgia) College of Art and Design
- The Art Institute of Pittsburgh (Pennsylvania)
- Sheridan College (Oakville, Ontario, Canada)
- Vancouver (British Columbia) Film School
- Pratt Institute (New York)
- New York University

These schools illustrate that a top-notch education in 3D arts is now available in many places throughout North America.

Another good resource for information is *Gardner's Guide to Colleges for Multimedia and Animation* (Garth Gardner and Co.), which details the programs at over 400 nationwide schools.

In such a huge and confusing field, how can you possibly choose the best school, and once you choose, which ones are going to accept you? The decision to attend a school can be made after first dangling your feet into the water by taking classes, as did art school student Nathan Taketani, and then deciding to enter a school full-steam ahead:

> *Actually I did take a few courses at a community college to cement my decision in going to art school. As to how I picked my school, it was both on a recommendation and a little research on my part. The thing that most interested me was the staff and their credits.*
> —NATHAN TAKETANI

It's impossible for anyone to recommend a school without knowing you, your talents, and your goals, and it's beyond the scope of this book to advise anyone on choosing a particular college. However, we can point out some of the important questions you need to answer before you choose a school:

- Do you need or want a few courses, a certificate, or a four-year degree?
- How much time and money can you afford to spend?
- Do you want a general education or total immersion?
- Are you planning to attend as a graduate student?
- How good are the instructors, and what is their industry experience?
- How current and relevant is the program you're considering?
- What is the school's reputation in the industry, and does it have solid connections to the industry?
- What is the school's reputation with students?
- Have you seen the school firsthand, and do you like what you see?
- What geographical region do you want your school to be in?

Geography is probably the first consideration many people think of when trying to find a school, and it might be best to begin with that criteria, as did Daniel Gutierrez:

> *When I was looking for a school the most important attribute was location. I was most interested in getting into a city that had an attractive and bustling art/animation scene. My two choices were primarily New York and Los Angeles, although I've since learned that San Francisco is also a good location.*
> —DANIEL GUTIERREZ

If you can narrow down the geographical region you prefer, what type of program you want, and how much you can spend, you'll go a long way toward closing in on the right decision. For instance, if you know you're limited to schools in a 100-mile radius, you can probably narrow the field down to a dozen campuses or fewer. If your budget for tuition is $15,000 per year, you can forget about the prestigious private universities that cost five times that (unless you're convinced you'll land financial aid to see you through). If you want to be working on a hit game or a film in two years, you're better off finding an art school that's going to immerse you in your area of interest right away and send you off with a certificate of completion, rather than a liberal arts program in a university that's going to put you through two years of general education requirements before you're even allowed to launch a copy of Maya in a classroom. If the cost of education is a real road block, consider community college programs, which often offer top-notch training in arts and technical subjects like 3D for a fraction of the cost of any private program.

Degree vs. Certificate Programs

Do you need a degree in art or computer graphics to get a job in the games and film industries? It can't hurt, but there's no guarantee it will help. Of the 30 or so people interviewed for this book, few mentioned a degree or certificate as a significant factor in hiring new talent at their studios. Overwhelmingly, they said they were more interested in an artist's portfolio, demo reel, and on-the-job experience than in school records. Even so, a degree may come down to a personal preference for one's future, as graduate Charlie Lac sees it:

One reason I went to an art school as opposed to a short-term non-credited class was to get a bachelor's degree.   —CHARLIE LAC

Some recruiters do use academic records as a distinguishing factor when hiring fresh talent right out of school, and several recruiters said they recruit from select schools that have a reputation for turning out highly skilled talent. (These schools are generally in the same city or area as the employers; some employers have established relationships with the schools to help the schools structure a genuinely relevant curriculum.) When you're considering a school, be sure to question the admissions counselor about their connections in the industry and if they've collaborated with those connections to develop an up-to-date curriculum that includes internship opportunities for their students.

You may decide you need a school with a strong reputation for turning out well-trained talent to help you craft your own skills. Keep in mind, however, that realistically, the market for new talent is so tight that your chances of getting hired straight out of school just because you earned good grades from a particular school are slim. Unless you graduate with a great demo reel and portfolio and you've made some friends and developed your chops, your diploma won't be worth its weight in sheepskin. On the other hand, if you attend a ho-hum college and you emerge with a great body of work and some friends in well-chosen places, you're just as likely to get hired as graduates from the more prestigious Savannah College of Art and Design or the Art Center in Pasadena.

What your tens of thousands of dollars in tuition will buy you, if you play it smart, is a solid education in art fundamentals and a working knowledge of the technology of 3D.

Just as importantly, it should also give you the best chance you'll ever have to network and get a toe in the door of the industry. The most reputable schools get their reputations by earning and cultivating industry relationships. It was a tough decision for Daniel Militonian to make but ultimately a wise one:

I would have to say at first, when I just got out of high school and all my friends wanted to party, I really didn't want to go to school any more and just wanted to start working, but thanks to my dad (I say this now) he made me go to school. The first year I wasn't really impressed and wasn't really learning anything new, but [once] I got past the beginner classes I realized that what I knew was absolutely nothing. I learned so much at the Art Institute from all the teachers there that without them, I wouldn't be one-third of the artist that I am today. So, yes, it was a very wise decision to go to art school. —DANIEL MILITONIAN

Doors to certain fields are closed if you don't have that degree, no matter where you've been or what you've got to show for yourself. Fortunately, the games and animation industries don't work that way.

If you don't want to invest in a two- or four-year program, however, certificate programs, such as those offered by many private teaching facilities and community colleges, are ideal for working students who may have already gone to college or full-time students who want to get trained and go on to the working world as quickly as possible. Schools may offer certificates of completion in a short course of study, such as 3D animation, or even in a very specific topic, such as the use of a certain software package. If you've already got most of the skills you need to land a job but need boning up in certain areas, a certificate can be a good compromise to a full-blown degree.

How Much Can You Spend?

Schooling is something that most of us take for granted when we're kids, but when it's time to pony up for college, it suddenly becomes a precious commodity. Families save, often from the day a child is born to high school graduation day, just to pay for a college education. Many students must work at money-making jobs to help support their college habit. Others are already working for a living and must weigh college courses against necessities like new tires or college funds for their own kids.

Like anything that costs a lot of money, school is something that you can't necessarily choose based on the merit of the institution alone. You're going to have to decide what fits into your budget.

Throughout the United States, community colleges are almost always the best deal in town. At De Anza College, in Cupertino, California, for example, you can take a full load of art, animation, and computer graphics courses for about $200 a semester, parking included.

Though you'll find a higher concentration of schools in California, many community colleges across the country offer some animation classes if not impressive full-blown animation curricula. Piedmont Community College in Yanceyville, NC (Figure 4.2) offers an in-depth CG curriculum for an inexpensive tuition. In-state students can expect to pay less than $600 per semester; out of state students pay about $3,000.

In comparison, Cogswell College, a private school with an intensive program in computer graphics, a single course will cost you about $1,600 (with the fifth course free if you pay for four). That's about $15,000 per year for full-time enrollment, and Cogswell is cheap for a private school: the Academy of Art in San Francisco charges over $2,000 per class. According to Cogswell's admissions office, the following are typical annual tuition costs for eight months of schooling, plus books and supplies (not including an average of $4,000 per year for room and board for students living away from home):

Public community/technical college $7,900

Public four-year college/university $9,021

Cogswell Polytechnical College $15,654

Private four-year college/university $32,231

Figure 4.2

Piedmont Community College in Yanceyville, NC is one of many community colleges that offer a complete course of studies in CG.

Keep in mind, these are only estimates of the cost of education. But it's safe to say that it will cost less to take a full load of courses at a community college than a single class at most private schools.

Given the low pay earned by most teachers, many instructors teach at multiple nearby schools, both private and public, with corresponding differences in the cost of the instruction but nearly identical subject matter and course work. There's no reason to believe you're going to get a better education just because you pay more for it. When comparing nearby schools, be sure to compare the list of teachers and the subjects they're teaching at each. It's always smart to do a Google search on teachers; you might be surprised what you'll learn about where they've been and what they've done, and it will give you some relevant things to talk about as you work to build a relationship with potential mentors.

General Education or Total Immersion?

State colleges and universities typically fall somewhere in between community colleges and private technical schools in tuition price because, like community colleges, they're subsidized by the government. However, there are two significant factors that may color your interest in these schools. The first is that state colleges and universities require that you meet certain academic standards for admission, and there are often far more applicants than openings, making admission intensely competitive. The second is that state colleges and universities won't let you choose your curriculum. You'll be expected to follow a course of study that will include many general education courses in addition to whatever you take to support your career in art. While this may hinder your pursuit of 3D arts, a broad education can take you places you never knew you wanted to go.

Alternatively, you can find programs that will exclusively groom you for a career in art, animation, or 3D, at private schools, such as the Academy of Art (which has campuses in many cities nationwide), and in training centers, such as The Gnomon School of Visual Effects in Los Angeles or dvGarage in San Francisco. To varying degrees, these schools may offer minimal general education but focus on visual arts. Other schools specialize in short courses designed for working professionals and don't bother with the formalities of degrees or the complexity of general education. Particularly common are training facilities that teach you specific skills in tools like Maya and then send you on your way without also teaching background skills like drawing or painting. These programs are great in teaching you the specifics of using a program or mastering a technique, but they tend to leave out the broader education colleges offer. These courses are best taken to brush up or expand on one's skill, while a broader education at a college or university is more important in the long run for those just graduating high school. Joseph Bowers reaffirms his decision to totally immerse himself in school:

> *I would recommend a school that focuses strongly on the fundamentals: anatomy drawing, sculpting, principles of animation, etc. If a school focuses only on teaching the programs then I think it's a waste. It would be like learning everything about a car, but not knowing how to drive it or the rules of the road.* —JOSEPH BOWERS

Considering a Master's Degree?

If you already have a college degree, then attending a school of animation, whether you're a full-time student or taking only a few classes, is really about finding someone to mentor you, guide your work, and provide training in the specific skills you need to learn to create a professional portfolio. True, plenty of people do pursue advanced degrees and research in the field of computer graphics, but this is almost exclusively at the engineering end of the field. There are masters degrees available in art, but if your goal is to work in the 3D industry, the value of an advanced degree in "3D graphics" may not be equal to the cost of obtaining it unless you wish to teach in the future.

ESCAPE: BEYOND NORTH AMERICA

With the growth in CG jobs in Europe, especially the United Kingdom, several formal training opportunities have also emerged there. The effects and animation industry has experienced unprecedented growth in the past five years, according to James Huggins of Escape Studios (www.escapestudios.co.uk/), a privately funded training facility in London. For example, The Framestore, a London post-production house, grew in four years from 80 operators to more than 450, Huggins said. As a result, training houses like Escape have emerged to fulfill the appetite of those striving to break into the business. Even in its short lifespan (Escape opened in 2001), Escape graduates, or "Escapees," have gone on to work at such companies as The Mill, The Moving Picture Company (MPC), Jim Henson's Creature Shop, and Cinesite. One of the great advantages of getting your CG training at a facility like Escape is that you learn from practicing industry professionals. "This ensures that the techniques and practices passed on to students are both current and relevant to today's production environment," Huggins said. In smaller training centers, you may also get more individual attention. Escape's class size is limited to 10 students. For more information on CG education abroad, a good resource is Animation World Network's database, available at http://schools.awn.com/.

Rather than pursuing an advanced degree in 3D and animation, chances are you would better spend your time and money devoting yourself to creating animation, since that's all you'd be doing as a graduate student anyway. Nobody's going to hire you over another animator simply because you've got a master's degree in animation. If you've got a bachelor's degree, you should probably take a few classes and devote most of your time to building a top-notch reel.

How Good Are the Instructors?

Schools invest money in creating a compelling curriculum and purchasing state-of-the-art equipment, software, and training materials, but the best reason to attend a given school is its faculty. Many schools are strategically located near major animation or game studios, and if the schools are worth anything, they'll have lured some of the talent from those studios to come and teach. Former students like Joseph Bowers found that to be a major plus in choosing a school:

Most of my teachers were working in the field and they helped me understand how the industry works, what is attractive to employers, and what turns them away. The teacher of mine who eventually hired me was extremely helpful to me when it came to learning about modeling. He would show work that he has done and it would change how I approached my own models. He raised the standard, making me work harder and get better. Before that, I felt of modeling as a technical thing, adjusting wireframe until it looks okay. Now I see it more as an art. …I see my models as sculptures.

—*JOSEPH BOWERS*

In addition, some schools have full-time faculty with a special passion for teaching. They may or may not have worked in the industry, but they stay current on techniques and tools and have a real devotion to the success of students. In either case, the best teachers are connected to the industry through their former students and friends who respect them.

Here are some things you can do to evaluate a school's faculty:

Find out who they are Most schools provide a list of faculty, including brief bios that will give you an idea of where they've worked and what they've done.

Google them Use what information you get from the school to perform an online search to find out anything you can about teachers' backgrounds, or if they've been mentioned favorably by other artists. Many teachers also have their own websites, and if they moonlight as professional artists, these sites may host versions of their own demo reels and portfolios, or even complete resumes. With some luck, you may end up with a very clear picture of who your prospective teachers are and what they've done.

Talk to an advisor Every school has an admissions counselor and program advisor who can brief you on the core faculty you'll be taking classes from. Take this information with a grain of salt, however; remember, the school is trying to sell you on attending. Advisors and admissions counselors won't deliberately mislead you about what a school has to offer, but they're very likely to emphasize the positives and omit any mention of the school's failings.

Talk to the teacher There's nothing like a face-to-face conversation to give you a feel for whether you'll like working with a teacher, although you should keep in mind that who you like working with isn't always going to be the person who teaches you the most. Try to evaluate your teacher as you would an art director: what can you learn from this person? Will he or she push you to new levels of skill and understanding? Will they inspire you to dig into your creative reserves?

Audit a class Try to get permission to sit in on a class or two with the teachers you're interested in. Usually they'll agree. This is a good opportunity to learn about their teaching style, as well as to see what kind of students you're likely to be collaborating with and learning from in-group projects and in workshop environments.

Talk to students While you're auditing the class, get the names and numbers of some of the students. They'll give you heartfelt reviews of the qualities and qualifications of a teacher. Remember, however, that other students are artists with their own egos and emotions. How they fared with a given teacher may affect their recommendations. Be sure to get a big enough sample that you can arrive at a composite picture you can trust.

A school can teach only as well as its teachers. In the CG field, having a solid teaching base that is rooted and kept up-to-date in the industry can make the biggest difference to a graduate like Daniel Gutierrez:

Every so often, you will take a class or learn something that just clicks. The planets align, tides shift…or you have an instructor that you work well with and understand thoroughly. When this happens, take advantage of it, because excellent instructors are not the norm, they are the exception. Seek their knowledge and don't be afraid to ask dumb questions. The most important part is to show a genuine interest in what they are explaining and what you are trying to accomplish. On two occasions I've had instructors that were so exceptional that even after doing well in their class, I took them again. This did a few things for me: it gained me the respect of the instructor and proved that I was serious about the task at hand, it gained me notoriety among my peers, and I gained knowledge.

—DANIEL GUTIERREZ

How Current and Relevant Is the Program?

Schools have to shell out a lot of cash to stay current in technology and techniques, and many schools are simply too small and poorly funded, despite their chronically high tuitions, to stay ahead of the curve. If you're going to school primarily to learn fine art, there will probably be a couple of fine art teachers ready to teach you to draw with chalk, and you'll be in great hands.

But if you're going to school to learn technical direction for film effects, you're going to need access to Maya, SoftImage XSI, LightWave, Shake, Houdini, Mental Ray, MTOR, RenderMan, and many others. Ideally, you'll also have a render farm you can work on and a choice of Unix, IRIX, Linux, Mac, and Windows platforms. You're going to need scripting instructors who know MEL inside and out and rigging teachers who can set up muscle influences and other advanced effects and teach you how to attach your rigs to state-of-the-art motion-capture systems. In short, you'll need a school that's as state of the art as the studios where you want to work. Chances are slim that you'll find anything quite that comprehensive, but if you know where to set the bar, at least you'll have a standard with which to measure each of your potential schools. Be sure to inquire about what versions of the software the school is using and be wary if it's one or two full cycles behind.

Also, take a close look at the school's library. Does it have the latest teaching materials, such as DVDs and a current and extensive selection of books on the topics you know you want to learn about?

What Is the School's Reputation in the Industry?

It's almost impossible to get accurate feedback on a school's reputation in the industry. Employers are reticent to mention specific schools by name, apparently to avoid showing favoritism that might hurt them down the line, and they're even more unlikely to level criticism at any school. But if you can find a company recruiter in your area with time to talk, you're likely to get some useful information about where that company goes to recruit and why.

One good source of information is online discussion boards, such as those at High-End3D.com, AWN.com, and Gamasutra.com. These sites attract many working professionals who are likely to answer a polite question about a particular school or schools in a specific region.

If you talk to placement officers at your candidate schools, they'll be more than happy to tell you what companies come to them looking for employees on a regular basis, and they may also let you know about recurring internship opportunities these companies offer, which can be a good indication of the school's standing with that company.

One way to confirm this information is to look at the school's job listing board—almost every technical college offers some kind of placement service consisting of a website or bulletin board—and see who's advertising and what companies may be attending upcoming recruiting events.

What Is the School's Reputation with Students?

As with getting objective feedback about faculty, getting student opinions about a specific school is difficult, especially if you want the opinions of recent graduates who have seen the school's program all the way through. Probably the best way to solicit this information is on websites where working artists are willing to answer questions about the schools they've attended. You'll find links to such sites on www.3djobs.net.

Does the School Have Connections?

In the animation and 3D effects field, some schools have a pipeline to entry-level jobs in certain companies. Usually, this is because an instructor works in the company or because a number of alumni of the school have ascended to hiring-level positions and they look for recent graduates of their alma mater. If you can get recruiters in a situation where they'll talk openly about who they hire and why, they're likely to spill the beans about which schools they work with on a regular basis.

You can also grill the employment placement person at the school to which you're applying. Ask what kinds of insider connections the school exploits on a regular basis, but keep in mind that these connections are often informal and can pass from student to instructor to hiring manager without any official involvement of the school.

Have You Seen the School Firsthand, and Do You Like What You See?

While it may seem like an obvious step when evaluating a school, you need to go there and check it out firsthand. Go to the school armed with a list of questions that you can ask advisors, teachers, and students. Get a tour of the facilities, ask questions about what equipment is available (and how often there's a waiting list for popular tools), and meet faculty and students. Do a reality check by asking the same questions of different people. Check out the school's job board to see who is posting openings there. Sit through a few classes if teachers will allow it. You'll know enough after such an inspection to decide if the school is right for you.

Getting the Most Out of School

When it comes to school, there's nothing truer than the old saying, "what you get out of it depends on what you put into it." Getting the most out of school principally means using the many resources available to you to their utmost advantage. Sammy Studios' Lean Artist Sean Miller echoes this sentiment:

When I talk to students at colleges, one of the most important things is you're paying for your education. Use those teachers. Ask the questions. Don't wait for them to come to you. Go to the teacher. And never take "that's good" for an answer. Ask why it's good. Get that clarification. If someone says something is bad, make them tell you why they don't like it, because you'll never understand what impact your art is having on someone unless you ask those questions. And those people are being paid to answer those questions.

—SEAN MILLER

For the would-be technical director, Craig Lyn advises a course of study that includes not only a breadth of art, but some very focused specialization in key areas of the field, such as modeling, lighting, or animation, and a specific end goal that few artists actually achieve in school: the creation of one truly representative piece of work.

And then the last thing, which is the most important, which is the reel. [Job applicants] should be concentrating more. They try to put volume in there, they try to tell a story, which is really nice, but as a technical director, I don't care about that.

It goes back to the whole theory of the guild system, at the end of it, they have to create their masterpiece, which is what proves that they're able to go out there into the world, and they're not doing that. They're doing all these small little haphazard bits and pieces of things. They should just concentrate on one specific area of the industry. For example, animation; for example, modeling, lighting, technical direction, compositing. Do something like that rather than getting lost in putting all these half-baked ideas onto their reel.

—CRAIG LYN

Getting the most out of school also means taking advantage of the many opportunities it offers: clubs, networking, collaborative projects, and perhaps most important, internships.

Internships

Perhaps one of the best opportunities you'll have as a student is an internship with a game or film studio. Most schools post internship opportunities along with other job offerings, and many schools have ongoing internship programs with specific companies, so your chances of getting into one of these positions are pretty good.

Although the work you'll do as an intern won't be glamorous, it's a practical way to get your foot in the door, learn about the company and its pipeline, and make a few friends who might mentor you or even hire you down the line. Most employers will want to see your portfolio when you apply for an internship, so it's also a good chance to practice your real-world job-hunting skills.

INTERDEPARTMENTAL PROJECTS

No matter what program of study you choose to enter, it's always a good idea to connect to similar departments in the school and establish contacts with their students. A way to gain valuable experience is to try to contact student filmmakers to see if they need some title animations or compositing for their films. As effects pervade the medium, they've become almost a given for student projects. Bold student productions make ample use of green screens and even CG characters, and they will always welcome a helping hand. It may not give you credits toward graduation, but it will give you some experience and perhaps some shots for your student reel. More importantly, it will help you establish contacts with future directors and filmmakers who may just contact you with paying work someday. The art of knowing someone is primary, and it's never too early to start developing that mindset.

If you do land an internship, be sure to go the extra mile and take advantage of the opportunity. While your employer may only be interested in your ability to organize digital files, scan reference drawings, or make coffee, if you do your job well and make sure you're liked, you'll probably have an opportunity to show the work you've produced on your own and to get feedback from real pros. Remember, you're working for little or no pay; you'll need to stick your neck out and get noticed if you want it to be a worthwhile experience.

Interning also affords you the opportunity to get hands-on time with professional equipment. The facility you're interning with may let you run through a tutorial or two if you stay late and practice on your own. This is usually true at smaller boutiques that don't run night shifts rather than large studios, but it's always ultimately up to the people who run the place. Who knows? You may eventually strike it lucky at an internship and find that one of their employees is more than happy to sit with you and show you the ropes once you've been there a short while. Just make sure you make good coffee and you do your intern work well!

Teaching Yourself

If you have a good grasp of fundamentals of art or animation, teaching yourself 3D and effects is certainly possible, especially if you're willing to focus on one area and don't try to bite off the entire spectrum of the technology. If you do choose to teach yourself, there are several things you're going to need:

- Tools
- Books and learning materials
- A mentor
- Time, patience, and diligence

Assembling the Tools: Hardware

Only a few years ago, running a high-end 3D application meant working on a 3D work-station that could easily cost as much as a new car. The hardware was highly specialized and difficult to find. At the time, one of the best reasons to attend an art school was that these schools provided the hardware on which you could learn 3D skills, which was otherwise nearly unaffordable on a student budget. But all that has changed. The $1,200 desktop computer and 3D graphics card you use for playing Splinter Cell probably has as much processor performance, memory, storage space, and 3D graphics rendering power, as a $20,000 SGI workstation from 1998. For $2,500, the computer you can buy today is far more powerful than the $100,000 proprietary systems used to create movies like *Jurassic Park* and *Terminator II*. And hardware is only getting faster, better, and cheaper by the day.

MORE THAN ONE PROCESSOR

Having two processors in your computer is sort of like having two computers. Much of the time, the second processor sits idle, but when you go to render an animation, the second processor kicks in and does almost all the work, while you continue to plug away on the first processor. If it's a really big rendering job, you can let both processors join forces, which nearly doubles your rendering speed. With Linux and Mac OS X, the impact of multiple processors is even greater, since the operating systems themselves use multithreading and multitasking to get more done simultaneously, with the aid of additional CPUs. Do you need to have a dual processor system to work with 3D? Not at all, but it's definitely a major factor in boosting productivity when it's time to render. However, most home users should channel their budgets toward getting a better video card, monitor, or more system memory than a second processor.

One alternative to a multiprocessor system is to have more than one computer, so that the extra machine(s) can work as render servers that you can send your rendering jobs to. However, to use this setup, you'll need multiple licenses for your software, which can easily cost more than the price of an extra CPU for a single workstation.

A popular setup is to have one system act as the sole 3D station, where all of your 3D work is accomplished. The second system can be the do-all box that can boost render power (using a distributed renderer such as Smedge software, included on this book's CD, you can send render jobs across a network of machines to utilize all the CPUs you have) or serve as a compositing station. You can also use it as a video editing box with DVD burning, not to mention as a web browsing and gaming station.

So what do you need to run Maya and other high-end 3D applications? Consider some suggested minimum specifications:

- 1 GHz or faster CPU
- 512MB RAM
- 40GB or larger hard drive
- Accelerated 3D graphics card with 128MB texture RAM with analog or digital video I/O (The video card is probably the most important component and is discussed in the next section)

Of course, in computers, faster is always better and by the time you read this even these specs may be outdated, but as this book goes to press, here's what's considered a dream machine for working in high-end 3D:

- Dual 2.5GHz or higher Xeon processors or equivalent for Windows and Linux. Dual G5 Macintosh for Mac OS X (see Figure 4.3)
- At least 1GB dual channel DDR RAM
- High-speed SCSI system hard drive at 36GB
- 200GB ATA-100 or serial ATA storage hard drive
- Professional workstation dual-screen open GL card with 256MB on-board memory for a PC, or ATI Radeon 9800 Pro for Mac
- One Trinitron tube 21″ CRT monitor capable of 1600×1200 resolution and one 20″ LCD at 1600×1200 native resolution
- IEEE 1394 (FireWire) port for digital video I/O

Figure 4.3

Apple has billed the G5 as the world's fastest desktop computer. With dual 64-bit processors, it may qualify as the next generation of 3D workstations.

Grappling with Graphics Cards

While the CPU—the main brains of the computer—has a linear effect on performance (double the CPU speed results in roughly half the time to complete a software operation), the impact of the graphics card the system uses can be much greater while you work. Modern 3D graphics cards contain chips that are specifically designed to speed the intensive geometry and number crunching involved in 3D rendering. These 3D graphics operations are handled by the Open GL and Direct X software components of desktop operating systems, which is why you'll often hear the 3D hardware referred to as variations of *Open GL cards* or *Direct X hardware*. Unlike the computer's CPU, which handles all software operations, the 3D card is exclusively responsible for the rendering and display of 2D and 3D graphics *on the screen*. Current manufacturers of the 3D chip sets include ATI, NVIDIA

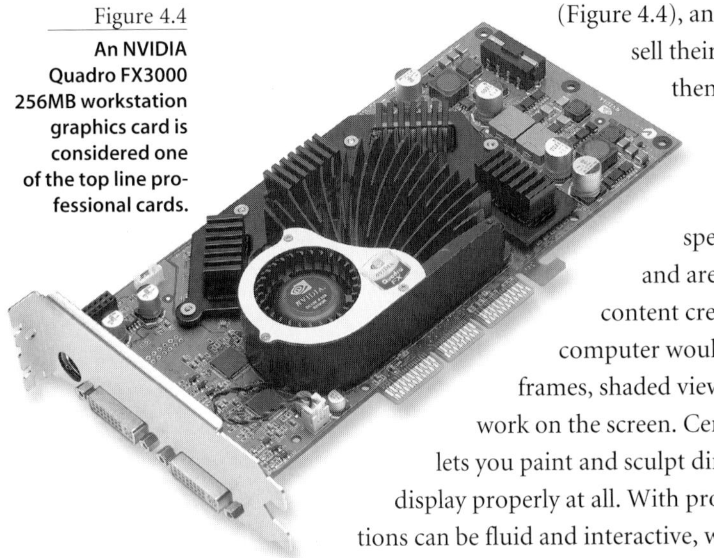

Figure 4.4

An NVIDIA Quadro FX3000 256MB workstation graphics card is considered one of the top line professional cards.

(Figure 4.4), and 3Dlabs, although these manufacturers also sell their chips to other manufacturers who bundle them with their own cards and drivers.

Many consumer brand gaming cards can run 3D applications like Maya very well. However, workstation cards and drivers are specifically made to handle this type of work and are generally more stable and robust for 3D content creation. Without good video hardware, your computer would be achingly slow at drawing 3D wireframes, shaded views, and texture-mapped shaded views of your work on the screen. Certain Maya features, such as Artisan, which lets you paint and sculpt directly on rendered surfaces, may not even display properly at all. With professional-grade 3D hardware, such operations can be fluid and interactive, which is vital to the creative process. Often, a computer that works well for general business tasks and web surfing can be transformed into a capable 3D workstation by simply upgrading the graphics hardware.

Many computers are advertised as having "blistering 3D performance," but beware of such claims. Some of these computers use 3D graphics cards that are optimized for *playing* video games, not for creating 3D graphics from scratch. Of course, if your primary focus is to create real-time game art, real-time game cards might be fine for your needs. The difference is that video games are highly optimized to occupy minimal texture memory and to have as few polygons on screen at a time as possible. When you're creating models and animations, your needs may be very different. For example, you may want to set up an animation for cinematic rendering containing far too many polygons and textures to work smoothly in a video game, but that are ideal for the creation of realistic finished renderings.

If you're creating 3D graphics with complex scenes, high-resolution models, and many high-res texture maps, stability and quality should take vast precedence over "blistering 3D gaming!" Consider a higher-end product advertised as a workstation graphics card. In general, the higher-end cards have more custom circuitry for features like geometry preprocessing and frame buffering, and they carry far more memory for storing texture maps and z-depth information, as well as custom tailored drivers. The truly high-end professional workstation graphics cards will cost two to three times as much as high-end gamer cards, but you might be surprised at how affordable some of the low- to midrange workstation cards are. Many manufacturers offer lower-end, reasonably priced, but still bankable video cards like ATI's FireGL T2 (Figure 4.5) that compete with similar gaming consumer cards such as the GeForce FX or Radeon series.. Keep in mind that not all cards will work in all systems. The high-end cards require high-end motherboard specs with workstation-class chipsets like Intel's 875p.

If you're not sure if the computer and graphics card you're considering has what it takes to run your applications, check with the software manufacturer. Most companies post a list of qualified hardware on their own websites.

For the most part, however, most video cards manufactured in late 2002 and beyond will be able to handle the most common 3D tasks in animation programs like Maya, at least to some degree. Getting the equipment you desire will ultimately depend on how much you wish to dedicate yourself and your time to learning and producing 3D.

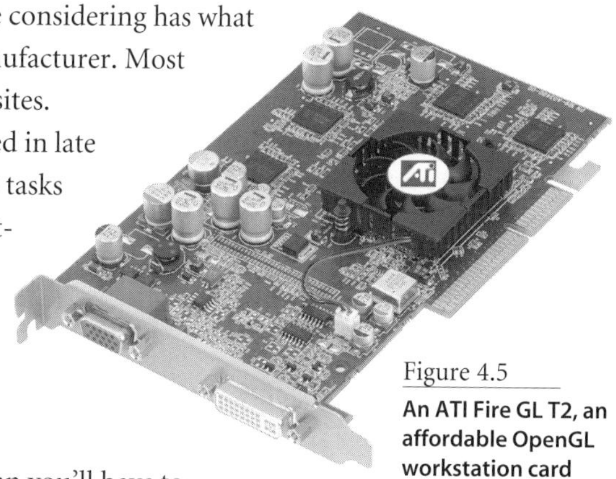

Figure 4.5

An ATI Fire GL T2, an affordable OpenGL workstation card that will speed up Maya work without requiring a huge budget

Prebuilt Systems

Putting together your own 3D system for yourself doesn't mean you'll have to assemble the machine yourself. Though you can do that, it can be a daunting and sometimes time consuming task, and is not for the inexperienced. Many system integrators, such as Dell, that build home and office computers have workstation systems prebuilt for sale, in addition to their typical home and gaming systems. Furthermore, some manufacturers like Boxx Technologies' 3D Boxx and RackSaver's NemeSys systems (Figure 4.6) specialize in workstation machines that incorporate the workstation graphics just mentioned and other solid components tailor-made for 3D and Digital Content Creation work.

Buying a system can save you the hassle of assembling the parts yourself or trying to get a home PC to stretch to customize a system for workstation use. Because these companies have been building systems for studios and professionals for some time, they can get the best performance out of their machines. There is however, the factor of cost to figure into the final equation, as you will pay a slightly higher premium for that convenience.

Figure 4.6

Some vendors specialize in creating systems specifically for 3D creation, such as RackSaver's line of NemeSys 3D workstations, that can save you the trouble of building your own system.

Mobile Alternatives

Yes, the day has come when *workstation* no longer implies a hulking tower of metal connected to a 21-inch ray-tube monitor. You can now throw a laptop in your backpack and do 3D modeling in the park, on a plane, or at the beach. Try that with a dual-processor tower! We have been using several laptops successfully with Maya and other high-end 3D apps, including a Dell M60 (Figure 4.7), a Compaq N800w and an Apple Power-Book G4. It's no surprise that the secret to making these mobile workstations, rather than mere laptops, is the graphics hardware they contain. Each of these systems uses a mobile 3D chipset by either ATI or NVIDIA, and the performance they provide, while not equal to what you can extract from a dual-Xeon Intel box with the latest 3Dlabs Wildcat card, is still plenty usable for modeling and character animation with low- to mid-res models. The amount of time you can work, however, will be limited by how fast your notebook battery depletes itself under a heavy workload.

For a better rendering performance, though, you'll likely want to move your files to a tower system, especially if you have two processors and bigger, faster hard drives.

Input Devices

You'll also need a CD-ROM burner or DVD-R or DVD+R burner for storing large project files and renderings or to output your work to video DVDs. Both can come in handy when it's time to distribute your work to employers. Luckily, they're now standard on most computers.

A Wacom pressure-sensitive tablet (it's impossible to paint well with a mouse) or one of its poorer substitutes, is virtually required for painting textures (Figure 4.8). For example, in Maya, the tablet helpful with tools that use the Artisan interface, which lets you sculpt geometry, paint weighting on characters when working with skeletons, and even distribute particles in particle systems.

Maya also requires a three-button mouse, which is common on Windows systems (and mice that have a scroll wheel can usually use their scroll wheel as a third button), but it's something of a novelty for die-hard Macintosh users who are used to a single mouse button.

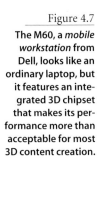

Figure 4.7

The M60, a *mobile workstation* from Dell, looks like an ordinary laptop, but it features an integrated 3D chipset that makes its performance more than acceptable for most 3D content creation.

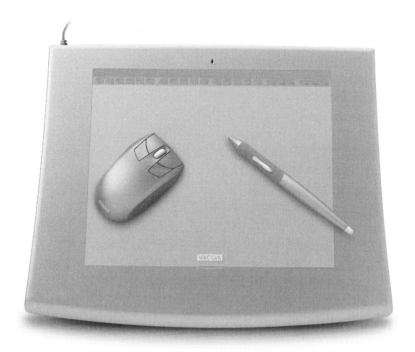

Figure 4.8

Wacom tablets have become a de facto standard for 3D artists. Their pressure-sensitive input is idea for texture painting, applying weight maps, and sculpting surface geometry.

Cameras

Another item that's a near necessity is a camera for capturing textures. A film camera and scanner work okay for this purpose, but a good digital camera of at least 1 megapixel or more will make the work much faster and give you a lot more freedom to build a library of useful and interesting textures. Higher-resolution cameras won't necessarily take better pictures, but they will give you more freedom for zeroing in on small areas of a picture that you may want to use as a texture.

One recommendation: the Nikon D100 SLR works well with the lenses for older film cameras and gives you unlimited creative control over lighting, focusing, and exposures. The different lenses let you get up close for shooting small detailed textures or shoot very wide-angle or telephoto pictures for background elements or environments. A useful accessory is a spherical panorama rig from Kaidan, a beautifully machined piece of specialized hardware that lets you capture environment maps and high dynamic range lighting maps for use in realistic renderings. But if you're just learning, you can do much of the same work with improvised homemade rigs, some trial and error, and a basic tripod.

One final but important piece of hardware that we recommend is a mini-DV (digital video) camera. This camera makes a fantastic, relatively cheap animation recorder that you can use to output finished animations prior to copying them onto VHS or burning to DVD. The camera simply plugs into the FireWire port (a.k.a. IEEE 1394 port) on your computer and lets you dump animation to DV tape. At that point, you can dub an unlimited number of copies onto a VCR. Alternatively, you can use the camera for gathering source material when researching animation. If you're animating a character running, for example, you can go to the local running trail, shoot a dozen different runners in their different strides, then come home and quickly stitch together the styles that work best for your animation.

Eventually, you're going to need to get your animations from your hard drive onto a VHS tape, and you'll either need something like a DV camera to use as an intermediate format, or you'll need to get a graphics card that can output an analog NTSC video signal (or PAL format in Europe) to a VCR. We have found the DV route more versatile because even the laptops we use all have FireWire built in, and we can move video both in and out of the computer.

Some DV cameras feature digital still camera functionality—usually limited to about 1 megapixel—which means they can stand in for a separate digital camera when it's time to gather a bunch of texture source images. Unfortunately, we have yet to find one that works as well in this respect as any dedicated model, primarily because the DV cameras just don't offer the same level of exposure control as even basic point-and-shoot cameras.

If you're planning on combining live-action video with 3D animation, especially if you want to do green-screen work where live action characters are superimposed on 3D rendered backgrounds, you may want to consider investing in a more expensive 3CCD DV camera, since these units produce fewer noise artifacts and better color separation in their images. As such, they're better suited to demanding compositing work. But at anywhere from $1,000 to $4,000, these are definitely a luxury item, and good quality compositing software, such as Apple's Shake can solve many of the problems created by using cheaper alternatives.

Typical hardware costs:

- Computer and monitor, with 1 GB RAM, FireWire, CD-RW or DVD-RW burner, and workstation-caliber Open GL: $2,000 and up
- Wacom tablet: $200 and up
- Digital camera: $400 and up
- Digital video camera: $400 and up
- Total cost: about $3,000

BURNING TO DVD

While it's easier to make DV tapes of your work, you can also burn your video or animation directly to a DVD-Video with a DVD recorder (either DVD-RW or DVD+RW). Using your DVD player, you can then make VHS copies from the DVD master, or even just distribute copies of the DVD. A growing number of animation facilities are now accepting demo reels on DVD as opposed to requiring only a VHS. As a general rule of thumb, it's best to send a DVD video as well as a VHS to make sure you cover your ground.

Assembling the Tools: Software

The price of top-end 3D software has plummeted in recent years. Two years ago, the cheapest seat of Maya you could buy was $7,500. Today, it's $2,000. But you don't even need to buy Maya to learn it: the company offers a free Maya Personal Learning Edition that you can obtain from the Alias website or this book's CD. The software looks and works just like the regular Maya Complete, but has some limitations. You cannot write standard Maya software files (.ma, .mb); only the Maya Personal Learning Edition file format (.mp) can be saved. However, you can import standard Maya software files

If you're serious about learning the software and showing your work to employers, eventually you're going to have to break down and buy it or enroll in a school that has done so.

For texture painting, you'll need Photoshop (Figure 4.9), Deep Paint, Painter, Body Paint, or another high-resolution painting software that lets you work in multiple layers and export your files in a variety of formats.

You'll also want at least a simple video editing tool (many of which are free, such as iMovie, which ships with Mac OS X, or Microsoft Windows' Movie Maker, which is included with Windows XP). These programs will let you combine your animation clips into cohesive sequences and export your animations to tape. If you intend to create more elaborate tape with titles, transitions, and music and audio tracks, or if your goal is to produce a reel on DVD, then you'll need to consider more advanced video editing software, such as Adobe Premiere, Final Cut Pro, or Pinnacle Systems' Liquid Purple.

Typical software costs:

- Maya Complete: $2,500
- Photoshop: $400
- Movie editing software: $100 or less
- Miscellaneous compositing and utilities: about $500
- Total cost: about $3,000

Figure 4.9
Adobe Photoshop is the industry standard for texture painting tools. The fast, efficient use of layers and multiple alpha channels and effects make it easy to create realistic complex images.

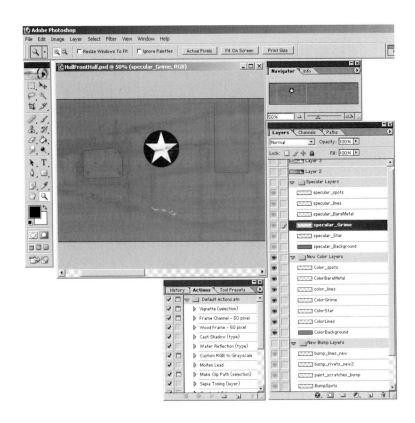

EDUCATIONAL DISCOUNTS

Good news for students and teachers: If you're enrolled in a college or high school, or if you work for one, you're probably eligible for deep discounts on software and hardware, everything from Adobe to Wacom. For example, Alias offers a student version of Alias Maya for $599. Discounts are available on software and hardware from almost every major manufacturer. Keep in mind that some student licenses may restrict the way you can use the software. Support is often limited to installation only, and there are usually restrictions on upgrades to new versions (the student version of Maya is not upgradable.) However, it's a practical alternative for budget-strapped students. Some schools may offer these deals through their own stores, and the software vendors themselves, as well as many e-commerce websites, also offer these student discounts. Try the following:

www.ccvsoftware.com

www.gradware.com

www.creationengine.com

For about $6,000, you can assemble a complete 3D animation studio, including hardware and software. That may sound like a lot of cash, but consider that Maya alone cost $1,500 more than that only two years ago!

Finding a Mentor

What money can't buy you is a mentor. If you're serious about learning 3D on your own, there's almost no hope that you'll succeed in catching up to people who have years head start on you, unless you have someone to critique your work and point out what you should learn.

If no one's volunteering for this position, you're going to need to go trolling. Offer to do filing or to take out the trash for a working 3D artist. Volunteer for work on an independent film and become best friends with the effects supervisor. Hang out at users groups and talk to lots of people; ask them if you can send your stuff to them for some feedback. When they tear it apart, do everything you can to learn from what they say and try any of the techniques they offer, then send back your revisions. Put your project on a laptop and take your mentor out to lunch: with luck he or she will teach you a few things while chewing on the Kung Pao chicken.

Many students of 3D approach active participants in discussion groups for feedback and advice. But buyer beware: sometimes people with the time and inclination to dispense free advice to strangers can do more harm than good. How much do you really want the opinion of unqualified strangers? The best approach is to find people whose work you truly admire—magazines and online publications that feature the work of talented artists and production teams are a good resource. E-mail people whose work you admire for their opinions and advice about your work and ask them questions about techniques they used to create a certain effect. With any luck, you'll establish a rapport and will be able to return to these mentors time and again. Don't forget, however, that people are busy, so you should avoid wasting their time with questions you can easily find the answer to elsewhere. One dumb or obvious question may be enough to get your e-mail filtered into your would-be mentor's Recycling Bin. But staying in touch politely can lead to benefits, as with the Orphanage's Emmanuel Shiu:

I went to a lot of the company parties and all of that, and I met a lot of the people, and guess what, I met a guy, a modeling supervisor, at ILM, and I started sending him my tapes, and sending him my progress…and he said, "Looks great." You know, "Cool, but we're not hiring right now." The most important thing: keep updating those people. Because when you do that, they will remember you…I would keep sending him models I had made, like every two weeks, I would send him a new model, and he would appreciate that because he would see my skill more, and he would see my motivation more.
　　　　　　　　　　　　　　　　　　　　　　　　　　—EMMANUEL SHIU

Books and Training Materials

The next thing you're going to need if you want to teach yourself is a good collection of books (Figure 4.10) and training materials. There are numerous publishers of excellent materials on Maya (we're partial to Sybex and Alias).

When you're first starting out in CG, consider a beginners or fundamental book to show you the essentials of CG and the basics of whatever program you wish to learn. These books will often touch upon a wide range of topics of a program, but leave the more detailed exploration to more advanced books. Therefore, once you've gotten your feet wet and you feel comfortable with the basics, strike out on your own and try a short animation based on your basic knowledge base. Then, get into the intermediate level and advanced books to give you the details you'll need.

Some recommended Maya books (see www.3djobs.net for a more extensive list):

Figure 4.10

You are what you read. There is a mind-numbing number of books available for learning the art and technology of 3D.

The Art of Maya (**Alias**) Not only is this an excellent overview of Maya features, it's just plain cool. It's a coffee table book featuring four-color illustrations of Maya in action, with very clear descriptions of its core functionality as well as some of its potential power.

Introducing Maya: 3D for Beginners; **Dariush Derakhshani (Sybex)** This is a comprehensive primer to familiarize you with Maya and 3D workflow by using step-by-step tutorials and clear explanations of functions and tools, covering almost all of Maya.

Learning Maya Foundation (**Alias**) This is an excellent collection of tutorials you can use to familiarize yourself with the Maya interface and tools, as well as its basic capabilities.

Maya Savvy; **John Kundert-Gibbs, et al. (Sybex)** A collection of tutorials and a fairly comprehensive reference that goes well beyond the lessons in *Learning Maya Foundation*.

Maya Character Animation; **Jaejin Choi (Sybex)** This book is more about character modeling and rigging than character *animation*, and that's what we like about it.

Training Tapes and DVDs

When it's time to learn specific aspects of the software, such as modeling, texturing, or rendering, you'll have to seek out resources that are specific to the topic. One of the best collections of such material is Alias's DVD library (Figure 4.11), which covers everything from modeling for games to Mental Ray rendering. Although these training materials aren't inexpensive, they feature top-notch professionals teaching subjects they know extremely well, and they're well worth the cost.

These DVD authors have lots of real-world working knowledge. If there's a down side, it's that even these in-depth tutorials have to rush to cover the vast ground of materials they're intended to cover. The authors are invariably forced by time constraints to skim through a lot of material, but the included course notes and project files give you plenty of opportunity to back up and step through the concepts they present. Overall, they're some of the best training materials you can get for the money.

Another valuable source of specific and useful training materials is the DVD library produced by Gnomon (www.gnomon3d.com).

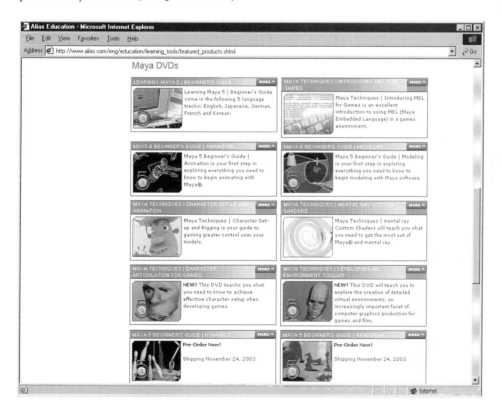

Figure 4.11

Alias' training DVDs and books are prepared by industry experts with lots of first-hand experience. You can get them at www.alias.com.

Training on the Web

The Web is a rich source of information on 3D techniques, tools, and resources. There are too many sites to list even a representative sample here, but the book's website contains updated links to many of the best resources.

Here are a few favorite sites for online training materials, just to get you started:

Learning-Maya (www.learning-maya.com) This site has an incomparable listing of current tutorial links to sites all over the world for all aspects of Maya education, easily structured by categories. It also has a comprehensive listing of Maya resources, books, videos, and so on that you can explore.

Digital Tutors (www.digital-tutors.com) This site has loads of free Maya tutorials, as well as lessons devoted to other applications. It's a good place to get your feet wet without a big investment. Some of Digital Tutors more advanced materials are also for sale, and their prices are very low.

Highend 3D (www.highend3d.com) A site with a very active forum for discussing tools, techniques, and portfolios, as well as lots of downloads of plug-ins, shaders, and resources. Probably the best site for discussions and sharing of advanced 3D techniques.

3Dcafe (www.3dcafe.com) An excellent site for tutorials and online discussions of 3D in general, downloads of models, and other resources.

Gnomon (www.gnomon3d.com) A subscription service with downloadable tutorials and a number of free sample lessons. These augment the DVD collection you can buy from Gnomon.

Maya3d.dk (www.maya3d.dk) Features a small but valuable library of tutorials.

Training in Art

It's essential not to forsake your traditional art skills while you prepare yourself with CG work. Don't forget to keep improving your drawing, painting, sculpture, and/or photography work as you learn more about how to run an animation program. That is perhaps the toughest part of training at home for a CG job, but that is easily tackled with diligence and an earnest willingness to become a better artist.

As a matter of fact, many employers are more keenly interested in your fundamental art skills than anything. Joseph Bowers points out:

Strengthen your fundamentals; if they are weak it will all come crashing down. You can be a great modeler but if you don't understand what you are modeling then it won't look good. You can understand how to animate in Maya, but if you don't understand how people move, it will look weak. I see many people who believe all they need is to learn a program and be good with computers and they will succeed. It doesn't work this way. You must become a strong artist and it will strengthen your work. You may be able to build a strong house, but if the ground it's on is unstable it will be a disaster.

—*JOSEPH BOWERS*

Summary

There's a lot to learn before you can work in the 3D industry, but there are also lots of ways to learn. Schools are a viable option if you've got the time and money to invest in your education, and they're certainly the best way to go for anyone who has not yet entered the work force. Part-time schooling or do-it-yourself training with the help of books, DVDs, and online learning is a practical alternative for people who already have a college degree or who are too busy working to go back to school full time. Whether you go to school or self-train, a mentor is an invaluable asset who can advise you, critique your work, and help steer you toward industry openings.

Above all, your education, however you get it, will prepare you to build a top-notch demo reel and portfolio, the two elements that will do more than any resume or degree to prove that you're ready to join the 3D workforce. Chapter 5 will tell you what you need to know about this all-important body of work.

CHAPTER 5

The Demo Reel, Portfolio, and Resume

There are many elements that contribute to a successful 3D job search, starting with education and training. But apart from personal connections, nothing will affect your chances of landing a prized production job in the industry like the trinity of resume (or *curriculum vitae,* often called the CV), portfolio, and demo reel.

The resume or CV is the paper *and* electronic document of one or two pages that summarizes and chronicles everything relevant to the job for which you're applying.

The portfolio is a collection of 2D images that shows what you can do as an artist. It may include drawings, paintings, illustrations, and photographs of sculptures, as well as stills of your rendered 3D artwork. Any artist hoping to be taken seriously for employment will need one. While printed portfolios are still common and useful for interviewing, it has become a prerequisite at many companies that your portfolio be available as an online web page as well.

The demo reel is an animated version of your portfolio on VHS tape, DVD, or CD-ROM and may also be posted on the Web. It is a required demonstration of your skills and aesthetics as an animator, effects artist, or compositor. Most studios will even want to see a reel if you're a modeler or texture artist because 3D turntables—simple animations showing models revolving through 360 degrees, as if on a potter's wheel—and animations are very revealing of your process and technical mastery.

Here's what we'll be looking at in this chapter:

- **Preparing a resume**
- **Building a portfolio**
- **Crafting a demo reel**
- **Delivering the package**

Preparing Your Resume

There's a good chance that at least some of what you've been taught about a resume is wrong. Pick up any number of resume guides from any number of respected publishers and you'll be told to build a resume in this order: summary or objective, experience (with emphasis on responsibilities), education, skills and tools, and references.

In fact, there are hundreds of books on preparing resumes and cover letters, and they all offer varying advice on the best way to create this vital document. Remember that the resume is your primary sales tool it should inform the reader about you and make you look good. If it fails to do either, it will fail to achieve its objective, which is to get you hired. With that in mind, a good way to present yourself to your future employer may look more like this:

1. Summary

2. Skills and toolset

3. Experience (with emphasis on projects)

4. Education

5. Personal information

6. Project history

There's a good reason for this revised order. As studios become increasingly swamped with resumes and demo reels, they rely more on semi-automated systems for prescreening potential employees. They do this by entering your resume into a database (or having you do it for them online) and then performing keyword queries on the database. For example, an HR recruiter might search for the words *modeling, texturing, lighting, Maya,* and *games.* If your resume doesn't have the keywords the search engine is looking for, you won't come up in the search. When a recruiter finds a set of resumes that matches her search criteria, she'll scan the first few paragraphs for relevant skills and experience and move on if she doesn't find what she's looking for. Only then will she actually read the resumes to get down to who you really are and what you've done. It's not very sophisticated or necessarily an accurate reflection of whether you're qualified for the position, but it's the way it is. Formatting your resume with your skills and toolset up front will make you a lot more likely to stand out in this process than someone whose resume lists skills under education and just above extra-curricular activities.

General or Targeted Resume?

One decision you'll have to make when preparing a resume is whether you want to target it at an individual employer. This can become a time-consuming chore if you're sending resumes out to dozens of employers. The other option is to create a single generic resume and save the personal treatment for the cover letter accompanying your resume.

There's no doubt you will do better with individual employers by tailoring your resume to each. This is especially true if your resume is being submitted to database engines because queries by recruiters will exclusively target the content of the resume, and you'll fare better in these searches if your text is loaded with relevant keywords and emphasizes specific skills the employer is looking for.

On the other hand, if you're submitting your resume to services like FlipDog.com or posting it on sites that list available contractors, you'll need a generic version of your resume that gives proportional weight to all of your skills, with the hope that whoever sees it will find what he or she is looking for in your experience (Figure 5.1).

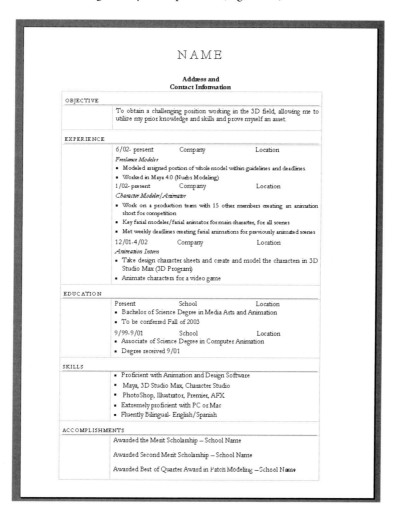

Figure 5.1

A sample resume from an artist fresh out of school. The layout is quick to inform the reader of the artist's skill set.

The Summary of Your Parts

The resume's summary is a single paragraph that tells the company why you should be hired over everyone else. What notable films or games have you worked on? Have you won any awards or been recognized at any festivals? Have you mastered both modeling and MEL? Have you faced a big problem and arrived at an elegant solution? This paragraph should be a well-crafted representation of your best attributes, your key skills, and your most relevant experience as it applies to your prospective employer. It will take 15 seconds to read, but it may take you hours to write and edit, which is time well spent. This is your best pitch; throw a strike, and you could be well on your way to landing a job.

Remember, you've only got 15 seconds to make your pitch, so you should probably spend as much time editing this paragraph to its bare essentials as you took to write the rest of your resume. While it might sound easy, it can be quite a chore to include the five "Do's," below in three or four well-worded sentences (Figure 5.2).

Do:

1. Include the objective of your career search, including the job title if you know it.

2. Include a summary of your most relevant career experience, including specific positions, accomplishments (such as films or games you have completed), and education.

3. Be specific about your desirable qualities that will be relevant to the employer (flexibility, adaptability, creativity, intensity, hard work, technical savvy).

4. Identify special qualities, skills, or aptitudes that make you ideal for the position.

5. Be sure to use keywords that employers are likely to search for, such as leading a team or lead artist, concept artist, Maya, Mental Ray, NURBs, UV mapping, character rigging, lighting, particles, technical direction, Perl, painting, dynamics, cinematics, real-time games, and compositing.

THE 15-SECOND RULE

One cold truth we discovered in our research is the *15-Second Rule*. Whatever you do to sell yourself in this industry, and whatever form it takes, you've got about 15 seconds of a prospective employer's attention to make it work. That's the time it takes to watch a single shaded and wireframe view of a model rotating 360 degrees or an animated character lifting a box and setting it on the table; it's the time it takes to flip through the first two or three pages in your portfolio; it's the time it takes to read a single paragraph that summarizes and sells who you are and what you can do; and it's the time it takes to recite that paragraph from memory when you pitch yourself to a recruiter or director at a job fair. If it takes you longer than 15 seconds to communicate your essence, you've already lost the game. Succeed in capturing somebody's interest in that first quarter-minute, and you'll get another minute or two to push the deal to the next level.

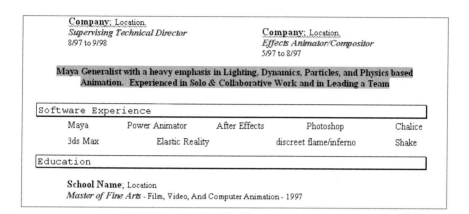

Figure 5.2

An example of a very concise and to the point summary in an otherwise full resume of just the artist's skill set and talent base is positioned to attract an employer's attention quickly without sacrificing much space, though it leaves out broader points useful in a longer summary that would benefit a less experienced resume.

Your Skills and Tools

The skills section of your resume doesn't require a lot of fancy writing. It should be made up of three lists:

- Core skills
- Tools and programming languages
- Platforms and operating systems

These lists must be specific and easy to read. Databases and employers will scan them to see if you have the skills to work with minimal training. Yes, everyone wants an artist with a great fine arts background, but the reality is that there are lots of such artists out there. While no one magic keyword is likely to make you a standout, your chances are slim of getting hired without the one skill the hiring company is focused on.

When listing your core skills, be specific: painting, drawing, illustration, sculpture, photography, character modeling, level design, texture mapping, lighting, matte painting, technical direction, scripting, and so on.

If you're primarily positioning yourself as a 3D artist for games, break down your skills even further: character, hard surfaces, and architectural modeling; low-poly modeling; NURBs; subdivision surfaces; UV mapping; normal mapping; character rigging; MEL scripting; lighting;; clay maquette sculpting.

Be just as specific in listing your tools, whether it's software packages and programming or scripting languages: Maya, 3Ds max, LightWave, Paragon, Photoshop, Deep Paint, Perl, C++, After Effects, Combustion, Match Mover Professional, etc. As Microsoft technical recruiter Marc Marrujo notes, having those key terms on your resume could separate yours from the others:

> *The key thing is to have key terms on your resume because I query on them. So hypothetically, if I'm looking for a developer with AI background, with C, C++ background, with a bit of Maya and hypothetically API background, then I'll go ahead and punch those words up with specific terms that I'm looking for and then what will happen is, hopefully, they'll populate and then they'll come up and I look at their resume and background and see it maps out to the specific role.*
>
> —MARC MARRUJO

Are You Experienced?

If you're fresh out of school, your resume may have little to offer in terms of on-the-job experience, but that doesn't mean you have nothing to offer in this section of your resume. List internships, officer positions in game clubs, directing a student film, or anything that represents a major body of work over an extended period of time. If education has been your only job for, say, the past 15 years, your summary of skills and tools will have to suffice as experience, so be sure to expand upon them to give them as much weight as they deserve.

List your jobs, starting with the most recent and going back as far as you think is relevant to show your ascent up the ladder of responsibility. If you've been promoted or changed jobs within a company, be sure to list those roles as separate jobs. Even if you've worked at jobs that aren't directly relevant to the studio work you're pursuing, it will show where you've been and what you've done with yourself. You'll be surprised to discover where your background reveals common interests and points of conversation with prospective employers. Even the fast food restaurant you worked in after high school can count for something. For instance, in writing this book, Sean discovered that he wasn't the only person interested in 3D who had worn the Chuck E. Cheese rat suit early in his career: Randy Nelson, Dean of Pixar University, was the original corporate rat, as well as the original programmer and animator of the Chuck E. Cheese Pizza Time Theater. The discovery was worth a mutual laugh and something both will remember.

When describing your work experience, include in the first line the name of the company, your job title, and the dates worked. In the description, describe projects you worked on and your major responsibilities, as well as any major accomplishments you achieved in this role.

In this highly competitive job market, employers are particularly interested to know if you have experience that's directly applicable to the project they're hiring for. PDI or Pixar probably won't want to hire you if you've been building space ships for five years, and ILM and ESC may pass if you've been animating children's cartoons. Companies will want to know in general if your responsibilities included modeling with NURBs and subdivision surface tools, but the specific projects you've worked on will give them a world of information about whether that modeling involved creatures and humans or ships and buildings.

Similarly, if you've been working on a game project, you should point out the game's genre and scope. It can matter whether that project was a first-person shooter or a graphically intensive massively multiplayer environment.

Experience: The Catch 22

Everyone wants an answer to the ultimate Catch-22 question in 3D employment: how do you get experience if you can't get hired without experience? It's true that big companies with deep pockets and great working conditions have the pick of the litter in terms of experienced employees, and they simply don't need to dip into the well of new, untested talent. Amy Bendotti, senior technical recruiter with Nintendo of America, confirms that.

> *What we look for is experience, 100 percent. We hardly ever hire entry-level just because we don't really have to. For artists, we don't really look at anybody that doesn't have at least two years experience and hasn't at least published one title.*
>
> —*AMY BENDOTTI*

In many cases, the answer is to get your start at a smaller startup company. Small game companies and boutique effects studios don't have the big budgets or ideal working conditions of the big firms, but look at the bright side: you'll get to do and learn more. Get one good game or a film project under your belt, and not only will your resume show you've got real-world experience, but your portfolio and reel will suddenly swell with professional, bona fide art.

WHAT KIND OF EXPERIENCE

It's often said that a company or client will only hire you if you've already done exactly what they're looking for. Employers like to be sure that an artist will be able to accomplish the job without the worry and fear of late deadlines and blown budgets.

When you're angling to get a specific job, it's always a good idea to tailor your resume (and even sometimes your portfolio and reel) to that job. Find out everything you can about what they're looking for and try to show off all the experience you've had with what they need. If the job is for a character lighter, tailor your resume to show off all the character lighting you've done, as opposed to listing just your lighting experience. The more the employer feels confident that you can do his or her exact project, the better your chances that you'll land the job.

KEEP IT SIMPLE

As important as what you put on your resume is its layout. Although you want to be careful to include all the relevant information and experience you have, you also want to balance that with a layout that's easy to scan for information. A too tightly packed resume is daunting to read when there are one hundred others in a pile also waiting to be read. A well-thought out, concise, and well-designed resume is easy to read, presents information logically, and pleasing to look at. Don't think using small fonts and tight line spacing to cram everything in will impress the employer—you're more likely to give them eye strain, and they'll miss half of what's in there anyway.

Another possibility is to work with recruiters, such as Jo Ann Pacho, an artist's representative with ArtSource, who may be able to help you compensate for your lack of on-the-job experience:

They come to us because maybe we have connections with a client they don't have. Maybe they want to work for a company that is shown on our site to be a client, and maybe we can help them get a foot in the door. Another reason some candidates come to us, especially right out of school, is for resources. They call us up and they ask us: "I have no experience, but I have this degree. How do I get experience if nobody wants to hire me because I don't have any experience…" So in tough times, we offer resources to our talent and it costs them nothing.

—*JO ANN PACHO*

Internships are also outstanding opportunities to get your foot in the door of a studio where you can land some real-world training, as well as a chance to be noticed. Be sure to list them on your resume (Figure 5.3).

Education

When describing your education, keep it simple: where you went to school and what degree or certificate you earned. If you won awards or achieved some other recognition, mention that as long as it's in line with the job you're going after. Many people interviewed said they really didn't care what you did in school—that your experience, portfolio, reel, and personality, were far more important. While some employers do give preference to graduates of certain schools, they're not likely to hold it against you if you spent your time in an institution they've never heard of. Employers care far more about the quality of your work than the name of your school, though they certainly appreciate well-rounded graduates who have studied a broad curriculum, no matter where they studied. As ILM's Ken Mariuama points out, a school's reputation is garnered through its graduates:

We've found that the schools that have a curriculum focused in traditional animation and also one in computer animation—the marriage of both of those disciplines—seem to turn out well-rounded students and people who can sort of almost step right in and be productive….There are several schools out there that have a really strong—I feel—a very good animation curriculum. We're finding a lot of good reels coming from those schools.

—KEN MARUYAMA

Figure 5.3

A sample resume from an artist fresh out of school. This time the layout focuses on showing off the artist's experience.

Name

Street
City, State Zip

Phone Number
E-Mail Address

Background

Skilled as a maya animator and modeler with a focus on MEL scripting and software/tool development for a production pipeline. I have written tools to ease the process of nurbs and polygonal modeling, texturing, character setup and rigging, data management and other tools based on production needs. Ability to work well in a supporting role to help and instruct others in a constantly changing production enviroment. Animation experience in both traditional and CG mediums.

Computer Experience

Maya 4.5	MEL Scripting Language
Adobe Photoshop 7.0	Houdini 5.5
Adobe After Effects 5.5	Renderman/MTOR
Flash 5.0	Quark Xpress 5
Adobe Premiere 6.0	Adobe Illustrator 10
Ultra Edit 9.0	Windows 2000/NT/XP
MacOS/OS X	

Education

2000 - 2003   School Name   Location
Bachelor of Science, Media Arts and Animation

1996 - 2000   School Name   Location
High School Diploma

Work History

2002   Company Name   Location
Look Development
- Look Development for Design and modeling of characters
- Developed various story points and ideas
- Created software tools for modeling, texturing and numerous interface tools

2001 - 2002   Company Name   Location
Graphic Designer
- Created design and layout for custom orders
- Illustrated various covers and images
- Organized file system and data management network

2000 - 2002   Company Name   Location
Web Designer/Animator
- Animated introduction sequence and various interface elements
- Designed overall look and theme of website
- Managed and maintained website and content

Personal, Not Private

Surprisingly, it can't hurt to include some personal information on your resume. There are numerous reasons to keep your private life private, particularly at this stage of the job hunt. However, while some types of personal information can hurt you, there's a flip side to revealing more of yourself than your quantifiable skills and experience: most employers look for people who are a good cultural fit for the team they'll be working with.

The other thing is knowing what they do in their free time. That's something I always ask. If I know a particular department at a company is looking for a designer, and they're all snowboarders or they're really physical people, then I might want to try to find somebody that's a similar type of person, because then they'll be like-minded and they'll mesh better. —JO ANN PACHO

You're going to put in some long, high-pressure hours with your coworkers(sometimes laboring late into the night and through weekends), and having a compatible temperament, similar interests, and a copasetic working style are key factors to making sure everyone will get along. Anything you can show on your resume that supports this objective will go far in your favor. So, while you shouldn't reveal information about you that could be a liability, don't hesitate to list some of your avocations that might shed light on your personality, especially if research reveals that other members of your prospective team have similar interests (but be sure you can back it up in an interview!). Do you restore classic cars, sing in the opera, or play semi-pro ice hockey? A potential employer can get a much better feel for you as a person if you've spilled some of these personal details at the bottom of your resume.

Matt White of LucasArts brings up a great point when he talks about spending long hours with your coworkers under high-stress demands:

This company, compared to many I've worked for, tends to keep a pretty civilized work environment, but we aren't immune from the crunch. I mean, we do find ourselves in positions where we're just having to really work hard to get stuff out. And when we hit those times, there will be periods where people spend more time sometimes at work than they do with their friends and family. And you want to make sure that the people that you have aren't jerks. [You] really want to make sure that they can work well with a team, and our interview process is something you screen for as carefully as you can for the fit factor. —MATT WHITE

Showing off your interests is one thing, but you don't need to reveal your skin color, age, sexual orientation, or whether you've got a family of quintuplets. It's illegal for employers to ask you questions about these "demographics" in interviews, and for good reason: they're discriminatory. For example, one dot-com boom-era company was famously quoted, then sued, after citing the "drag factor" as a reason for not hiring older people and those with families, the theory being that such employees wouldn't work the obscenely long hours and unpaid weekends the company routinely demanded of its employees. While the entertainment industry is generally more civilized—for example, it normally rewards overtime work with overtime pay—there are undoubtedly recruiters with all sorts of prejudices that you don't need to expose yourself to. Such prejudice is carefully guarded against in big companies with well-trained HR staff (who have plenty to lose in the event of a lawsuit), but your chance of being shunned by smaller startups because of such intangible factors is much greater.

Your best approach to putting personal information on your resume is to simply list some of your strongest interests, certifications, or affiliations, in particular those you think might appeal to the group you'll be working with. At the same time, it's best to avoid references to religion, politics, and other potentially inflammatory subjects that could count as much against you as in your favor. A touch of personality goes a long way, but too much gets in the way.

Tailor Made

Whenever you are preparing any materials for a potential employer, do your research and know what an employer is looking for. That way, you can tailor your resume, reel, and portfolio to that company's wants. A modeler crossing over from games to film is going to need to de-emphasize low-poly modeling on the resume and reel and focus on high-resolution modeling techniques. But it pays to be even more specific, as Emmanuel Shiu at The Orphanage notes:

When I went to look for a job, a lot of times what I would do was try to find out—you can do that on the Web—what they're doing, what are the upcoming projects that you think you may be hired for. Like Tippett now, they're hiring for Hellboy, *which is a WWII picture. Well, if you show some WWII stuff, you're much more likely to grab their interest than if you were showing some futuristic airplane.* —EMMANUEL SHIU

Having an interest in a specific niche occupied by the employer is a definite advantage, as long it's sincere. Amy Bendotti of Nintendo of America echoes the sentiments expressed by many employers: "We want people who are really passionate about Nintendo."

Before you proclaim your faith, be sure you can support it with a detailed discussion of what you love about *Star Wars*, or what you like about Nintendo vs. PlayStation 2 vs. Xbox, which games you love to play, and what it is about the artwork or other relevant aspect that sets these games apart from those on other platforms. According to Brian Freisinger, modeling supervisor at ESC, you don't want to smack of the starry-eyed fan:

…If you're obsessed with the film, if you're a Star Wars *nut, or a* Matrix *nut, get a job at a different studio, because nobody's going to like you. You're going to be one of those guys: "Dude. DUDE, this is so cool!" Just shut up. We've been working on it three years. We know.*
—BRIAN FREISINGER

More Resume Resources

A guide to crafting the perfect resume is beyond the scope of this book, but there are hundreds of texts available (every library has dozens), and there are numerous helpful websites, as well. Monster.com, FlipDog.com, and Careerbuilder.com have excellent tutorials and libraries of sample resumes you can download and modify for your own use. All of these sites also features links to commercial services that can prepare a resume for you for a fee. On the book's website, there are links to other valuable resume writing materials and books.

The Portfolio

Art school graduate and recently employed modeler Charlie Lac thinks "a good portfolio and a connection in the company is probably the most important thing." And indeed he's right, showing off your work is hugely important, and using a portfolio can be a big part of it. Unlike a resume, which has to communicate many aspects of who you are, the portfolio has a singular purpose: to illustrate your artistic skill and aesthetic style. Anyone who wants to work as an artist needs a portfolio to have a prayer of landing a job. Unlike a resume, the portfolio should only show about a dozen or so examples of your very best work if you're including a demo reel with it, or perhaps twice that amount if it's only the portfolio.

AVOID SYCOPHANCY

One thing that will turn off employers is a sense that you're trying way too hard. Admiring a studio's work is one thing, but effusing about them can get grating. It's important to know about the place your applying to, to know their strong works as well as their weak ones, and to be able to talk objectively and informed about them. The more you suck up, the less chance you have to land the job. There is sometimes an inverse relationship between how much someone absolutely *loves* this kind of work to how well they can perform it.

CREAM OF THE CROP

Don't let your attachment to your work impair your judgment. The worst thing you can do to sabotage your portfolio is leave works in that are not your best. It is better to have a small, fantastic portfolio than to have a large, mediocre one. If you also spend time tailoring the portfolio to the type of work you're applying for, you should create a sharp statement of your work potential. Keep in mind the portfolio shows your prospective employers the work you are *capable* of doing, not just the work that you've already done.

While there's no limit to the amount of material you can have in your portfolio, only you can decide if everything you include is up to your highest standards. This is a good time to lean on a mentor or friend with a well-developed eye to give you some honest, unequivocal criticism of your work. If someone else calls a particular piece into question, consider pulling it from your portfolio, particularly if you've got plenty of other A-level stuff to show.

Show only your best work. Ask yourself honestly, "Is this my best work, or is it just okay?" If it's just okay, or if it's not quite finished, leave it out until it really shines.

Organize your work in a way that is immediately recognizable and sensible to an employer. If you're applying for a job with a portfolio, arrange your work in an easy to understand manner, whether in a printed portfolio or an online portfolio. For example, you can arrange your models all under a menu item on your web page named Modeling, and then include examples of lighting, texturing, and other specialties under separate headings. You can also separate different kinds of your work in a printed portfolio using tabs or binder separators or even just on different pages.

Be creative, but be sensible in your organization. Many artists just put thumbnails of all of their images on a single web or printed portfolio page and expect the employer to know what they're looking at, but an employer might not be able to tell if that human head is an example of your best modeling skills or just a so-so model that shows off what an awesome texture mapper you are. If you force an employer to ponder this question, you're killing your chances of an interview.

Many recruiters, especially in game companies, use the terms *portfolio* and *demo reel* interchangeably. For example, they'll often ask for an online reel, meaning they expect to see still images, animations, turntables, or all of them. Pay close attention to what the hiring company *says* it wants to see. In film, a demo reel means a videotape of animations or turntables, generally on VHS, although DVD is also acceptable in most cases and can show your work in better light if it's professionally produced.

Even if you're applying for programming or technical director positions that require more technical than artistic merit, you can find creative ways to present your work. In Figure 5.4, the artist, knowing that the job required some technical MEL skills, displays them in his art portfolio. The portfolio shows he has both the ability to script viable tools and to creatively show them off.

That said, the portfolio should reflect a range of styles and techniques that represent the job you're applying for. If you don't have work that covers the entire range, you're better off providing fewer pieces and letting the employer ask for more. In all the interviews conducted for this book, nearly every person who was responsible for reviewing portfolios and reels offered a caution similar to this one from Sean Miller, lead artist at Sammy Studios:

You tend to judge them by not only the strongest piece on the reel but also the weakest piece on the reel. Very often, the thing that gets you put into the No pile is going to be the weakest piece on your reel. If you've got something that's really great, and something that's really bad, we don't know which one we're going to get. We expect people to be able to tell the difference between good and bad. If you put something on your reel that's bad, it becomes something we have to consider. —SEAN MILLER

Figure 5.4

Even MEL scripts can be creatively displayed in a portfolio, as shown here with Art Institute of California— Los Angeles student Daniel Gutierrez's graduating portfolio.

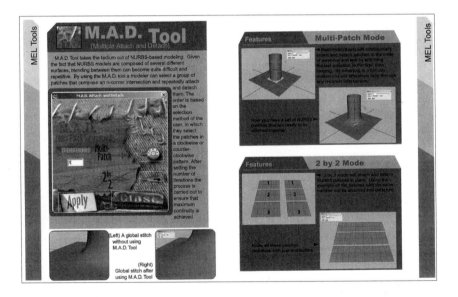

Credit Where Credit Is Due: The Breakdown Sheet

The breakdown sheet is a simple description of your contribution to the work you're showing, and it can be a crucial part of the interview. If your portfolio includes images or animations that you collaborated on with other artists, you need to tell the employer what part of the shot you are directly responsible for. For example, if you modeled the characters used in an animated short, your breakdown sheet should explain what characters you modeled and how you modeled them. As a rule of thumb, it's best to include a credit sheet listing every segment of the reel with a simple breakdown of what you did and if others were also involved.

This sheet is usually attached to the resume and accompanies your portfolio or reel. The temptation to claim a shot as your sole creation may be strong, but don't do it. Here's something we heard from almost every supervisor interviewed for this book:

The things I always get suspicious of, especially in a small industry over here, when you see this shot, and you ask them what they did, and they say, "Oh, I did all of it."

"Really? I just had someone in here three days ago who said the same thing about the same shot." It's a small industry, and someone will call you on it.

Apart from that, there's really nothing bad. What's always a good thing, though, is if you're able to sit there and talk someone through your shot. This is what I did, this is how I did it, this is what I was looking at, and this is what I was thinking when I did it. I had guys who said, "Yeah, I just put it in there and I lit it." —CRAIG LYN

Printed Portfolio Mechanics

There are two kinds of paper-based portfolios you're likely to need in your job search. The first is a book that you maintain and lug around yourself. If you've been to art school, you've probably spent a lot of time discussing this collection; if you haven't, you're going to need to find some other artist portfolios to look at to get a feel for what works and what doesn't.

CREDIT SHEETS

You might be surprised at how many people put shots on their demo reel that they've hardly worked on or simply lifted from another person's reel or from a movie or show. Employers in most large studios require a credit sheet so they can confirm the role of the applicant on the reel.

Many interviewers will sit with you as you watch your reel and go down the credit sheet, not your resume, to ask you questions. That way they can be assured that you are capable of the work you're displaying.

In general, this portfolio includes your best artwork and should be augmented by your sketches and working drawings that show the thought process you went through to arrive at the finished piece. In addition to art that's relevant to the employer, this book can also contain a collection of all kinds of artistic work you've done: photographs of sculptures and paintings, illustrations for publications, and anything that shows your range as an artist. The primary purpose of your personal portfolio book is a record of your original work and your capabilities. It will be an invaluable resource when it's time for a job interview; for when you have to tailor make a portfolio that you can leave behind with an employer, since you will not want to leave behind your originals.

A physical portfolio you may want to create is a handout or "leave behind" that the employer can keep that includes duplicates of the best work from your collection or personal portfolio. An effective physical portfolio to hand-out for a modeling job for example, would include model sheets—8.5×11 sheets with images of 3D rendered objects, drawings, and illustrations from your personal portfolio and your reel—to give an employer an instant snapshot of your capabilities and style and art work that would quickly remind them of you and direct them to a website or your personal contact information (Figure 5.5).

Alternatively, you can create a sampling of your larger portfolio and print images on separate pages. Although color printing can run you a dollar or more per page, cheap photo-quality inkjet printers, such as those from Epson and Canon, produce output that's better than you can expect from a web offset press. If you're going to send a portfolio, print it on letter-sized paper so your images will fit in a standard filing cabinet. Make sure your images

Figure 5.5

Art Institute of California— Los Angeles graduating student Juan Gutierrez illustrates his strength in character modeling with these model sheets in his portfolio.

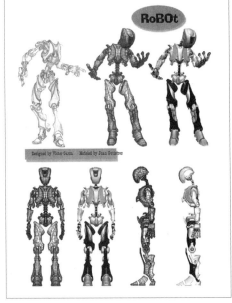

are nicely framed on the pages, that you use the best print quality, and that the prints will stand up to some rough handling. To that end, you should print your images on matte finish paper, which doesn't reveal smudges and fingerprints like glossy pages. Preparing printed portfolios for mailing to many companies can be brutally time-consuming and expensive, which is another good reason to consider a model sheet as an alternative.

> *I hired a person from the Academy [of Arts College, San Francisco], and all I saw was a printout, and it interested me because on that printout were multiple images of the models he could do, and the way he lit them and the way he presented it hooked me, and that was all it took. Of course, I investigated more after that, but it got me enough to want to see what else he had.*
> —EMMANUEL SHIU

The Online Portfolio

An online portfolio has become a helpful asset for landing a job in 3D. Everyone in a 3D studio is plugged in to the Internet, which means an online portfolio can be passed around the office at the speed of a few mouse clicks. Presenting your portfolio online saves your potential employer time and effort, and anything you can do to grease the wheels of the hiring machinery is a worthwhile effort.

Many companies, especially in gaming, now insist on seeing an online portfolio before they'll even consider you, and it's the first stop they'll make after pulling up your resume in a database query. However, some companies, particularly those in the film business, refuse to look at web portfolios and insist on getting a demo reel before they'll take you seriously because web animations need lots of video compression (and cause degradation of color and quality to boot) or can look off-speed during playback. Some companies may want to take a quick look at your work on a website and then see a CD-ROM, DVD, or VHS tape to get a close look at the level of detail in your work. Again, pay close attention to what the hiring company says it wants and follow directions carefully.

Aside from the fact that some companies require one, more good reasons to use an online portfolio is that they increase your exposure and save you money and time. An online portfolio is available instantly to anyone with an Internet connection, meaning 100 percent of your potential employers if you're going to work in 3D, anywhere in the world. If you rely on mail, your work may take a week to cross the country and many weeks to land in an international studio. If you're printing portfolios, duping VHS tapes, and burning DVDs, the cost of assembling and shipping portfolios can quickly drag an unemployed artist under, particularly if you rely on FedEx or DHL to get your package to a director in a timely fashion. Perhaps most importantly, you need time to work on new artwork and animations or to brush up on Perl or Python. With a web-based portfolio, you publish once and let the world come to you.

Animators commonly post video clips on their website, but be aware that bandwidth issues demand that your movies be scaled down and highly compressed for playback online. Using video compression to fit your movie online with a Sorensen or AVI-compressed movie at 320×240 pixels will make your movie download and play at acceptable speeds for most medium-to-high-bandwidth users, but the high-level of compression and small screen size will result in a lot of lost detail.

Mechanics of Creating a Web Portfolio

It's a safe bet that if you've got the technical chops to do 3D, you're also capable of the minimal technical exertion needed to produce an HTML portfolio. In fact, you don't even need to know HTML to do this. Many off-the-shelf software programs include templates and "one-click" publishing solutions that make it easy to produce this work. Or, chances are, for the price of a pizza, you can get one of your HTML-savvy art buddies to help you out.

You might be tempted to wow your audience with fancy, drawn-out Flash animations or a sequence of introductory screens. Resist the temptation and remember the 15-Second Rule. The employer wants to get into your site and see your relevant work. Unless you're applying as a Flash artist, the clock is ticking while your fancy Flash animation plays, and you're losing your chance at keeping the recruiter's attention.

There are as many ways to design a web portfolio as there are artists, but you should always make sure your web page calls attention to your artwork, not your lack of HTML skills. As with other elements of your presentation, a terrible-looking website can cast doubts about your skills as an artist in general. It's far better to keep it simple and show your art on plain, simple pages, than to create a busy, complicated site that detracts from your real work.

If you're going to post animations on your site, make sure they're in a format that downloads quickly and plays smoothly. Many video editing programs, such as Adobe Premiere, provide automated settings for saving files suitable for web playback, and tools such as Discreet's Cleaner are made especially for this purpose. If you are posting large files (over 1MB), it's a good idea to label the thumbnails with the size of the full-resolution animation. This will give lower-bandwidth users some idea of how long they can expect to wait for the download. You should also advise prospective employers to contact you directly for a VHS or DVD to get a better look at your work. The online portfolio (Figure 5.6) may get them salivating, but you'll probably have to close the deal with your reel.

If you lack the expertise to create efficient QuickTime, RealMedia, or AVIs, pick up a book or enlist the help of someone who can prepare these files for you.

Sites such as Highend3D.com, CreativePlanet, and many others listed on the book's website have excellent resources for browsing the portfolios of other 3D artists. This is a great way to find out what other people are doing.

Figure 5.6

A reel can be compressed and put online for employers to reference. Though you lose quality with online video, it can be a good point of reference for an employer before or after they see your DVD or VHS reel. This still is from an online reel displaying CG created for a USC student film.

The Demo Reel

For animators, compositors, effects artists, or anyone creating moving 3D images, the demo reel exceeds the resume in importance. Unless you've worked at a top shop with an eminently droppable name such as Digital Domain, Weta, or ILM, no one really cares where you've worked as much as they do about what you did there. What they want to see is your reel. If you're still not clear on what a demo reel is, it's a VHS video tape—or in growing cases, a DVD—or an online facsimile of one, containing samples of your very best work, most of which is at least minimally animated. It can include shots you created for films, commercials, or video; movies or screen captures of video games; or even simple turntable animations of models and environments you created. Typically, a demo reel will have a short title screen (Figure 5.7), and maybe closing credits at the end, but you should waste no time jumping right into your work. Music and other forms of audio are entirely optional.

Because so many supervisors and recruiters have very specific opinions about what should and shouldn't be on a reel, we'll let them do most of the talking here.

First, there is the animator's reel. More than other artists, the animator needs a reel that communicates as a single work of art, rather than a series of unrelated moving images. The best animation reels are short films, where the character being animated tells a story and moves through a range of emotions. We asked Randy Nelson, Dean of Pixar University, what it takes to make an animator's reel stand out from the crowd. He explained that Pixar is far more impressed by good visual storytelling than by an elaborate command of computer graphics. Or as he puts it, "There are great storytellers, and there are great stories, and you don't always get the two of them together. So what you are looking for is somebody who has got technique in the service of ideas."

The thing that jumps out of certain portfolios is, here is a communicator who's got ideas he or she wants to communicate and has mastered a technique that allows them to be expressed, and we see those three elements present. A communicator, ideas, and technique, all coming together—you know you've got somebody who's thinking about the same thing you are, which is how to delight an audience, how to scare an audience, how to put an audience on its edge and release that expectation with a laugh. That is always what we are looking for. So that may mean that the tape is very rough. It could contain no computer graphics whatsoever. That's a really important thing for people to understand. From our point of view, we care about the ability to express ideas, not whether you use a computer to do it.

—*RANDY NELSON*

DEMO REEL MUSIC

Picking out just the right music to accentuate your demo reel can be a difficult decision. Music often drastically affects how someone views imagery. The beats and timing of the music can help or hinder the timing of the animation and edits in the video.

You should choose a piece of music that best reflects your imagery, something that is upbeat and keeps a good pace with your work. If your best work is in subtle character work, then hard-driving techno music is probably not your best choice.

However, keep in mind it's not necessary to include music on your reel. In some cases, supervisors will turn off the sound altogether when they sit down to watch reels. They prefer to focus on the timing of the imagery entirely.

Not all studios are looking for storytellers. Some may simply want artists who can breathe life into animated characters. In studios that focus on effects, rather than on all-digital character features, the expectations are more technical and have less to do with telling a story than with making a visual impression. There's also the fine line between impressing a potential employer and offending someone with different sensibilities.

Figure 5.7

A simple, legible screen with an elegant animated background is quite ample for the title screen for a demo reel.

If your reel is going to ESC Entertainment, however, neither the fantasy world of CG adult films nor the expressive world of children's character animation may be quite the right approach. In some studios, it's far more important to be able to reproduce a convincing version of reality than it is to be a storyteller. In ESC's work, 3D animation is almost always composited with live-action plates to create an altered, often spectacular, but sometimes very nearly ordinary-looking simulation of reality. Making things look ordinary is surprisingly difficult because we're all so keenly knowledgeable about the world around us. In some ways, reproducing reality is harder than creating the most spectacular science-fiction effects. Modeling, texturing, lighting, or animating ordinary, everyday objects and scenes can help shift the focus from your artistic eye to your mastery of technique. It's one thing to model a fantastic-looking futuristic car that could look like, well, anything, but it takes a keen eye for proportion and detail and some precision and refined skill to make a model of a BMW that really looks like the one your potential employer drove to work this morning.

Here's how Brian Freisinger approaches a demo reel:

Honestly, what I look for in a reel: I've seen some of the most blitzing reels that have come in, that have some of the most fantastic structures and creatures and architecture, but you know, this guy sent in this thing, it was this really cool creature set, this really cool demon, but what the hell's a demon look like? You can do anything you want. It may look cool, and I can break it down structurally, would it really walk like that, would it look like that, but at the end of the day, I have hired people who had like, coffee pots and phone booths, and it looked real. But it was something that I could recognize: tanks, guns, you know, that's what we do. When creature work comes along, there's like two or three creatures in the film…

My boss, Kim Libreri, says, "We don't try to re-create reality, we try to capture reality."

…One thing though, that I do like to look at besides a demo reel: when I'm interested in somebody, I often ask to see the mesh, if they'll send you the file. When I started the job at Manix, I just sent meshes in. That's kind of how I think. It's actually pretty easy

to cover up screw-ups in a reel, but if you have a talented modeler looking at a mesh, it's pretty easy to see how they think structurally, by what they sent me in mesh... Did you microbevel it, did you do this, did you do that? How's your poly count? Did you hide the thinner section with this thing, or did you actually bother to put that bevel in? Are they going to be hard or easy to train? I actually think the mesh often is more important than the reel.

—*BRIAN FREISINGER*

Freisinger's point about including your project files is well taken. While a director can get a sense of your skill and technique through your demo reel alone, including a disc along with your project files is going to clearly reveal how you achieved your effects. Be aware, however, that this will backfire if you used sloppy technique or didn't go far enough to organize your projects in a clear, logical way. Be sure to take the time to go through your scene files and name objects and texture maps using a sensible convention and to purge your files of redundant geometry, unconnected nodes, and other junk that could cast doubt about your work habits.

Also, make sure you are not violating any agreements if you are using scene files from projects you were hired to make. Quite often sharing these files with others will breach an unspoken, if not legal, agreement with your previous employers.

Different Reels for Different Jobs

There is no right or wrong thing to include on a demo reel, but it's vital that you focus on your core skills and the job you're applying for. If you're after a modeling gig, show your best models and leave out the character animations and particle effects. If you're after an effects animator's job, you're going to need some well rendered and composited animations where you pull out all the stops to create realistic explosions, smoke, fire, flocking, motion blur, and so on—no one's going to look to see how cleanly you modeled the upper lip of the character that's firing the bazooka. Here's how to present some of the things you might include:

Modeling Turntables are a great way to show off 3D models of objects, although they don't always do justice to interior sets. One popular approach is to set your prop in standard three-point lighting, then animate the object to rotate 360 degrees over five seconds or so (Figure 5.8). Render this animation in both shaded and wireframe views to show what your model looks like when rendered and to give a good idea of how you modeled it. Do models have to be well lit and textured? Yes. While a visual effects modeling supervisor can look at a simple-shaded render, or even a wireframe, and see what you can do, the recruiter who's screening your application is likely to be a lot more impressed by a good, realistic rendering. And in games, you're most likely going to be texturing the models you build. Even though texturing may not be central to what you'll be doing as a modeler, it's essential to the presentation that's going to sell your skills to a recruiter.

Figure 5.8

Typical turntable positions for a modeled character from a student reel by Juan Gutierrez, printed out for a flat portfolio presentation.

Texture painting A texture mapper's job is to create visually interesting, texturally rich, and realistic surfaces. Your demo reel should show rendered models as well as the untextured shaded models and 2D maps that you used to create the surfaces. If you're applying for a film job, be sure your textures are of sufficient resolution and detail to be absolutely convincing, and pay special attention to details like specular maps, attenuation of specularity, reflections, bumpiness, and displacement. Be sure to fix any texture stretching with tricky UVs and hide visible seams as much as possible. Of course, if you're texturing for games, the requirements are quite different: you should limit yourself to a minimal number of textures in any scene and keep them small (512×512 pixels maximum). This is your opportunity to show how clever you are at tiling and reusing textures in creative ways. Try to avoid visible seams in tiled textures and disproportionate scaling of reused textures. Do use textures to enhance the sense of geometric detail in low-poly objects, for example, painting rivets, dents and seams into the welded metal texture that's applied to a simple rectangular box. You might be hired to work on games for a third-generation console, and this is a good chance to show off your bump, specular, and normal mapping skills. Even if the games you'll work on can't use these features, employers will be happy to know that you know how to use them down the line.

Character animation The days of animating walk cycles for a demo reel are long gone. Although realistic walks and a good sense of weight and timing are still vital skills, if you want to be taken seriously as a character animator, your character is going to have to reveal personality, express emotions, and convey thoughts and motivation (Figure 5.9). Characters don't have to do very much, but they have to do it with feeling. At the least, characters have to demonstrate a clear sense of purpose and go through some transition of emotion. Typically, you'll want your reel to include *cinematics,* short scenes where your virtual actor performs for the camera.

Student Joe Bowers puts it very well when asked about how his demo reel is progressing and what he thinks he'll need:

For animation I think I will need a short and sweet animation reel that is blunt and to the point. Here is my character animation, here is what I have to offer you, can I have a job... please?
—JOSEPH BOWERS

Effects animation If you're after a job in special effects animation, you're going to need to show not only cool effects, but cool effects composited with live action. This means in addition to rendering your effects, you must take the time to bring the renderings into After Effects, Shake, Combustion, or some other compositing application and seamlessly blend them with motion blur and lighting and color correction. It's a great idea to include the source footage, rendered plates, and composited clip on the reel to show your technique as well as your mastery of the art.

Figure 5.9

A still frame from an animation-oriented reel from Daniel Gutierrez. Animation reels focus on the ability to tell a story and emotion through the use of simple characters and settings.

Technical direction A technical director's reel needs to show a variety of work that clearly illustrates the ability to solve a variety of 3D problems: modeling, compositing, texturing, lighting, effects animation, and character rigging. If you have created user interfaces with MEL or other tools, it's worth showing screen captures of these in action as well.

Crafting a Demo Reel

The mechanics of creating a demo reel should be old hat to anyone who's been working in 3D animation. In fact, creating a demo reel is a piece of cake compared to the grueling, months-long task of creating and rendering all of the scenes that will go into the demo reel. Then you'll need to edit all of the clips you plan to use on your reel into a continuous sequence.

As far as the hardware required to edit your reel, there are numerous ways to output to video nowadays. You'll need access to a computer that can either output to a DV camera through FireWire or has a video output board and enough speed to play the video back at full speed while you record directly to a VCR. The simplest way to output video now is by burning a DVD, though you may have to burn a few versions to preview how the final images look on your TV if you don't have one of the other video output options.

For editing, programs like iMovie, FinalCut Express from Apple Computer, Adobe Premiere, and Pinnacle Edition are ideal for creating a reel from the animated clips and video on your PC or Mac. The documentation that comes with this software will step you through the relatively simple process of copying your animation to tape as well.

Like other aspects of your presentation, bad editing and bad choices of music can hurt you. No one's looking for fancy editing or audio in your reel, so it's better to leave them out. Craig Lyn said that he always turns off the sound before he sits down to watch demo reels, and other managers expressed irritation at the poor choices artists often make in the sound they add to their reels. Audio is a matter of personal taste, and your chance of sharing your hiring manager's taste in music is slim. On the other hand, you may be including some clips that have original soundtracks, and it is useful to include the audio track with these clips because it will help recruiters see how well you worked with audio. This is particularly true of character animators doing lip-synch animation. The down side of including audio is that sudden audio edits from one track to another are far more jarring than their visual equivalent, and you may have more trouble incorporating existing audio than simply washing over it with an alternate track of canned music.

LABELING

It's always best to print out a label with your contact information clearly typed out. Don't bother with fancy label designs, simple can be just as striking. Often glitzy labels and tape sleeves or DVD inserts seem like they're trying to cover up for something. Let your work do the talking.

The same goes for fancy video effects and transitions. It's great that you've got a video editor with 7,000 out-of-the-box effects like a sweeping wipe. But you're applying for a job in 3D, and that's what your prospective employer is looking at. Cuts-only edits with simple text credits at the end are more than ample for a reel. Our advice: unless you're really good at audio and editing, leave out the audio and skip the whiz-bang edits. If you are going to include audio, consider skipping the music and instead including a voice-over narration that describes your thought process and techniques for each of the included clips.

Do whatever you want for credits at the end; we suggest a simple screen with your name and contact information. Leave the credits for what you did for each shot on the credits sheet you included with the reel. If you're lucky enough to get your video watched to the end, chances are you've already made a good impression and what you put in the credits won't matter anyway. For end credits, just the facts—name, e-mail, phone number—are enough, but do make sure to include a credit sheet with specific information about what you did on the shots shown in the reel.

Once you've recorded a reel to tape, put a label on the cassette with your name and contact information. It's likely the cardboard sleeve will be lost or discarded moments after the tape gets its first viewing.

A DVD Demo Reel

With the proliferation of cheap DVD burners and good DVD authoring software, the temptation to create a demo on DVD is great. It's possible to break your project into chapters, with menus for different types of work, such as modeling or texturing and to create tracks that are optimized for NTSC or PAL video, as well as for playback on a computer (which has better color fidelity than a TV). DVD video quality is leaps and bounds better than VHS tapes, too. You can also create hybrid disks that contain both your video reel and resources such as model meshes or MEL scripts that directors may want to inspect to confirm your skills.

TESTING YOUR DVD

Your favorite consumer electronics retailer is a great place to test your DVD for compatibility. They can have as many as 50 or so DVD players hooked up and turned on at any given moment. You can quickly go down the aisle popping your disc into every player in sight and get a pretty good idea of the odds that it will play on any employer's hardware and that the menus work as expected with various remotes. While you're at it, you can also put it through every computer DVD player you can find, including a couple of different Macs and PC workstations. It's a couple of hours well spent, considering the impression you'll make if you ship out a nonworking disc. Just make sure this is ok with the store before they have security boot you out. Most store managers would be happy to help you out.

Be sure that if you take this route, you test your disc extensively on multiple brands of DVDs because home-burned DVDs may not play on all types of DVD players and you want to be sure your disc loads and plays quickly, with no user meddling required. An advantage that VHS has over DVD is that you can be pretty sure exactly what will happen when someone puts the tape in the drive and punches Play. That's why it's a good idea to always bundle a VHS tape with a DVD, just in case.

Although it still seems like new technology, DVD is slowly starting to be preferred over VHS as the medium for distributing demo reels. The discs are smaller, lighter, cheaper, easier to store, easier to transport or mail, and much better quality than VHS. The burners are already faster than the 1:1 speed of VHS, so you can knock out four ready-to-ship DVDs in about the time it takes to dupe one copy of your reel on tape.

Whether you decide to print a fancy label for your disc is your own choice, but remember it's what's inside the disc that counts.

Delivering the Package

Shipping your reel to a recruiter is something like a Hail Mary pass in football. You throw it up in desperation and pray that it will land in the hands of someone on your team. If you've done your homework about what the company is looking for, your artwork shows your talents, your resume is well prepared, and you've gone through the correct process to submit your work, you've done all you can. The sad truth is that your reel may arrive on the same day as 200 others and that your work may be evaluated in batches of 50 or more at one sitting. That it isn't a pretty picture:

> *I was at Siggraph four years ago…and one of my friends worked at Pixar at the time. They had this little room behind their booth. It was floor-to-ceiling reels of character animators —people were dropping off reels —and it was floor to ceiling of just character animator demo reels.*
> —BRIAN FREISINGER

The market has been extremely competitive for years. In the corner of Pixar's old studio space, they had a museum where hiring managers kept extraordinary creative relics of hopeful animator's efforts to get noticed. Some animators strive to improve their chances of getting attention by creating elaborate packages and hand-crafted boxes in which to ship their reels and resumes, such as Chinese puzzles and inventive mechanical contraptions to spring video tapes onto unsuspecting recruiters. However, according to Pixar's Randy Nelson, the attempts didn't necessarily achieve their objective:

> *But the important thing to note about that is that there is an inverse relationship between successful candidates and coolness of presentation. That is inevitably what recruiting would tell us—we would all go, "Wow, how clever, that is so amazing, what*

a great thing"—is that great reels come in sort of plain old beat up Sony 6-hour tape cardboard packages with hand-written labels scrawled on them, because film makers are too busy making films to have time for all that neat stuff.

And so recruiting would tell us that the sad thing is that the enormous creativity that showed up in the packaging of the presentation was rarely reflected in the thing presented.

It became axiomatic in fact that one of these, "I am so damn clever, you can't believe how neat this thing is, this is the best box you have seen in a year," inevitably that was all there was to see. The really great folks just sent their work in, and their work spoke for them. And folks whose work wasn't this great figured out some way of putting some creativity into it, and unfortunately it should have just gone into the work on the reel instead of the package the reel came in.

—RANDY NELSON

Summary

Preparing your resume, portfolio, and demo reel is the process of communicating and presenting what you've done and what you know. This sounds simple, but the art of the deal is a delicate balancing act in which you must emphasize the right blend of talents and skills, aptitudes and potential. Most importantly, it means preparing your materials to show employers what they want to see. Like most works of art, it's not something you can do overnight with any expectation of success, but if you follow the advice in this chapter you'll be well on the way to having a presentation that's going to impress potential employers.

CHAPTER 6

Finding Jobs

Where do 3D artists find work? The answer is that there are jobs for 3D artists and technical people in almost every major city in the U.S., and in most cities in the developed world. This book's DVD and website list companies around the globe.

The epicenter of 3D opportunities, of course, is in the entertainment and media industry: cities such as Los Angeles, San Francisco, San Diego, Chicago, New York, Boston, Austin, London, Sydney, Toronto, Vancouver, and Hamburg spring to mind. However, you can find 3D jobs anywhere where television shows and TV commercials are produced; where architects render building designs; where lawyers sue over traffic accidents and manufacturing liabilities; where industrial designers, biotech engineers, and manufacturers visualize new products and packaging; where illustrators are coming up with the latest magazine covers and infographics. Even the entertainment industry is branching out. Many game studios, especially smaller ones on a shoestring budget, operate as virtual studios, with artists, game designers, and programmers spread all over the map.

If you're willing to relocate to find work, you can focus your efforts on the major entertainment industry hubs. Even if you've settled somewhere off the beaten path, you may still be able to land a job doing the type of work you enjoy, as long as you're not too rigid in your expectations. In this chapter, we will explore the following:

- Hollywood jobs
- San Francisco jobs
- Jobs on the Web
- Job search engines
- School job boards
- Job fairs and conferences

To Hollywood (and Beyond)

There's no doubt that the best place to get a job in 3D and effects is Hollywood. By "Hollywood," however, we're not referring to the literal town of Hollywood, California, so much as a state of mind—and a network of interdependent businesses. The center of the world's entertainment industry is still located in the Los Angeles basin, but that encompasses an area about 10,000 square miles beyond the boundaries of Hollywood itself. It includes the cities of Santa Monica, Burbank, Culver City, Glendale, Venice, Marina Del Ray, Pasadena, Van Nuys, Torrance, Irvine, Long Beach, Sherman Oaks, Los Angeles, Beverly Hills, Universal City, Costa Mesa, Newport Beach, and, of course, Hollywood. Among the various entertainment-related businesses are, of course, game and effects studios. It should come as no surprise that this is where most of the entertainment-related 3D and effects jobs are located, since most of the world's film, television, music, and many games companies are based here, such as Disney, DreamWorks, Paramount, Vivendi-Universal, Time-Warner, and so on. Working on film effects requires frequent face time with the directors, art directors, and production companies that run film projects, which means big effects houses tend to be near the big film studios. Most big film companies these days have spun off countless television, online, and video game enterprises that also fuel the industry. Add to this the small boutique shops that specialize in certain types of effects, from character animation to compositing to animated title sequences to TV commercial production, and you've got an industry with hundreds of branches, offshoots, and potential places of employment.

Keep in mind, however, that the Hollywood web of influence is too big to be contained by specific geographical boundaries. When someone mentions "Hollywood jobs," they are often referring to work whose financial backing and creative impetus originated in Los Angeles, but that work might actually get done in locations as far afield as San Francisco, Great Britain, or New Zealand.

There are 3D job opportunities in the entertainment industry almost everywhere if you're looking to work in the video game business. Depending on whom you ask, the video game industry now produces something like ten billion dollars in annual revenues, which rivals the money made by movies, again depending on who you ask. While a very small percentage of the people working in movies are engaged in 3D and effects, a huge percentage of the creative talent in games are artists and engineers working in the 3D medium. Chances are good that if you want to work in 3D, you'll end up working in games at some point. Game companies are springing up all over the globe, and even though times are tough for small startup game studios, game budgets are booming as game revenues increase.

The San Francisco Bay Area

Given that 3D and digital effects are a spin-off of computer and software technology, it's no surprise that the San Francisco Bay Area has become a center of digital effects in its own right. As with Hollywood, the term "San Francisco Bay Area" is a broad one and can mean anywhere from San Rafael and Novato in the north to San Jose in the south (the heart of what is known in general as Silicon Valley). Companies such as Pixar, Industrial Light and Magic, Pacific Data Images/DreamWorks, Tippett Studio, and ESC Entertainment were fermented in the same brew of technical genius that produced Apple Computers, Hewlett-Packard, Silicon Graphics, nVidia, 3D Labs, ATI Technology, and others. Pixar's largest shareholder, for example, is Steve Jobs, who famously co-founded Apple Computer in a Silicon Valley garage. Although the directors and artists that provide the vision behind the Bay Area studios have Hollywood pedigrees, most of the engineers who wrote the software and built the render farms that power these companies made their start in Silicon Valley. Games, which are even more technologically dependent than film effects, also have a major base in the San Francisco region. Electronic Arts, Sony Electronic Entertainment of America, Sega, LucasArts, Stormfront Studios, 3DO, and a host of smaller game companies call the Bay Area home. Shrek, Nemo, and The Hulk, may all have a Hollywood address, but their heart— PDI/DreamWorks (Figure 6.1), Pixar, and ILM— is in San Francisco.

Figure 6.1

PDI/DreamWorks' headquarters, several inches above sea level, near the San Francisco Bay.

BUT I HATE L.A.!

All this should not be taken to mean that you have to live in L.A or the San Francisco Bay Area, or even in a big metropolis, to get a job in the 3D industry, although it certainly helps.

If your taste runs more toward working in paradise (and everyone's got an opinion of what qualifies), you can find occasional openings in game studios in clean-living towns like Boulder, Colorado (Anark Studios); Bend, Oregon (Sony EEA); Oakhurst, California (Sierra Tel, near Yosemite); and even Honolulu, Hawaii (Konami). Television graphics, product visualization, forensic animation, illustration, and corporate multimedia work is available in local markets in every country in the industrialized world. There's a list of links to some of these companies on www.3djobs.net.

Finding 3D Jobs on the Web

There are many places to find 3D jobs, and one of the most obvious (although, in some ways, least effective) ways to find a job is to search the opportunities advertised online. The Internet job market has exactly the same mix of advantages and disadvantages offered by eBay and other online auction services. These sites reach tens of thousands of users—in the language of economics, they're *efficient markets*. (In such markets, prices are quickly bid up to the very maximum amount that the market will bear.) That's good for employers, but not so great for hopeful employees because employers can expect hundreds of applicants for any advertised job. While online job searches make it deceptively easy to find job openings, you can be sure you'll be vying for these positions in an intensely competitive environment.

You've probably heard it before, but the best leads come from personal networking and who you know, which is something that I discuss in greater detail in the next chapter. However, if you simply want to see what's available, websites are a fine place to start.

Be aware that printing links to websites in a book like this can be risky; it's common to see the sites and links appear and disappear within the same week. However, the sources I discuss in this chapter have been around for a while, and with any luck, they'll still be posting job ads when you read this. There's a much more extensive index of links on the website for this book (www.3djobs.net). You'll also find links to some of the major corporate job boards on the website and the book's DVD.

When commencing an online job search, keep in mind that there are three major types of job resources you'll find there: job databases, such as Monster.com and FlipDog.com; job bulletin boards, such as those on Highend3D.com (Figure 6.2), Gamasutra (Figure 6.3), Creativeplanet.com, and AWN.com; and company websites, including those of recruiting agencies and the studios themselves. Each of these has its own unique utility in your job hunt.

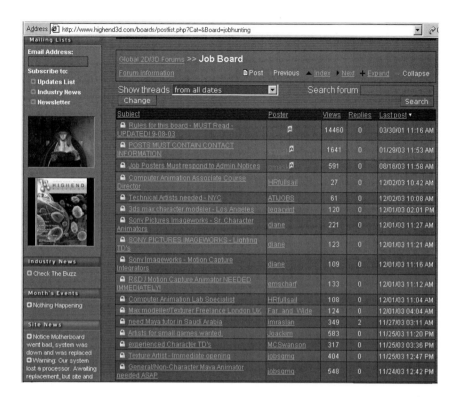

Figure 6.2

Some of the best resources for new openings are online job bulletin boards, maintained by special interest websites devoted to 3D and animation. Highend3D's job board is one of the most active for visual effects.

PRINTED RESOURCES

The Internet has become the overwhelmingly favorite place to post job classifieds, but it's also possible to find useful 3D job information in printed publications. It's tough to find specific job openings this way because print periodicals have a lead-time of weeks or months that are far longer than the hiring cycle at most studios. However, well-connected print publications, such as *Cinefex* and *Game Developer*, are a good source of information about studios winning contracts to work on new films and staffing up for major projects. When you find these nuggets of news, it's worth checking out the company online or through personal connections for news about opportunities. Occasionally, studios will advertise in local papers for 3D talent, but this is very rare. 3D is a highly specialized skill, and most studio recruiters are savvy enough to turn to specialized markets for their recruiting efforts or use word of mouth referrals. On the other hand, if you're looking for alternative gigs, such as architectural rendering, forensic animation, or illustration jobs, newspaper classifieds and their online counterparts are worth trolling since these old-school industries may not be as well tuned to the favorite haunts of 3D talent.

Figure 6.3

Gamasutra's board should be a first stop when searching for game-related openings.

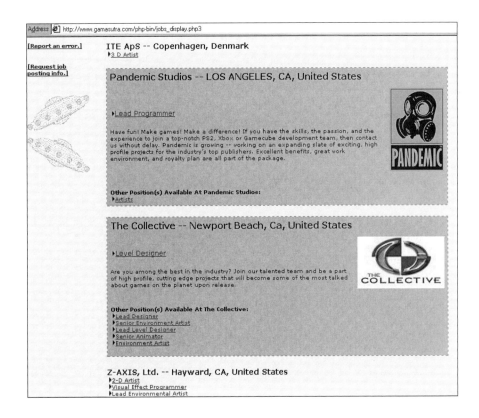

Favorite Online 3D Sites

The following table includes sites that have been around for a while and provide a steady stream of useful job-hunting information and specific job listings. See www.3djobs.net for a more up-to-date list.

SPECIAL INTEREST SITES	COMMENTS
highend3d.com	Highend 3D's job board is very active for film jobs. The site focuses on high-end 3D applications and the film and broadcast industries. The job listings, quite a few of which are international, tend to reflect this bias.
awn.com	Animation World Network (AWN), affiliated with *Animation Magazine*, posts all kinds of domestic and international job listings from the 2D and 3D animation world. The listings are sortable by date posted, location, company, and title.
cgchannel.com	This site has lots of postings, primarily for film CG jobs.
cgtalk.com	This is a great job listing board for film and games jobs.
creativeplanet.com	Creativeplanet is a great site to find job listings in 3D, motion graphics, broadcasting, and compositing.
gamasutra.com	Gamasutra, operated by CMP, which also publishes *Game Developer* magazine, has the most active listings of new jobs in the gaming business. You can post resumes and search through resumes of other users.

General Job Search Engines

General employment sites have nearly eclipsed newspaper classifieds as a place to search for jobs from A to Z. Monster.com, HotJobs.com, FlipDog.com (Figure 6.4), and a dwindling number of smaller competitors have become the de facto place for big, corporate HR departments to post their job listings. Even entertainment companies like Electronic Arts, Sony, and Microsoft use these databases to promote their openings, despite the fact that listing on Monster.com is likely to invite hundreds of unwanted resumes from people who are only vaguely interested in a 3D career.

The advantage of such sites is that they do a lot of the work of job-hunting for you. The way it works is this: you create a profile of yourself by answering their job-related multiple-choice questions. You then submit this profile and a text-only version of your resume to the database, which actively searches for jobs that match your skills. When it finds a match, you get an e-mail with instructions about how to contact the employer and how to fulfill the employer's requirements (these usually include submitting a traditional resume, demo reel, and so on.) Of course, you'll get lots of weird and highly suspect matches, and you'll end up throwing away many e-mails you get from such search engines. Occasionally, employers will search the database to find employees and contact you if you're a match for an open position, but don't count on this happening frequently in a down economy.

Figure 6.4

At FlipDog.com, you can set up an automated job search through the Job Hunter feature. When FlipDog finds a match, you get an e-mail.

The following job sites are all good places to mount a general online job search:

GENERAL JOB SEARCH DATABASES	COMMENTS
flipdog.com	FlipDog is now owned by Monster.com, but it appears to operate a separate database and use separate search agents. For some reason, FlipDog seems to be a better place to find 3D jobs than Monster. See my notes on Monster.com about search agents.
www.hotjobs.com	HotJobs.com is operated by Yahoo!. Like Monster and FlipDog, HotJobs lets you save searches and search agents so you can be notified when new jobs are posted. Also like the other big job databases, HotJobs gets a lot of ads from large corporations, including some games companies, but they receive few job listings from film effects studios.
www.monster.com	Monster.com is the best-advertised job resource in the world, but it has no traction in the film industry. It is, however, likely to run many ads from the games and effects industry, and it's a good place to look for openings in industrial design, architectural, software, graphic design, and engineering firms. For best results, you can create search agents that alert you by e-mail of new openings that match your search criteria. Monster.com has great general information about preparing resumes and interviewing.

Corporate Job Sites

The most current source of publicly available information about the openings at any company is its own website. Companies such as Sony Entertainment, PDI/DreamWorks, ILM, Pixar, Digital Domain, and other really big shops have so many jobs open at any one time that it's unlikely you'll see ads for most of their openings in classified ads or even on online job boards such as Monster.com. However, smaller companies *are* likely to post their most current openings on the Web.

Large companies such as Electronic Arts (Figures 6.5 and 6.6) and Microsoft maintain their own online submission databases that closely resemble those on Monster.com or FlipDog. Just like those sites, you submit your resume and fill out a multiple-choice form, then sit back and wait for notification when the database finds a match. (If you do receive an alert to an opening, the ball's in your court. You'll need to be ready to quickly submit a resume and reel to the listed recruiter.)

We have posted links to many corporate job sites at www.3djobs.net. It's important to remember that even if you've seen an ad for a job posted elsewhere, you should visit the company's website to see if there's more information about the listed job, what other types of openings are available that you might fit in, and what specific qualifications the company is looking for. Many corporate websites post requirements and tips about submitting resumes, portfolios, and demo reels. Following their instructions won't guarantee that you'll get a job, but failing to follow the instructions almost certainly guarantees that you won't.

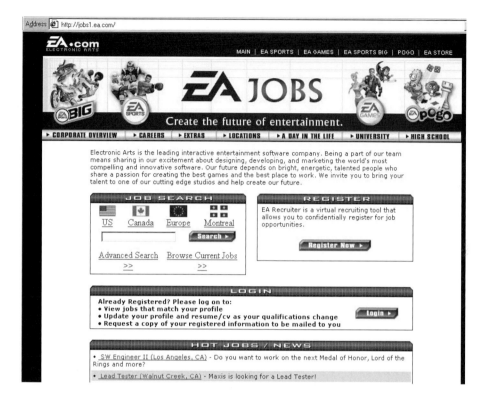

Figure 6.5

Like the general job boards, Electronic Arts lets you submit a resume and fill out a survey. When a new job opens up that matches your key words, you get an e-mail.

Figure 6.6

Electronic Arts' corporate headquarters is among the biggest and best in the business.

You should not rely on corporate websites to inform you about what openings are out there. However, if you do, you may never hear about an opening that's tailor-made for you. It's common to hear that so-and-so is looking for modelers, animators, and 3D texture painters and rush to the company's website only to find no information about those openings but plenty of ads for tenured art directors, CG engineers, and vice presidents of sales.

TIPS FOR WORKING WITH ONLINE JOB SEARCH ENGINES

- Prepare your resume for uploading to a database. Convert your formatted resume to plain text format, then comb through it for places where the formatting doesn't make sense or looks awkward. With an online resume, it's not important that it fit on a single page. It's far more important that someone reading it online can read it easily and that the formatting works in plain text. Make sure you follow the guidelines for listing your skills and toolset, because these are crucial to a database query.

- If you're going to apply for different jobs in the same company, be sure your resume works for both positions—another reason to list your skills and toolset up front. You probably won't be allowed to post multiple copies of your resume in your personal profile. If the database finds a matching job, you can send in a more tailored resume for that position, but keep in mind that a recruiter may see your more generalized resume before you get a chance.

- Follow instructions carefully for posting your website URL.

- Remember that even if you come up in an HR database query, you won't necessarily be called in for an interview. With Electronic Arts jobs, for example, you'll get an e-mail notification that you've matched a new job description, but you'll have to apply for that job and send a resume and reel before you'll actually be considered.

- Check your profile on the company job site fairly frequently. The rules and submission formats and guidelines can change without your knowledge.

The reason for this is that really high-level jobs for seasoned managers and credentialed technical people are tough to fill, and companies sometimes search many months to hire the right candidate for these positions. Between the time there's an opening for this type of job and the time the job is filled, there's plenty of time to place ads on corporate and third-party websites. However, the entry-level and even mid-level artist positions are often filled through personal referrals, long waiting lists of past contractors, or from a long list of possible hires waiting in the stacks of unsolicited demo reels, so many of these are never advertised. Just because a company has no jobs posted online doesn't mean they have no openings. If you do hear about one of these unlisted openings but don't see it on the company's website, use your contacts to find someone to look at your reel. Chances are good that your word-of-mouth information is more current than the web page.

School Job Boards

If you're a student at a school that teaches 3D and effects, chances are good that the school has the inside line on nearby industry jobs and internships. Typically, at least some of the teachers in such schools moonlight from industry jobs, and they're likely to throw a few employment bones to the school. 3D companies like to keep plenty of interns on hand for thankless jobs like render wrangling and by law, these unpaid (or meagerly paid) positions have to be accompanied by credit and supervision from a qualified teaching institution (or they're called "slave labor" instead of internships). Many 3D artists have gotten a foot in the door through render wrangling and other mailroom-type jobs. Students with suffi-cient time and financial security to afford a few months of such sweatshop labor can par-lay internships into real jobs if they're on their toes and have a good portfolio or reel to sneak into their bosses' in-boxes when no one's looking.

(A render wrangler is a person who baby-sits rendering jobs on render farm servers, making sure the servers don't crash, that the rendered images come out looking like they're supposed to, and that all the little rendered bits get shuffled into their proper bit holes. This is a job that usually takes place late at night, when the other 3D artists, techni-cal directors, and parking lot attendants are home drinking chai and watching reruns of *The Poseidon Adventure*.)

A few schools have such a great reputation and strong connections in the animation industry that they get raided regularly by studios in search of new talent, so, as discussed in Chapter 4, it's worth checking a school's hiring record and job boards before enrolling. Nearly every college has a career placement person who helps graduating students find jobs, and that person will also maintain a list of available internships. Most schools also have a job board or online job listing where they advertise jobs that have come to them through the grapevine. Often, these are jobs that won't be posted anywhere else online, so check these boards carefully. If you're not in school, you might still be able to gain access to job boards of nearby colleges, and these might offer valuable leads to local jobs.

Word of Mouth

One of the best places to get word-of-mouth information about who's hiring is through online bulletin boards like Highend3D.com. Even more valuable, however, is a network of friends working in the industry. Make sure to let them all know you're job hunting. They'll probably come to you if there's an opening. It doesn't hurt to remind them that many companies offer bounties for referring people who end up getting hired, so it's in their best interest to put your name in the hat.

It's also important to keep your ear to the tracks. Go to user's group meetings—find out if Siggraph has a local chapter, for example—and software demonstrations, and get involved in volunteer projects. You'll be surprised how quickly these can lead to strong job referrals.

Job Fairs

Many of the big computer graphics gatherings offer job fairs or recruiting events, although some of them do this simply as an informal part of their appearance at these events. Professional conferences like Game Developers Conference and Siggraph are fantastic opportunities because they are widely attended by the art directors and supervisors who might be responsible for hiring; there is usually an area at the conference dedicated specifically to recruiting.

Similarly, at Game Developers Conference, recruiters are on hand to talk to you and look at portfolios, and it's common to get introduced to art directors and other hiring managers if you have something worth looking at.

> When you prepare for one of these big job fairs, make sure you print plenty of resumes, get business cards, and burn lots of copies of your demo reel. You'll easily hand off 20 or 30 copies of each in a busy day.

If you do make a contact at these shows, be sure to follow up afterward. Companies may absorb hundreds of reels and resumes at one of these events, and there's almost no hope they'll remember much about you other than whatever notes they may have scribbled down while you talked. Assuming you got a business card from a recruiter or manager, you have an open door to contact them after the show, thank them for talking with you, and confirm that they've received your materials and are considering your application.

NO FAIR

The job fair portion of Siggraph's conference used to be particularly impressive, with push-pin bulletin boards where employers could look at portfolios posted by artists, artists could look at job openings posted by recruiters, and a highly organized system for dropping off demo reels and arranging interviews resulted in lots of people getting seen and hired. Even better, this was staged near the registration portion of the convention, so you could participate in the job fair without paying to get into the show. Unfortunately, the economy reached such a sorry state in 2003 that the show's organizers cancelled the job fair due to lack of support from attending companies. The substitute was an informal bulletin board with a chaotic confetti of thumb-tacked resumes and stapled-up job openings that offered no apparent advantage over electronic and snail mail communications. On the bright side, many production companies manned their show-floor kiosks where you could drop off resumes and reels. If you are lucky, you will find a loitering recruiter. For schmoozing alone, Siggraph is always a worthwhile event.

If you do plan to attend trade shows, be sure to choose wisely. There's a big difference between professional events, such as Siggraph, and consumer/retailer conventions. Shows such as E3 and CES (The Consumer Electronics Show), which are geared towards hyping new products to retail vendors and distributors, are not nearly as useful for job hunting. These tend to attract more salespeople, retail buyers, and hardcore fans from the general public and fewer developers and art director types. While it's fun and educational to go to these shows, and you'll learn a lot about what's new in the market (and who has money to blow on monolithic booths, stadium-class sound systems, swimsuit models, and the coolest tchotchkes), you should weigh the advantages against the cost of attending. Shows like these can cost hundreds of dollars a day, if you consider show admission (usually over $100), travel, hotels, parking, and meals. If you do attend the retail shows looking for work, plan to focus your attention on smaller studios, which are far more likely to administer their booths with people who may be involved in the hiring process, such as artists, art directors, developers, and HR people. Big companies, with the money for dedicated PR and sales teams, usually won't pay their creative employees to attend such events. Typically, they'll send key people only to the professional conferences, such as Siggraph and Game Dev, where they might actually learn something useful.

Even the annual expo hosted by the National Association of Broadcasters (NAB) is a mediocre event at which to hunt for 3D employment (see Figure 6.7). As with other wholesaler/retailer shows, this gigantic expo, covering acres of conference center, is mostly about selling hardware and software to broadcasters. During the job fair offered at the 2003 NAB show in Las Vegas, many of the broadcasters who were supposed to be on hand to recruit never showed up and simply left a cardboard box on a table where you could drop your resume. The odds at the blackjack table were much better!

Figure 6.7

NAB is a sea of manufacturers and broadcasting companies, but your chances of finding people you can talk to about a job in 3D are slim.

Summary

Finding jobs in the 3D industry is a challenge. Companies list new openings all the time. Some of these will be to fill a large number of seats for upcoming projects, in which case your chances of landing a gig are good, but more will be for hard to fill specialty positions. The key to landing a job is not only applying for the easy to find jobs, but also expanding your search to look for jobs that aren't advertised. Never sit back and hope that a search engine or recruiter is going to bring a job to you. Diligent searching using a variety of sources and jumping on leads when you find them is your best shot at success.

Use online advertising, web search engines, special interest bulletin boards, school job posting sites; be a regular visitor to company job boards; read industry press; attend users groups, conferences, and film festivals; and above all, keep in touch with your contacts in the industry. It will take all of your resources and energy, but eventually, you'll find a job with your name on it.

CHAPTER 7

The Real Goods: Who You Know

You'll hear it in any job hunt in a difficult market: It's not what you know, but *who* you know that will make the difference between getting the red carpet treatment and getting the door slammed in your face. It's not fair, it's not pretty, and it's not supposed to be that way, but it *is*.

The equation is simple: given 100 artists with more or less equal talent and qualifications, the guy with a buddy on the inside is going to land the job every time. What's worse, you might never even hear about the job, since the guy with the inside line is going to be settled in and hanging out at the water cooler swapping tales of special effects conquests, while you're still pasting your resume into FlipDog.com. The truth is, the best jobs are never even advertised because these cherry gigs are almost always filled from a company's Rolodex of personal connections.

Okay, so you weren't born on a block where all the kids grew up to be famous animators; your uncle is a plumber, not an executive at Disney; and your college roommate isn't the technical effects supervisor on the next *Harry Potter*. You might as well go jump in the lime pit and get it over with, right? Well, maybe. But there are a few things you can try first, beginning with tapping into the connections you may not even realize you have, and networking, networking, and ever more networking. This chapter explains:

- Why personal connections are so important
- How to identify and tap into your connections
- Other resources for networking
- Informational interviews
- Other opportunities for making yourself known

Friends in the Business: The Job Hunter's Hotline

It's fairly obvious that somebody with personal connections is more likely to get hired than someone without, all else being equal. But there are a number of reasons for this that you must understand if you want to crack this most difficult of job-hunting nuts.

Put yourself in the shoes of the recruiters. Their job is to find a perfect match for a given position. This means someone who has all the requisite skills and talent, certainly, but also someone who is a reliable, productive worker and a good cultural fit for the group he'll be working in. In other words, someone whose personality, interests, and values complement those of existing employees. There are many intangibles in this list. It's one thing to know 3D tools and skills and show this on your reel, but how can a recruiter evaluate your capacity for good cheer and a positive constructive attitude when deadlines call for working late into the night and through weekends to finish a shot? You might say you're a "quick learner" on your resume, but who will vouch for such a claim? The success of any group can depend on these intangibles, and only someone who knows you personally—especially someone who has been down in the trenches and working closely with you—can truly make a judgment call about what you're like under pressure. When someone on the inside recommends you, they aren't simply verifying the accuracy of your resume, they are offering **a reliable, first-person testimonial to your character**. Such a person is not just a witness, but also an advocate on your behalf. This is the golden ticket: find one and the Chocolate Factory is yours, Charlie.

If you don't believe us, listen to Matt White at LucasArts:

Some of the most successful hires we make are through people that work here who already know the environment, who know what's required and know somebody who fits that mold, so it can cut to the chase pretty quickly. —MATT WHITE

And to Brian Freisinger at ESC:

When you're in the industry, it's nepotism, it's all nepotism. Three guys I hired out of school, and three other guys I hired, I knew. Two of them I'd worked with before, and one was a guy I'd known in the industry, and another guy I recently hired was a friend of a friend who came highly recommended. And you glance at the reels and make sure they're good, and then you hire them…usually when he's recommended by friends of yours in the industry, you grab 'em. You cut through 90 percent of all the other stuff you've got to deal with. They've got a track record. —BRIAN FREISINGER

Of course, if you're the bridge burning type, there's a risk to being known in the industry. (You've seen *Star Wars*, right? There's a Dark Side to everything.) If you've made a mess of things in other jobs, your past is likely to come back to haunt you. The world is full of people who can't get hired because nobody wants to work with them ever again. In a comparatively small and surprisingly interconnected industry like the 3D business, where employees change companies as often as they change the oil in their Minis, your reputation is going to precede you. If you find yourself in this boat, don't count on being able to list only your remaining friends as references; the damage you do can lead to some long-lasting memories. Don't burn your bridges, no matter how badly your bosses need to hear what you have to say. Always leave on a good note.

Several recruiters and artists we interviewed recalled rejecting an otherwise qualified candidate because of past experience and a lingering bad taste in their mouth. Or, as Brian Freisinger puts it plainly:

You're going to work with other people, so you may as well learn to get along with them, because that's the rest of your career. And it gets around quick if you're a jerk.

—*BRIAN FREISINGER*

Again, it's not enough to have someone just say they know you or know of you. What you need is that all-important *reliable, first-person testimonial to your character.*

Now that you know why personal connections are so important to your job hunt and what you need them to do for you, the questions are who do you know who is in a position to vouch for you, will they vouch for you, and if not, what can you do to get them to become your champion? At first glance you might not be able to identify anyone obvious, but sometimes the help you need can be found in unlikely places. And sometimes turning a casual or distant acquaintance into an active advocate on your behalf is less difficult than you might think.

Who Do You Know?

If you're already job hunting, there's a chance that you've already made a mental short list of people you know in the industry, but if you're in school and a year or more away from seriously looking for work, it's the perfect time to make a thorough list of people you know who might be able to help you find a job in the future and throughout your career. It is of the utmost importance to make solid connections with your classmates and professors and make a good impression on them to which Joseph Bowers can attest:

Definitely, most of my friends who have already graduated have gotten jobs, working on some impressive stuff. I know if I ever need work they will be there to help if possible. The most important contact is my teacher who hired me. Mainly because I now work for him, which is great.

—*JOE BOWERS*

In 1967, a Harvard sociologist, Stanley Milgram, conducted a simple experiment that showed that people almost anywhere in the country are connected to almost every other person through a short chain of acquaintances of acquaintances. Milgram gave a letter to several hundred randomly selected people around the country with instructions to deliver this letter to a "target" in Boston. If they didn't know the recipient personally, they were to give it to somebody who might be closer to that person, and so on, until the letter got to someone who actually knew the recipient personally, and could hand it over. What Milgram found was that it took about six people, on average, before the letter arrived at its destination. This experiment led to the coining of the phrase "six degrees of separation." Although there are more people in the world today than there were in 1967, in a world as small as the 3D industry, it's likely that you are separated by only two or three degrees from any other person in the industry. You may not know it, but John Lasseter, George Lucas, and James Cameron are practically your best friends.

But the real question is, who are those people and who do they know? What you need to do is dredge up every person you know and figure out which ones have connections in the industry that might help you find the job you're after. Start with the following exercise:

Make a chart, or a spreadsheet, with four columns. In the first column put the names of all of your former employers and coworkers, teachers, and advisors, all of the 3D students you know (including those who have graduated), and any friends you know with even the faintest hope of having even second-degree connections in the industry. Don't be choosy at this stage. Include your close friends and family members on this list, especially if they have any dealings with the entertainment or tech industries.

FEEL OUT YOUR TEACHERS

As important as a teacher can be in your job search, it's important to gauge your teachers accurately. Some teachers may be against the idea of helping students into companies for fear of a conflict of interest or some such. Others are so inundated with students who want help, they may refuse everyone flatly. As recent graduate Daniel Militonian puts it, "You can't really count on teachers too much in school, because you have to understand that every student wants them to get them a job and they just can't, so I would never ask a teacher to help me get a job. So in school you have to make as many friends as possible and make sure they remember you when you are working in the field and help you out."

Feel out your teachers to be sure they are receptive to helping students get jobs. More often than not, you'll find them eager to do so. Some even will approach their better students with work over the course of the semester.

In the second column of this chart, put a number from 1 to 10, for the level of influence this person has in the 3D industry. If it's a teacher, who also happens to work in a 3D studio, make it a 10. If it's a teacher who has taught lots of students who have gone on to work in the industry, maybe an 8 or a 9. If it's a teacher who teaches life drawing, but might have students who have gone on to work in the effects or games industries, make him a 6, and so on, until you come to students who have yet to form any close bonds in the industry—rate them a 1.

In the next column, rate each person from 1–10 on how you think they would rate *your character* as a potential employee. Use 10 for anyone who you know would not only vouch for you, but also act as an advocate for you in their company or another company that is hiring, and use a 1 for someone who may have serious reservations about recommending you. Try to be honest with yourself as you fill in this column. Have you worked with the person? Did you get along well? Did you agree on the types of things that had to be done and work together to do them? Just because you exchanged friendly banter at the water cooler doesn't necessarily mean someone has a high opinion of you as a worker. This score is really about evaluating yourself through their eyes. If it's a teacher, did the teacher consistently express admiration of your work, offer encouragement about your prospects, single you out as a star pupil?

In the last column, score how each of these people are likely to rate your technical skills and talent, with a 10 meaning they'll score you as a consummate and talented professional. Do they think you have the chops to make it in the industry? Have they seen your work and evaluated it with a critical eye? How likely is it that they will praise your skills to a potential employer?

Once this list is complete, total the three scores for each person. Then sort the list with the highest scores on top. Anyone who scores 25 or higher gets an "A" and is a valuable *A list* contact for you; these should be on the top of your list of people to tap into in your job hunt. (You can think of the A list as your *advocate* list.) Anyone in the low 20s should get a "B" and is very likely someone you can cultivate as an advocate (we'll cover how to cultivate a connection later in this section.) Finally, if someone scores below 20, consider the reasons. Have you failed to show this person what you're really capable of? Perhaps it's a teacher whose class hasn't inspired your best efforts or someone with seemingly distant connections in the industry who is otherwise completely sold on you as a talented and upstanding artist. In this case, have a chat with them and find out who they really know.

If it's a contact who is not as impressed with your work as you would like, consider putting some serious effort into raising this person's score. For example, if it's a teacher, find out how you can improve your standing in his or her class and better your work in an effort to impress them more. If nothing else, it will help you sweeten your body of artwork in the end run.

MAKING CONNECTIONS THE EASY WAY

The hands-down best way to make connections is to simply be pleasant and outgoing with your workmates and classmates. Getting to know people and having them get to know you puts you in their mental Rolodex. If they like you and if they respect your work and abilities, your phone calls about potential work will be welcome. This is a very personal business, so be careful about how you cultivate your friendships. Don't ever get to the point where you try to use people for their ability to get you work. That, like nothing else, will burn you and your bridges to a cinder. Just be cool and make sure to stay in touch with pals you meet along the way.

Cultivating an A-List

If you're a student or new to the industry, you probably have a very short A-list, and lots of people who score a "B" or below, even though they're well connected in the industry. You'll have to work to bring these people up. How you do this depends on the nature of your relationship. In general, you'll need to demonstrate your character through hard work, dedication, and good spirit, and you'll have to show them that you have the skills and talent to deserve their attention.

The Web of Trust: Tapping into Friends of Friends

During the dot-com boom, Epinions.com came up with—and even explored patenting—an elaborate system to tap into a simple and ages-old concept that we here will call the *web of trust*. What it boiled down to was the expression, "Any friend of yours is a friend of mine." If Mary trusts you, and you trust somebody else, then by extension, Mary is more likely to trust that somebody else than a total stranger. It was a powerful concept and, though it didn't turn it into a viable business model, in the real world this concept is used everyday by almost everyone. You use it when you ask your friend to recommend a dentist, or a mechanic for your Honda, and you may even use it when you're looking for a date for Friday night. But you can also use the web of trust to get connected in the 3D industry. Nathan Taketani, who is graduating from art school, now knows his web of trust very well:

I am searching for a job now, the online thing seems to have the most listings but in reality there is not a lot of opportunities for recent grads. The real trick seems to be hitting up my friends to see where they're at, and talking to my teachers and getting involved with their projects. —NATHAN TAKETANI

Once you've identified your A-list of industry contacts, it's time to start taking each of them to lunch. Be persuasive and persistent. Few people who rate an "A" on your list are likely to turn down your invitations to lunch more than a few times, no matter how busy they are, especially when you insist that you're buying at their favorite restaurant (it will be the best $30 you spend in your entire job search). It doesn't hurt to appeal to their ego: "I know you're well connected in the industry and you have a lot to teach me. I would really like to pick your brain about the business." And this isn't going to be just a small talk kind of lunch. You should bring a notebook, or even better, a tape recorder, and you should use the opportunity to pepper your contact with key questions, such as:

Who do you know who is working in the industry?

How do you know them?

Do they trust your opinion?

What do you think they would think of my work?

What are they like; do we have anything in common?

Would you put me in touch with them?

Would you introduce me to them?

Do you think I would be a good candidate to work for them?

If so, would you recommend me?

If not, why?

How far you want to go down this list will depend on how comfortable you are with your lunch date. If you have cultivated a really strong relationship with this person, then none of these questions should be difficult to ask. If you feel some of these questions would be inappropriate to ask—or would put them on the spot—maybe you should think about improving your status with this person before you try to tap into their network of friends.

Immediately after your lunch, be sure to send a thank-you note, remind the person that they offered to put you in touch with such and such a person, and make sure to keep following up until they follow through.

Remember not to pester these people into being your personal advocate. The best kinds of relationships are formed through true friendships or teacher-student relationships. While most people will be more than happy to take some time to let you pick their brain, be aware of their tolerance level for this type of contact.

To that end, keep a detailed log of when and how you've contacted people, so you don't end up stalking anyone without realizing it. You will talk to dozens of people at all hours of the day all week long—forgetting that you already hit someone up for a lunch date is easy to do.

Informational Interviews vs. Networking Lunches

Unlike lunch with a friend or a friend of a friend, an informational interview is an opportunity to find out about a job in some industry or to get general information about a particular company. Although an informational interview might be a good way to develop job leads, its purpose is to help you find the right job in the right industry. In some industries, it is accepted practice to cold-call strangers in appropriate companies to hit them up for informational interviews, and many books on job-hunting specifically recommend this. Unfortunately, the 3D job market is so competitive that many studios now have a policy of flatly denying informational interviews, and many art directors and recruiters won't even bother responding to requests. There are simply too many artists trying to get in through this perceived back door. You will instead need a networking lunch set up through your personal contacts.

Assuming one of your A-list contacts has finally given you a name of someone at a game or effects studio, it's time to take the next step in your networking. Unless you're extremely lucky, the chances are slim that this new contact will have an open position just waiting for you to step into (if they do, your introduction from your advocate may get you hired on the spot). However, that doesn't mean the contact won't make time for you. It's time to make another lunch date, this time with your new industry contact. As soon as your A-list contact makes the introduction, you need to follow up and invite the new contact to lunch (or coffee or a beer, or go to the office for fifteen minutes if that's all the contact has time for—be flexible but persistent—but not too persistent!). Make it clear that you're not looking to get hired but would like to ask questions about the company and especially what he does at the company (again, appeal to the ego). Good questions to ask include how they got where they are, what type of skills and demo reel they have, what they look for when they hire people, or what other people saw in him that got him hired.

When you go to this lunch, bring your reel and portfolio. Any artist or art director will naturally gravitate to a book of pictures. Chances are that if you put it on the table, you'll get your stuff looked at without asking. If you bring your reel, you'll need a laptop or some convenient way to show it. Use the opportunity to ask for critical feedback, and take mental or even scribbled notes, if you can do it without impeding your conversation. After the meeting, jot down the important notes and comments so you can refer to them later. If the new contact offers specific criticism of your work, this is a golden opportunity to impress. Remember this feedback, because your next step should be to rush home and fix, to the letter, whatever the contact says is wrong with the work, and send it back in its new and improved state a few days later. If the contact is impressed with the changes, you'll have an opening to send more work. If you can show this kind of commitment and responsiveness, you may gain a new advocate in the industry.

Emmanuel Shiu, background artist at The Orphanage, says persistence can pay off:

I met a guy, a modeling supervisor at ILM, and I started sending him my tapes and sending him my progress… I sent him my stuff, and he said, "Looks great." You know, "Cool, but we're not hiring right now."

The most important thing: keep updating those people. Because when you do that, they will remember you…he remembered me because of that. I would keep sending him models I had made, like every two weeks, I would send him a new model, and he would appreciate that because he would see my skill more, and he would see my motivation more.

That's really important. Just because you don't get the job, doesn't mean you stop. You keep going, and going, and you will get it, because people will see that you're really serious.

—EMMANUEL SHIU

Even if such an opportunity doesn't come up, a networking lunch is a perfect opportunity to ask about other people in the industry, such as recently hired artists, whom you may be able to tap into as further contacts. While most people won't give out the contact information of other people in the company, if your contact likes you they may be willing to send an e-mail to someone suggesting they give you a call. If you network well, there is a certain exponential growth factor, and you can quickly go from knowing no one to knowing more people than you can stay in touch with.

Following Up

When someone grants you a networking lunch, they're doing you a big favor. Be sure to send them a thank you note within a couple of days—a handwritten note packs a lot more punch than an e-mail, but an e-mail is better than nothing. Then be sure to do anything you said you were going to do, such as sending more artwork or sending a version of your work that incorporates the contact's suggestions. You have put a lot of effort into lighting this fire, and you need to keep it stoked.

Be mindful, however, that most successful artists in this industry are busier than they want to be. Be persistent without being pushy. Be respectful of their schedule and try to be patient if it takes them an awfully long time to get back to you. But being too demanding can cost you in the future.

For example, I once had a person out of the blue contact me through one of my published articles to help them with some animation questions. I was more than happy to help when I could. I would receive at first an e-mail or two every few days, to which I would take a day to respond. When I became excruciatingly busy at work and home and couldn't get back to him to answer his questions, I received a torrent of e-mails asking why I wasn't responding to him. One e-mail came just short of demanding that I write him back and answer his question. I understand he was frustrated and needed help with his project, but this was clearly uncalled for. I replied to him, answered his question, and politely told him I just did not have the time to correspond with him anymore. I wished him luck and sent him on his way, referring him to some books I thought would be beneficial. I felt very bad about that, but honestly, it really chapped me to have him act that way.

Networking Opportunities

Even if you have many friends with industry contacts, eventually, your well of personal contacts may run dry. Where do you turn to find more resources? School clubs, software user groups, volunteer projects, trade associations, and Internet bulletin boards are all good places to find others with similar interests, and any of them offers opportunities to meet and befriend people who may become your lifeline to a job down the line. This is not something that's going to happen overnight, and if you contact people with the obvious intention of using them as a stepping stone to a job in the 3D industry, you're not likely to get the time of day. On the other hand, if you immerse yourself in these organizations, become involved, participate actively in their projects, and help other members when you can, you'll quickly earn a reputation as a person to keep in mind when opportunities arise, and that is when contacts become fruitful. In time, people in these groups may start to make their way onto your A-list of personal connections.

School Resources

Schools, by their nature, are social places. Students struggle through the same classes and subjects, face the same assignments and deadlines, and are often asked to work together on group projects. But if the classroom environment gives you limited exposure to people you connect with, consider joining a club or organization dedicated to 3D work. For example, some art schools have game clubs, where members work on developing a game together, and you can practice doing real-time art for a working game or prototype and get important experience working with engineers, art directors, and game designers who tie the artwork together. In fact, clubs are one of the few places you can get real-world game development experience without first getting hired to work on a game.

GET TO KNOW YOUR SCHOOL

Most schools have many programs that have at least a tangential connection to CG. Getting to know people in other departments and programs can open the door to solid contacts for you. For instance, if your school has a video production department, get in touch with their students and see if you can do some effects or CG work for their video projects. This can not only increase your body of reel-worthy work, but establish contacts with people who you may run into in your professional future.

Student films are also projects that often involve numerous students collaborating on a project. You may find yourself in demand to create special effects for an otherwise live-action film, or you might get involved in creating a fully animated short.

When signing on to work on any volunteer student project, ask lots of questions about who is producing it, who's in charge, what the timeline for completion is, and so on. In short, treat it as a job because such projects can eat up lots of free time that you could spend working on your own portfolio pieces or brushing up on new software or graphics skills. Also, consider whether the project will realistically get done while you're attending school, since it won't do you much good as a demo reel piece if it's only half done when you graduate.

Finally, make a real effort be social, to tutor and mentor other students, and generally to be a likeable person. Your contacts in school can be lifelong associates or friends. Many of these contacts may not bear fruit right out of school, but they can eventually blossom. Many artists have been hired through friendships they made at school, so get to know your classmates and be ready to learn from them. You'll sometimes find that you learn more from your pals than your teachers.

Volunteer and "Work-Now-Get-Paid-Later" Projects

If you troll through websites like Creativeplanet.com, Highend3D.com, AWN.com, and others, you're likely to find lots of opportunities to work for little or no pay on short films or games. You'll also find lots of game startups, effects studio startups, and television commercial production startups—the list is practically endless—who want you to do a whole bunch of work for no pay. The implicit promise from all of these companies is that if the project is successful you'll a) get a share of the profits, b) get a job when the company gets funded, and c) get great real-world experience. It is our understanding, as well as the anecdotal experience of other artists, that few such projects ever get finished or funded, turn a profit, or end up hiring anybody for pay. In other words, even though it's implied or even promised that you'll get paid eventually, you'll probably never see a penny for your efforts. That doesn't mean, however, that all such projects are worthless.

As a matter of fact, such projects do offer the opportunity to work on demo reel material, with the sense that you are contributing to a larger project. If you can get involved with a locally produced project, you may be able to use it as a support group of other artists who are probably also out of work (or they wouldn't have time to be working on such an effort for nothing). At the least, you'll make some contacts, and that is key.

However, be wary of volunteer projects that are conducted as "virtual studios." There's nothing to stop someone from talking you into doing work for them and then forgetting all about you as soon as the project's done and they've moved off to greener pastures. If you are considering virtual studio work, be sure to ask if the "employer" is offering a written contract that spells out the promise of future compensation (be wary of verbal contracts—they generally don't stand up in court). There is nothing wrong with asking for such a contract. If a production company is serious and honest, they will be more than happy to consider offering a written contract that spells out the terms of your deferred employment. Those who balk at the mention should not be trusted.

If you can, try to check the backgrounds of the people running the project to help you get a sense of how realistic their plans are. This is another instance where your contact list is valuable. Call your friends and see if they know anything about this project or the people running it. If you have a good list of pals, chances are someone will know something. If you're lucky, you'll find out that these are credible artists with a history of creating successful projects on a shoestring. If that's the case, it may be a great opportunity to get some real-world experience while paying your dues.

Indie Game Development

There are a growing number of developers who have figured out how to produce games on their own with begged and borrowed help. If you're prepared to take on the financial hardship and burden of becoming an independent game developer, which means forming your own team, designing and implementing your own game, and managing your own business (no small list of "to do's"!), you should look at some of the online sites that discuss indie game development. There are numerous helpful articles, including one great one (that we hope will still be there when you read this) on Dexterity.com:

```
http://www.dexterity.com/articles/indie-faq.htm
```

IF THEY HAVE SHIFTY EYES...

This industry is full of people who need favors. Most of them are appreciative and genuine, but there are those who won't give you a second thought once they get what they want from you. It's important to establish some level of trust with the people you're about to volunteer for. Make sure you are valuable to the project without becoming a doormat. Clearly establish your own goals (that is, what *you* want out of this arrangement) and don't lose sight of them. You are giving your work, and you need to get something out of it in return.

It's important to figure all this out before you make a firm commitment. Completely bailing out on a volunteer project once you've committed to it for less than legitimate reasons will get you some bad karma.

And remember, once you've achieved professional status, treat volunteers who come to you with the respect you appreciated being given.

User Groups

User groups are fantastic places to meet and get to know likeminded artists and technical people. There are far too many such groups to list, since many of them are conducted at the very small local level, but a quick search on the Internet for "3D user groups" will bring up hundreds of possibilities. Look for groups that have an active membership (whether their website has current information will be one clue) and that host regular monthly or weekly meetings.

Some user groups are devoted to specific software applications, such as Maya, Max, or XSI, and others are more general and discuss techniques that span applications. You'll also find user groups that are primarily interested in effects work or games development.

User groups are also a great place to get critiques of work in progress, and many of them have the equivalent of "open mic" nights, where members can show their work and solicit the feedback of other members. Being in an open group setting, you're likely to get honest, well thought-out feedback. Doing this in such a public forum well help toughen you up to criticism—a valuable job skill in this industry.

One of the most valuable features of 3D user groups is that many of them publish a list of members' contact information. If you find such a group in your area, this list can become an invaluable networking white pages (Figure 7.1).

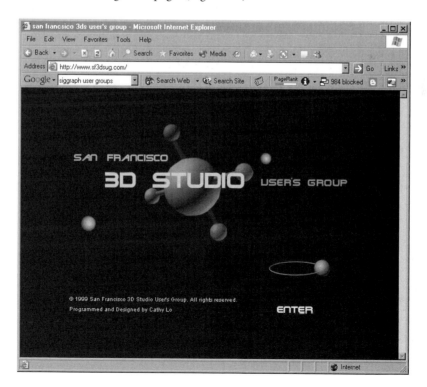

Figure 7.1

Many user groups exist around the country and are easy to find online.

Trade Associations

Trade associations are essentially like user groups in that they form an advocacy group in which members can educate each other and share ideas. However, professional trade associations are often far more formal and can host symposiums, support research, publish newsletters and trade magazines, involve themselves with hiring and pay practices, raise concerns over working conditions, and even lobby for special political treatment. In 3D graphics, the mother of all such associations is Siggraph. Here is how the organization describes itself: "In the span of 30 years, ACM Siggraph has grown from a handful of computer graphics enthusiasts to a diverse group of researchers, artists, developers, filmmakers, scientists, and other professionals who share an interest in computer graphics and interactive techniques. Our community values excellence, passion, integrity, volunteerism, and cross-disciplinary interaction. We sponsor not only the annual Siggraph conference, but also focused symposia, chapters in cities throughout the world, awards, grants, educational resources, online resources, a public policy program, traveling art show, and the Siggraph Video Review."

Of additional interest is that Siggraph's chapters include special student chapters and local chapters that network directly into the international organization. Everyone who works or plans to work in this industry should make the $27 a year investment for membership, if only for the potential networking opportunities.

The Siggraph website (Figure 7.2) is also a gold mine of information about companies and opportunities in the industry.

There are many other organizations related to 3D graphics, including those involved with architecture, engineering, robotics, digital imaging, and virtual reality. You'll be happy to know that you can find a great directory to most of those on the Siggraph website.

If your interest is in games, then you should also belong to the International Game Developers Association, which in the words of the IGDA membership web page, is made up of "...programmers, designers, artists, producers, and many other development professionals who see the importance of working together to advance games and game development as a craft."

Membership costs $100 per year (or only $35 for students with a valid ID).

`www.igda.org`

While it's not really intended for people at the artist or programmer level, the Entertainment Software Association is another important player in the games industry since they are devoted to the needs of video and computer games publishers (which accounts for 90 percent of the $6.9 billion entertainment software industry) and host the annual Electronic Entertainment Expo (E3), a gathering of video and computer game publishers and enthusiasts.

`www.theesa.com`

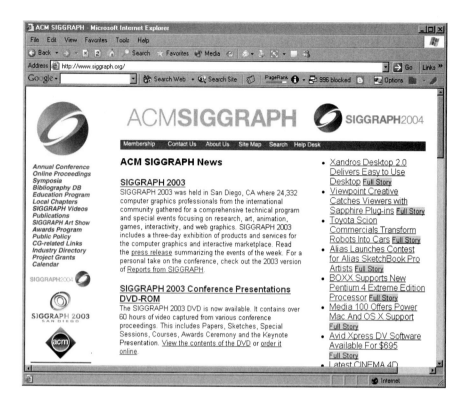

Figure 7.2

Siggraph's home page links to many useful areas and news in the graphics industry.

Online Bulletin Boards

Many websites feature online bulletin boards and forums where users can discuss any number of topics. These are a great place to immerse yourself in discussions of the industry, technology, and techniques; to review portfolios and get yours reviewed; and to strike up conversations that can lead to all kinds of interesting relationships. The book's website provides links to many such forums, and we wholeheartedly encourage you to seek them out as valuable resources.

However, be aware that the vast majority of these boards are unmoderated, and there is no requirement to join a forum other than registering on the site; there is no prequalification process to allow anyone to submit an opinion or "knowledge" to the fray. While it's great that anybody can join, the bad news is that you have absolutely no idea who you're talking to or who's talking to you. Be sure to check the background of people who critique your work or offer you advice. If they have a website of their own, that's a good place to start because you'll be able to see if they are in a position to judge. Also, make sure to find a community that appeals to your specific area of interest, such as Women in Animation (Figure 7.3):

www.womeninanimation.org

Figure 7.3

Many online com-
munities exist for
people to communi-
cate and share ideas
with one another,
such as Women in
Animation.

If you spend a lot of time on open forums, you may find that the LOUDER PEOPLE
TALK and the more frequent and voluminous their comments, the less qualified and
helpful they are. That probably has something to do with the fact that people who are
good at what they do don't have the time to spend trolling around Internet forums and
tossing in their two cents at every opportunity.

STICKING YOUR FOOT IN YOUR KEYBOARD

When you find yourself joining in a bulletin board or other such online discussion panel, it's
sometimes best to first sit back and get a general feel for who these people are and how they
will react to your comments before posting your ideas and opinions. Having been a part of
many discussion boards, we've seen how anxious people can get to voice their opinions,
which sometimes leads to miscommunication and even harsh reactions. Many of these
forums are attended by professionals and it's always a good idea to present yourself as one
yourself to avoid getting a bad rap. You'd be surprised how many of these people you'll meet
at trade shows and user groups. It's best not to flame people from the get-go.

Film Festivals and Trade Shows

Trade shows and conferences are potentially a great place to network and even to find jobs. If you can find a show that hosts a legitimate job fair (a vanishing species) or one that specializes in one of your particular fields of interest, it's a great place to meet and talk to people who may have similar interests or who are looking for people with your skills. Be aware, however, that attending conferences and trade shows can be an expensive proposition. The most interesting part of professional conferences is the seminars and workshops that go on in the back rooms, and since the organizers have to pay the teachers, not to mention the conference hall owners, admission to these workshop sessions is almost always very expensive. For example, admission to the full program at Siggraph 2003 was $825 or $1,100 (for members and nonmembers, respectively) or $425 or $550, for registered students. That's not accounting for travel expenses to San Diego if you don't happen to live there.

Siggraph

Despite the recent cancellation of Siggraph's job fair (as detailed in Chapter 6), the Siggraph show remains a great place to meet and greet professionals in the industry, and there are still recruiters and art types operating the main show booths and prowling the halls of the conference. You just have to look harder and keep asking for tips on who to talk to.

Even if you can't find recruiters looking to hire, the Siggraph show is probably the best single opportunity to network with other people in the industry. If you do attend the conference, consider signing up for the workshops and seminars and make sure you mingle at the film festivals and other semi-social events that happen there. These are great places to see the best and the brightest work from that year, and they are ideal for mingling and networking with other people in the field. If you do go to Siggraph, travel with a friend, not just to share expenses, but also because it's a lot easier to mingle at these events if you're not alone.

www.siggraph.org

SIGGRAPH VOLUNTEERS

One way many students make their way into the Siggraph conference is to volunteer to work for the show. Siggraph is usually receptive to volunteers and welcomes student help. This way, you get to hit the conference floor, meet some of the thousands of people who attend the show, and see what's the newest and greatest. Who knows, you may even make some powerful connections with your fellow volunteers while you're there, not to mention some friendships.

For information on how to volunteer for Siggraph, visit their website.

Game Developers Conference

The yearly Game Developers Conference (also known as GDC or GameDev) held in San Jose, California is as important as Siggraph if you're hoping to break into the games business. Like Siggraph, this is a professional show intended for people in the industry, and the focus is on techniques and technology rather than on showing off the latest wares (although there's a fair amount of that too, since this is where game developers and game publishers meet each other and form the deals that keep us all employed). Like Siggraph used to do, GameDev hosts a job fair where recruiters and other hiring managers man the booths and troll for fresh talent. You'll be amazed at how many copies of your resume and reel you'll need to have with you for this event. It's easy to drop off 30 or 40 of each, and you'll get ample opportunity to show your stuff and talk to living, breathing recruiters.

This is also a great place to meet and network with other people in the industry. There are generally lots of programmers and artists milling around, feeling slightly uncomfortable and wishing they had someone interesting to talk to.

For more information about the show, go to the website at:

www.gdconf.com

Electronic Entertainment Expo (E3)

Unlike GameDev, E3 is a "consumer" show. As such, the game companies are there in force, the volume of everything is amplified to near deafening levels, and the spectacle, including swimsuit models hawking the latest T-and-A games, is nonstop. At the last show, the U.S. Army, which publishes "America's Army," outdid itself with real-life commandos rappelling into the show's courtyard from an attack helicopter!

While it may sound like a lot of fun, this is a lousy place to do much networking. For every one game company person working at the show, there are at least a hundred game store employees and teenage boys crowding the booths. It's too loud to think, and the focus is really on selling games to distributors and retailers, not on professionals meeting to exchange best practices and to find new talent. However, if you're interested in getting more information on the show, go to their website:

www.e3expo.com

The National Association of Broadcasters (NAB) Conference

The NAB conference, held in Las Vegas every spring, is one of the biggest trade shows in the entertainment business. It's a purely professional event, featuring everything from television broadcasting companies (there are always keynote speeches by big-shot anchormen and other TV personalities) to camera manufacturers like Sony and Panasonic to companies that make boom microphones and helmet cameras, and just about anything you can imagine having to do with video or broadcasting. This includes all kinds of hardware and software vendors, even those who are involved with 3D. Unfortunately, 3D is only a tiny fraction of what goes on at this show and is not prominently featured. Even when it is, it's only the parts having to do with broadcast animation and little, if anything, to do with games. There might be 100,000 people at this show, but finding 3D people to network with is like finding a needle in a haystack. As far as graphics go, NAB primarily focuses on compositing and perhaps motion graphics. You'll also find vendors of green-screen technology and compositing and editing software at the show.

If you're interested in the compositing or motion graphics aspects of CG work, NAB isn't a bad place to hang around, though you'll find little in the way of job opportunities lurking around. If you're primarily interested in 3D work, NAB is not your ticket.

`www.nab.org`

Summary

Everyone you ask will tell you that it's not just what you know, it's who you know that will determine your ability to get a job. This is true of any industry, but it's particularly important in 3D graphics, where there are too few jobs to go around and the distinctions between one artist and another are often a highly subjective judgment that can be easily swayed by personal influences. For programmers and highly technical people, connections aren't as imperative, but they never hurt. To be successful at networking, you have to start now and keep doing it for the rest of your life. You never know when you're going to need friends, and they're not something you can make overnight. If you're serious about working in the 3D industry, you'll make a list of your contacts now and start cultivating your relationships into strong A-list advocates who can come to your rescue when times are tough.

CHAPTER 8

Working with Recruiters

There are two kinds of people who have the title of recruiter or something like it: the kind that want to find you work, and the kind that want to keep you out.

Those who want to find you work are third-party employment agencies, also known as staffing agencies, recruiting firms, and headhunters. These people work for you in the hope they can find you work. They do this because they get *paid* (by the employer) for tracking you down and guaranteeing your qualifications.

The recruiters who want to screen you out and keep you from bothering the people upstairs are in-house human resources (HR) employees. It's not that these people have anything against you personally, but they know that there's a 99 percent chance that anyone who comes through their door or whose resume and demo reel is in their hopelessly backlogged in-box is a waste of their time. Guilty until proven innocent. Of course, these HR people probably have other duties, like making sure their employees' health and dental plans are properly deployed and that the company picnic is planned to a T, but they are definitely the front line of defense when it comes to keeping unqualified, and therefore unwanted, applicants out of the hair of the people in production.

If you're going to attack the job market on all fronts, you're going to have to learn how to work with—and around—both types of recruiter.

- What staffing agencies want

- Working with agencies

- Getting agencies to work for you

- What in-house recruiters want

- Approaching in-house HR people

What Staffing Agencies Want

Staffing agencies, also know as *recruiters, outsourcing agencies*, and *headhunters*, are businesses that exist for the sole purpose of finding and hiring talented people to fill the needs of their client companies. Although most such agencies work for many different companies, a few specialize in finding talent for one or two specific companies that are simply too big and mired in their own bureaucracies to respond quickly enough to demands for quick hires. When staffing agencies are successful in placing a candidate, the company that does the hiring pays a fee to the recruiter. (The money comes out of the hiring company's pocket, not yours, but the amount is calculated as a percentage of your salary and the length of your employment, and recruiters sometimes get a bonus for permanent hires.) Although it costs companies as much as a third more to use recruiters than it would to conduct the search themselves, they make it up in time and expenses that they would otherwise have to incur.

The good news about this arrangement is that agencies really want to find you work. The bad news is that you are only worth their time if you can be made to look like a round peg that will fit neatly into a round hole. In other words, they want people with very specific skills— and preferably lots of on the job experience doing exactly the kind of work they're being hired for—so they can be sure you can step right into the job and get to work. If you decide to use a recruiter, it's important that you know what you want and where you want to go.

Because most companies that themselves don't have HR departments primarily use staffing agencies when they need to find someone in a pinch, they are usually only willing to pay the extra agency costs if the candidate can begin working on day one, with virtually no training or warm-up time. This means that you must have already mastered the exact job you'll be doing at the new company. Agencies would love to be able to send a person directly to these jobs and have everything work out immediately; that's what their clients need as well, as Jo Ann Pacho, Artist Representative with ArtSource points out:

Sometimes they call us and they don't even want to interview. And most agencies work that way. When the client calls you and says I need a production person, they start next Wednesday. And they just show up. That's the perfect relationship with the client because you've already got their confidence that you're going to give them just the right person.
                                                                                                —JO ANN PACHO

Recruiters extensively screen their candidates to make sure they have the skills, resume, and a portfolio that properly demonstrates their abilities, and they'll only advance you for a position if they're certain you're right for it. Staffing agencies stake their reputation on the quality of the workers they deliver, so if they offer you as a candidate to fill a modeling position at one of their client companies, they're going to be sure you've actually got the chops to do the work.

That's not to say that recruiters won't work with you if you don't have lots of on-the-job experience, as long as you can demonstrate ample skills. On the other hand, just because you're in their database doesn't mean they're going to find you work. In fact, many artists spend months signed with recruiters without ever being called up to work. There's a large number of people available for only so many jobs, including short-term contracts. If a recruiter has two people in the database and one has several years of on-the-job experience, all else being equal, the experienced person will get the job.

What Staffing Agencies Can Do for You

Not all recruiters are purely mercenary and looking to "pick the low hanging fruit." The better staffing agencies will groom you for possible employment, sort of like Henry Higgins prepping Eliza Doolittle to come out into polite society. A reputable talent agency will help you polish your resume, critique your demo reel and portfolio, coach you on presentation and interviewing skills, and even fill you in on technical areas you may be lacking. Further-more, a recruiter knows exactly what employers are looking for and how much they pay, so they are a great resource when it comes to educating yourself during the job hunt.

You may wish to contact recruiters who have established a niche in the CG market that aligns with the job you are looking for. These recruiters will be better able to guide you and target you to employers more efficiently than agencies that sling resumes for all sorts of CG or creative positions. This goes back to knowing what you want and being able to communi-cate that effectively to the recruiter. The better the recruiter, the more focused their specialty. For example, Prime Candidate specializes in gaming industry recruiting (Figure 8.1).

As long as you're working with reputable recruiters, they will usually increase your chances of finding work. However, consider this: if a company is under contract with a recruiter and the recruiter introduces you to that company, the company is obligated to pay a fee to the recruiter if they end up hiring you. While this might not seem to involve you, it effectively raises the cost of hiring you to the employer by 25 to 30 percent. That can be a big enough number to price you out of a job.

Reputable recruiters will offer you as a candidate to a particular company only with your explicit permission, but there are unscrupulous recruiters out there who will take your name and resume and blast it out to every client on their list. This impersonal approach won't do much to improve your chances of landing work, and imagine your surprise when you apply to that company on your own months later and find out that they won't hire you because you're too expensive! This doesn't happen often, but the sto-ries are common enough to make it worth checking out recruiters before you give them permission to promote you.

Figure 8.1

Prime Candidate specializes in recruiting some of the best talent for the gaming industry and has offices in key locations in the country.

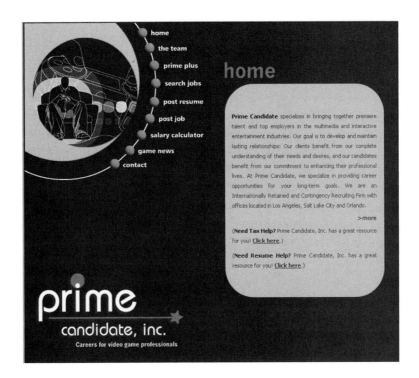

Another consideration is that when you are placed by a recruiting agency, you are usually hired as a temporary worker. You are actually under the employ of the recruiter, who gets paid by the hiring company and then issues you a check for your salary. As such, you won't be getting any of the benefits you might otherwise be entitled to as a regular employee. The better staffing agencies will pay you benefits, such as medical insurance and even 401K contributions, as long as you're working, but the fly-by-night recruiters won't. Such benefits can be worth 20 to 30 percent of your salary, so this is a major consideration.

A final caution about recruiters: many people put all their hopes for finding work in the one or more staffing agencies they've signed up with. Almost anyone who's been down this road will tell you it only leads to disappointment. While recruiters can be a useful prong in your employment strategy, you should consider them only one of several strategies you'll need to find work.

How to Screen Staffing Agencies

When you approach recruiters, ask these questions to help assess whether they're the right recruiter for you:

- What companies do you represent (who am I likely to end up working for)?

- How many people have you placed with my range of skills and qualifications?
- How many other artists/technical directors/programmers are you representing? How many of them are currently working?
- What will you do to help me prepare to find work?
- What benefits do you offer for people you have placed in positions?
- Will you obtain my permission before promoting me to any company?
- May I have any referrals of people you've placed so I can talk to other artists represented by you?

Employment agencies are sort of like professional matchmakers. When you, the eligible bachelor or bachelorette, come through the door, they give you a good going over, inspect your resume, your qualifications, your portfolio, and any other assets you may have in your dowry. They may also have you fill out an elaborate application and submit to a verbal interview. Once they have the measure of you, they'll excitedly set about looking for a match in the form of an employer. But don't make the mistake of believing that this first interview is the end of the process. Not long after you have your interview, the recruiter will be contacted by other out-of-work artists, programmers, and so on, and will forget all about you (although their database probably

Figure 8.2

Working with a recruitment firm such as ArtSource can help you tap into the companies out there.

won't). The recruiter will move on to look for positions for those people. If you want to succeed, you're going to have to assume the role of the pesky parent and continually remind the recruiters that you're still available. Better yet, if you can update the agency with new portfolio pieces and news of newly acquired skills, you'll remind them that you're evermore eligible!

If the agency is local, don't hesitate to drop in once in a while to show your face. You're a lot more likely to get special attention if you can appeal to a recruiter's human nature and put a face to your resume. Be sure to find out what to expect from any particular agency, too. For example, digital media staffing agency ArtSource (Figure 8.2) provides some good information on its website.

What In-House Recruiters Want

Many in-house human resources employees have the title of *recruiter*, a word that implies that they go out into the world to find the best possible employees to man their burgeoning company. The irony is that many of these people spend huge portions of their day doing the opposite: they screen *out* undesirable and unwanted resumes and demo reels from hundreds, sometimes thousands, of submissions, hoping to find a few that appeal to their standards. In other words, the talent the company needs to complete its game, film, or other mission, *is right there* in front of their eyes—yours might show that you're the perfect candidate—but getting through all of the submissions to find the right one can be daunting to an in-house recruiter.

Ken Maruyama, a recruiter with Industrial Light and Magic, agrees that the initial viewing process is to merely weed out reels that are not up to par with the work expected:

There's three of us in the recruiting area, but we're the first screening process and we look at them. Oftentimes, even in the screening process, we will sit with an artist to view some of the work. It's a screening out process. The ones that show a lot of promise, then we'll go into a more juried reel review process where we'll get several of the supervisors together in one room and go through the reels. —KEN MARUYAMA

There are only so many hours in the day for HR people to sift through submissions. Only the reels that catch their eye make it to the next level and are passed on to the decision-making people. It's up to you to get their attention with your submission and get them to linger on your resume long enough so they'll pass it up the chain for further consideration. Also, as we've said before, be sure to follow the instructions and submit your reel and resume they way the company requests. For example, ILM posts its requirements on its website (Figure 8.3).

Jo Ann Pacho sums up the feeling many HR and staffing people must have while they search for talent:

I do it all day long. I mean all day long. I may look at upwards of a hundred portfolios and reels in a day and it's mind numbing, but you really learn to spot the ones that are good and the ones that are bad. The ones where I get lost and I can't understand what is this person's core competency, I don't spend a lot of time on those. I move on. I try to find the ones that clearly define the skills that they have, the amount of experience, and how they've applied those. Those are the ones that come to the front, and those are the ones that I pass to the admin. —JO ANN PACHO

A word of caution: the only way to catch a recruiter's eye is with a solid and professional resume and reel that shows off your experience. Colorful gimmickry and perfumed resumes will only be irritating and count against you.

Figure 8.3

Companies such as Industrial Light and Magic have instructions on how to submit demo reels. Follow them, or yours might end up in the wrong pile.

How to Help In-House Recruiters Find You

Like staffing agencies, in-house recruiters are on a mission to find the perfect candidate to fill open positions, and they'd like to do this quickly and with a minimum of effort. After all, sorting through stacks of resumes and reels for the right person to hire takes many working hours, and when a job's needs are specific, it can take a long time to find the perfect candidate.

Unfortunately, the way in-house hiring managers tend to look for employees and the way potential employees tend to look for jobs is often exactly reversed. According to Richard Bolles in *What Color Is Your Parachute?*, hiring managers prefer to find people to fill open positions in this order, while misguided job seekers often start their search at the bottom of this list and work their way up.

1. **From within.** Promoting a full-time or part-time employee, contractor, or intern already working for the company is the primary mode of hiring. This is why it's a good idea to use part-time, contract, or internship work as a back door into full-time employment. As Carla Block (director of Sammy Studios) mentions, internal networks are key to finding new people:

> *We've had tremendous, tremendous success with our internal networking. I can't say enough about that. Employees do not recommend people that they wouldn't want to work with. It's really that simple.*
>
> —CARLA BLOCK

2. **Using proof.** Hiring an unknown person who brings proof of what he or she can do is the first thing most companies do if they have no potential in-house candidates. For 3D artists, that means having a killer demo reel and/or portfolio; for technical people, that means presenting examples of graphics scripting or programming.

3. **Using a best friend or business colleague.** Getting referred into a company by a trusted person is also a great way in (see Chapter 7 for more information on this). Andrew Pearce of ESC Entertainment says it very well:

I'd say 90 percent of the time it's from recommendations that come from someone else. That puts someone's candidacy up higher on the list quicker than anything else.

—ANDREW PEARCE

---

4. **Using an agency they trust.** This is why it's worthwhile to work with reputable staffing agencies.

5. **Using an ad they have placed.** Note that this method is pretty far down the list, which means looking through ads is a long shot. Especially in this industry, where needs rise and subside on a daily basis, ads are often scarce and shouldn't be relied upon.

6. **Using a resume.** Working from a stack of randomly submitted resumes or going through reels collected from the past is usually a company's last resort, so don't count on it getting you anywhere. Most companies prefer to look only at solicited submissions, too.

Even if options 1 through 4 are out of your reach, there are actions you can take to improve your odds with recruiters. Start by paying attention to what they say they're looking for. When you read a company's ad for an open position, you may be aghast at the improbable list of job requirements. Keep in mind, however, that the recruiter, who generally isn't a technical person, didn't make these things up. A recruiter usually starts the job posting process by interviewing or querying managers and art directors about what traits and skills they're looking for in the new hire, and then compiles this laundry list into the job description you read in the job posting. But that doesn't mean that all of those required job skills are really what the recruiter or manager is looking for.

When you submit your resume, reel, and cover letter, be sure that you target the specific requirements spelled out in the ad. The recruiter will only be looking for general answers to the difficult requirements. For example, if the ad calls for a technical director with Python scripting experience, it's okay to claim that you know Python, even if you really only know a little bit of it. Your objective is to pass through the recruiter's impossibly fine screen so that you can talk to the actual manager who will oversee your work and decide if your Python skills are up to snuff. If you're fortunate enough to make it to this interview, you'll find out just how much Python you're expected to have on the job; there's a real chance that it will never come up at all.

More often than not, recruiters are looking more for fundamental qualities, as Microsoft Technical Recruiter Marc Marrujo knows:

What I need is smart people that are in the industry, that are hands on. That's the type of people I need. People that are in the industry that want to take it to the next level, that definitely work and strive to be the best they can be. Those are the types of people. I don't care if you have been developing games in Siberia or on the beach in Cabo San Lucas. Whatever. I'm just looking for solid people that are smart.

—*MARC MARRUJO*

Finally, appealing to an in-house recruiter is your chance to demonstrate your creativity, enthusiasm, and eagerness to work. Showing that you're a perfect fit for the job as well as a standout person who will make the recruiter's efforts shine is an edge over merely having the verbatim qualifications for the job. Take it from Carla Block, at Sammy Studios:

I'm just looking for people that are about quality and not quantity when it comes to product. I go back to the cliché term—they're passionate about making games because that really makes the difference between a really great designer or a great artist and a great programmer and just an okay programmer, or an okay artist. There are a lot of talented, talented individuals out there, but we want somebody who really just understands what we're about and really kind of blends into our culture because we've taken a lot of time and careful calculation about the culture that we've tried to create here.

—*CARLA BLOCK*

OVER-INFLATING YOUR SKILLS

The idea of overstating your skills, such as saying you have more experience in Python script-ing than you actually do to get a foot in the door, is a double-edged sword. While it may be okay to stretch the truth a bit to get an interview, it is dangerous to overstate your abilities too much. You will, after all, be expected to perform at the level you say you're able to, and coming into a job and being unable to rise to that level will not only cost you the job, it will tag you with an unflattering reputation. The same holds true with doctoring up one's demo reel or portfolio. There's no better way to get a black eye, and people in the industry will be reluctant to overlook that. If you do stretch the truth to get the interview, make sure you can rise to the occasion and get your abilities up to snuff right away to make a good impression at work. There is nothing worse than hiring someone who swears that they know what they're doing and doesn't.

Persistence Pays

While nobody likes a pest, recruiters have to face an endless stream of candidates, many of whom look more or less alike on paper and reel. After you send a resume to a recruiter by e-mail, send a nicely formatted paper copy along with your reel, then call a couple of days later to "make sure they arrived safely." Assuming the recruiter takes the time to talk to you and confirm that they did, send another note thanking the recruiter for taking the time to help you and say that you're looking forward to hearing back about the position. These are small efforts, but they hugely increase your visibility in a world of look-alike anonymous e-mails and UPS packages, and they'll help your name stick in the mind of the recruiter. This may be all it takes to differentiate your resume enough from the cast of thousands to get you to the next level. Then, if you manage to get a job or internship, send a thank you card.

What if you don't get the job? Keep at it. It can be a difficult pill to swallow over and over again, but keep plugging away until you find yourself in a job so you can finally get the experience everyone else said you lacked to get a job. Andrew Pearce, pipeline supervisor with ESC Entertainment, maintains that a good attitude will help keep you going.

You can be very positive about the whole interview process and then it can just fall apart on you. Until they give you paper, don't assume you have the job. Keep positive, even when you get the rejections. That was the hard part. You want to be like, oh, but I can do anything, I can sweep floors. But no, hold back on that.

—ANDREW PEARCE

Persistence also requires a good measure of focus. It's true that breaking into a new industry can be backbreaking. A lot of people try to find secondary work to earn a living wage as they try to hone their skills and move into the CG market. While this might be a financial necessity, it is also crucial to stay focused if you want to finally break into the kind of work you want. ArtSource's Jo Ann Pacho has a warning about that:

For example, "I'm a game designer, and I'm not getting any game work, so maybe I want to be a Flash Action scripter. If I just diversify my skill set then I'll be more hireable." Yes. For the sake of argument, logic speaks to yeah, that may be true. But if you hate Action Scripting, don't go there. And that's the problem. [People] are giving up their passion to make money. And when they pick up a skill they hate because they think it's going to pay the bills, then they end up trapping themselves. Yeah, maybe [they are] going to pay your bills for six months to a year, but you're not going to be happy, and that's the crux of being an artist. You have to be motivated to create. And if you're not, then it's just a job, and then you're no longer an artist. So, how do you balance that? It's tough.

—JO ANN PACHO

It's best to find a more comfortable fit with the industry you want to break into, to find a job that is closer to your dream. Sometimes just to get into the industry you must take on a lower-level position than your current, more well paid, job, but at least you'll be in an environment closer to your dream, and that will help keep you focused until the day you do break in.

Summary

In-house recruiters are a company's first line of defense against an endless flood of resumes and reels and unqualified employees. Your best bet to penetrate their defenses is to approach your job search the same way they approach their employee search. One of the alternate ways of finding work is to go through staffing agencies, or headhunters, which get paid for helping you find work by sending out your credentials to companies looking for people, typically to fill in specialized jobs or short term projects. In either case, the more finely tuned your expectations and goals are, the better recruiters can help you.

CHAPTER 9

Interviewing for the Job

Assuming your resume, reel, and networking were sufficient to impress your prospective employer with your skills, background, and references, you will be asked to interview for the job. This is the moment you've been working toward: an honest chance to pitch why you're the best person for the job.

The good news is that preparing for the interview requires far less work than any of the other major stages of job hunt preparation. The bad news is that there is a different kind of work involved in the preparation. This final stage sends shivers of fear through many people, including seasoned pros: you've got to go face to face to sell yourself, something that many 3D artists and programmers are entirely uncomfortable doing. Like any fear, the key to overcoming this one is to educate yourself and prepare for the danger that lurks ahead.

- Preparing for the interview

- Interviewing

- Closing the interview

Preparing for Different Types of Interviews

Your primary objective when you go on an interview is to reveal enough of your desirable qualities so that the employer will decide that you are a good fit for the company. Of course, you also want to show that you actually have the knowledge and experience that your resume and demo reel implies, but chances are the employer is pretty much convinced of that already, or they wouldn't have called you in the first place. An interviewer mainly wants to see what kind of person you are, how you carry yourself, how you mesh with them, how you potentially mesh with those in the department you may be working in, and what kind of image you project.

Just as there is no right way for an employer to conduct an interview, there is no one right way for you to approach the interview, but there are important measures you can take to prepare yourself.

There are several possible types of interviews you might be subjected to, and each of these needs special preparation. In the best case scenario, the employer will want to go over your reel or portfolio with you, which will give you a chance to talk about your work. Most artists enjoy recalling creative decisions and the tools and techniques they used to achieve a particular look or effect, but be aware that an art director is going to use this opportunity to critique your work as well, and discuss what you might have done differently. Be prepared to take some criticism. Before you ever land an interview, you should get critical feedback from professional artists to thicken your skin and help you prepare specific answers to specific questions, as Sean Miller, lead artist at Sammy Studios points out:

> *Get feedback from as many sources that you feel could be reliable, and listen to it with a real eye towards whether or not it will make your stuff better. It doesn't mean you have to use every suggestion that person gives you, but it is nice to know what impact your art is having on other people. It helps you prepare for reactions you'll get in an interview situation.*
>
> —*SEAN MILLER*

Telephone Screening Call

Telephone interviews tend to get sprung on unsuspecting applicants after they send in a reel or resume. The recruiter who is calling you is armed with questions and will want to interview you on the spot, but if possible you should defer this call long enough to prepare for it. Try to buy yourself 24 hours (say, "I'm busy at work right now and can't talk."). Otherwise, this interview is like other one-on-one interviews, but you don't have to worry about firm handshakes and maintaining eye contact.

You do have to worry about stammering on the phone and sounding like you don't know what you're talking about. Prepare by going through your body of work, your reel and portfolio, and the pieces you think would be most applicable to that job. Go through possible questions in your mind so you can be quick to answer them. Above all, be relaxed and engaging and try to get a one-on-one interview at the end of the conversation by offering to come in to meet the folks on the phone at their convenience.

One-on-One Interviews

When you interview with an HR recruiter in person, it will typically be your first interview in preparation for interviews with other managers who will potentially oversee your work. As with resumes, this is a screening process, and the recruiter is looking to weed out the bad and pass the good to the upstairs managers. The good news about HR people is that they are primarily interested in your basic qualifications. They want to know whether you seem like a "normal" person (you don't have a crazy twitch in your eye and a gun in your pocket) and if you have an appropriate level of experience and your skills seem comparable to the work of people in the company. The bad news about HR people is they know all the tricks of the trade for questioning new employees, including zinger questions that will trip you up and reveal your weaknesses. Think of your interview with HR as walking through a minefield. You don't necessarily have to shine in this interview, but you need to watch your step.

Important things to remember:

- Dress well and look neat
- Smell good (but don't wear too much cologne or perfume)
- Look your interviewer in the eye
- Use a firm handshake
- Keep your hands away from your face
- Speak clearly and with confidence
- Have a sense of humor without being obnoxious or conceited

In short, use the skills you would use to impress a date.

If you make it through HR to a second interview with a director, then you've passed many of the company's basic requirements, but the art director or other manager is going to be more keenly interested in your technical ability and your artistic talent. He or she is probably going to want to go over pieces of your portfolio and reel with you and will expect you to explain why and how you achieved certain effects.

It is important to bring a copy of your reel's shot list with you. Be very familiar with the list and your reel so you can answer questions without hesitation. In addition to your body of work, you should impress the interviewer with your personality and passion for what you do. As Douglas Hare of The Collective demonstrates, really finding out about a person is critical to finding a good employee. Usually that depth of insight can only come with an in-person interview:

> *We're looking for people who are going to have the right sort of personality perspective. We're looking for people who are going to be able to collaborate, work with groups of people from different disciplines, be open to criticism, be pro-active, be able to follow direction, be able to understand that this is a very fast, evolving industry and there's always something to learn.*
>
> —DOUGLAS HARE

Interviews by Committee

Facing an interview by a panel of questioners can be utterly demoralizing, as numerous people volley questions at you as fast as you can answer them. Although one person will probably be running the interview, the trick is to take each question in turn, be sure to look everyone in the eye when you answer their questions, and try to relax. Imagine you are the center of attention at a cocktail party (without the cocktails, of course!), rather than the object of an inquisition. Remember that in group interviews, the committee is there not so much to pass judgment on your work as to see for themselves what kind of a person you are. They convene because everyone is too busy to give you one-on-one time. It's important to do your best to connect with each person in the room, pay attention to what they are asking and saying, and respond to people individually, without leaving anyone out. Avoid darting your eyes from one person to the next, which will make you look even more nervous than you probably are.

If you've done your homework and know ahead of time who's going to be at the interview, make a mental chart of who is sitting where so you can try to personalize your answers by using their names. If you're bad at remembering names, don't try to incorporate their names into your answers because you don't want to call someone by the wrong name. If you do though, laugh it off, apologize, and go on; it can be embarrassing, but it won't be a deathblow if your talent shines through.

TURN OFF YOUR CELL PHONE!

There's only one thing worse than your cell phone going off in the middle of the interview, and that's answering it. Believe it or not, it happens. Applicants will leave their cell phone on, it will ring, and they will have the nerve to interrupt the interview and answer the phone. Even a brief, "Hello, let me call you back," will be patently offensive to an interviewer. Either turn that phone off, or just leave it at home.

Research *Before* the Interview

When you are first contacted for an interview, by no means agree to be interviewed on the spot—say that you are tied up with work but that you would be happy to talk at a specified time in the near future. You need some time to prepare if you're going to have a decent shot at impressing the interviewer. However, do try to spend a few minutes on the phone with the person who has contacted you. If the person who has called or e-mailed isn't the one who will be conducting the interview, be sure to get the names and titles of the people who will be and write them down, and be sure to be polite and remember to say a hearty thank you. If you're bad at remembering names, be sure to spend some time committing the names of your potential interviews to memory so you'll have a head start, even if the list of people partially changes by the time the interview occurs.

Next, you need to do some research on the company or studio. Assuming it has a website, look it up and read everything you can. Find out what films or games it has completed, read post-mortems on those projects if you can find them, and track down any interviews with your interviewers or articles they may have published. (Search engines, such as Google, are the best place to start.) You may even find a white paper or two if the company has been around for a few years. If you can, find bios of the interviewers and study them carefully. You may find interests or experiences similar to your own that can help you establish a rapport in the interview. After a hard day working on your research, head down to the video store and rent the company's films or games, if you haven't already seen them, and spend some time studying their work and making notes about specific things you like and those you think could be improved. Just be careful not to offend anyone in the room should a conversation arise about it. Amy Bendotti, senior technical recruiter at Nintendo of America, said not researching can really hurt you:

> *Definitely research the company. Know the latest news and what the games are. If they're interviewing at Retro and they don't know that we do Metroid Prime, or they haven't played it, that's a huge strike against them.* —AMY BENDOTTI

Researching Yourself

Armed with this knowledge of the company where you'll be interviewing, it's time to prepare your self-knowledge, which will be the heart of your interview. A good exercise is to write down five or six short stories about yourself that you can recount in 30 seconds to two minutes. These should offer clear examples of your success at tackling a hard problem or an important assignment. Include the circumstances that made this a difficult assignment and the specific traits and skills you employed to overcome the difficulty, as well as how your success benefited your employer and the outcome of the project. Then spend enough time retelling and practicing these stories so that you have committed them to memory. During the interview, you'll have opportunities to talk about what you can do to demonstrate your problem-solving abilities, and these stories are going to be vital to showing that you have interesting and relevant experience in the trenches. Remember that recounting stories about your capabilities and successes in the context of a job interview is not bragging; these are the things that the interviewer is looking for when he asks: "So, why should I hire you?"

To that extent, it's important to know what you want from a job, and how you're prepared to handle it should you land the position. Tina Dickey, Artist Representative with ArtSource suggests you walk into an interview knowing what you want:

I would say to really research. If they want to get into game development, to really research the kind of genres that they want. For example, if they want to do a first person shooter and they love first person shooter...take a game and analyze it, and do some models or do a character or something that would fit with that style of game. So...if they get an interview or not, the manager can look at this and be like, "Hey, this person's really given some thought into this, and not only is their work excellent, but they're already immersing themselves into this kind of world, and that person might be a really good asset to this team." Rather than, "Here's all my schoolwork, yeah, it's good, I haven't really thought about first person shooters or whatever the genre is." It's just a little extra edge that could help sell that candidate as a good fit.

—TINA DICKEY

Questions to Expect

Of course, there are countless questions an employer might ask you in an interview, but, according to *What Color Is Your Parachute?*, there are only five that matter, and they definitely apply to finding a job in CG:

Why are you here?

What can you do for us?

What kind of person are you?

What sets you apart from the other qualified applicants?

Can we afford you?

The entire interview is an employer's exercise to learn the answer to these five questions, and every question is really an attempt to get to the bottom of the big five. At the same time, your objective is not only to give the employer answers they want to hear for these questions, but also to find out the corollary information for yourself. Do go into the interview prepared to give them the answers they want, but also ask the questions that will tell you what *you* need to know. Remember that asking questions in an interview is as important as answering them—it shows you are genuinely interested in the job, and that you want to make sure the job is a match for you as much as you are a match for it. Let's look at each of the employer's questions from the perspective of a 3D artist.

Why Are You Here?

Or, to be more specific:

- Why did you apply to this studio instead of the one down the road?
- Why did you decide to do games, rather than film, or vice versa?
- Why have you applied to be a modeler, when your resume says you also do character animation?

The employer wants to know why you want to work at the company because that has a lot to do with how interested you really are in the position, how long you're likely to stay, and how motivated you'll be to work hard when deadlines demand it. For games or film, you should describe your interest in the genre, your devotion to the art form, your eagerness to learn from others in the company, and the opportunity to contribute your own unique skills to the creation of successful projects.

The corollary question for you to ask is "*What does this job involve?*" You need to know exactly what your duties would be, what skills you need, what would be demanded of you, how many hours you would be expected to work, if you'll get on-the-job or formal training, and what opportunities there might be for you to be promoted. Sure, you've spent a lot of time and effort getting as far as this interview, but is this a job you actually *want*?

What Can You Do for Us?

Here you want to emphasize your hard work ethic, your dedication to the art form, your technical mastery, and your commitment to getting jobs done quickly, on budget, and on time. Studios want people who can come in and get to work right away creating production-ready assets, solving problems, and contributing creative energy to the project.

You should ask, "*What skills and attributes would I need to master this job?*" Pay attention to what the employer says. Are the technical requirements, the work habits, and the creative demands all things that interest you or that you want to strive for? If they say, "You need to be an ace Python programmer," does that repel you because you hate programming? If so, maybe this isn't the right job for you.

What Kind of Person Are You?

Chances are, the *right* answer to this question will come from looking at successful artists, directors, and programmers in existing game and effects companies and observing the kind of work ethic and personality that goes along with the job. Artists and technicians in 3D environments tend to work hard *and* play hard. They put in long hours in front of the computer pouring out creative energy, but they get some of it back by making art, playing games, listening to music, doing sports, driving fast cars and motorcycles, building haunted houses—the kinds of activities you would expect of companies with a primarily young, male-dominated demographic. Of course, there are exceptions. Some big studios may take themselves really seriously and have the kind of 9 to 5 hours and corporate regularity you'd expect of a bank or legal firm, while small studios may be dominated by engineers with a deadly serious case of workaholism. This question delves not only into your personality, but also into your work ethic: will you show up every day and put in the long hours (by the company's standards) and work hard to get the job done? Will you mesh with those around you? Industrial Light and Magic Recruiter Ken Maruyama says a big part of the interview is determining if you will play well with others:

We look for the personality of the individual. Since this is a real collaborative experience where you are working on a crew and you really are having to rely on other people to help get your work done, we look for people who gravitate towards that team experience. Sometimes you'll find people who kind of want to be the star and they want to be the person who is singled out, who wants to be the guy that everybody points to, and those are the people we tend to shy away from. But it's the ones that have a real passion and a love for their work, and who seem like they're the ones that really want to learn and they are really, truly interested in the type of work that we do here.

—KEN MARUYAMA

Obviously, the corollary question is equally important for you: *Will I like working here?* Finding the answer to that question is one of the most important things you can do in the interview process while you try to get the job. If you can figure it out early, your enthusiasm for landing the job after the interview will shine through during it.

What Sets You Apart?

Here's where your knowledge of the company, combined with your stories of personal success, is going to win the day. When you hear questions that allude to this big question, you need to show how your unique qualities and skills will serve the needs of the company. What you'd like to find is the opportunity to say something like, "Sure, there may be other character animators who can do this job, but I know that you're working on a film about animals right now and that is a particular interest of mine. In my senior project, I was able to study the expressions of animals and how they could be animated to better convey their emotions while still keeping true to their animal personalities. It's a nuance that I think few animators have even thought about, but I have received a lot of praise for the expressiveness of the animals in the film, and I'm sure I can bring those qualities to this project."

The employer wants to know what sets you apart, and this is a question you need to answer for yourself well in advance of the interview. If you are an environment artist, what particular skills do you have that make you better than other environment artists *for this job*? Perhaps you are adept at architectural modeling and lighting; maybe you have a great sense of urban landscapes or are particularly good at rendering outdoor scenery. Without knowing what the company has done and what it's working on, you won't be able to prepare yourself for this question going into the interview.

Also, you should know what your qualities are, as well as your qualifications. Douglas Hare, owner of The Collective, agrees that a person's formal qualifications count less than their abilities:

If someone came to us and didn't have any formal qualifications but gave a fantastic demonstration of their abilities, then that would actually count for more.

—*DOUGLAS HARE*

Can We Afford You? Negotiating Salary

The last question is about how much the employer has budgeted for the position versus how much you count on earning. This is a painfully difficult question to deal with, and there are countless books written about nothing other than negotiating a salary. The real trick to salary negotiation, like every part of the job-hunting process, is to do your research beforehand. Most 3D employers will give no hint of how much a position pays because the scales are always changing according to the market. ArtSource's Jo Ann Pacho says:

Right now, it's just so highly competitive that it's really a buyer's market. The employer can really set the bar much higher than they could in the past. They're getting more demanding and wanting to pay less because they think that with the economy dip that they can. But there are always highly specialized fields that tend to get a standard wage across the board no matter what.

—*JO ANN PACHO*

To get an accurate idea of the salary you can expect, you need to call up your network and start asking questions. If you know someone with a similar position in a similar sized company as the one you're applying at, find out how much they make so you have an idea of what the salary ought to be. Also, try to find out if the company offers benefits, which can be worth 20 to 30 percent of your salary and are often negotiable. (The best way to research a company's benefits is to talk to current employees, which will be easier to do when you tell them you're interviewing for a job there because that at least temporarily grants you insider status. However, the best time to *negotiate* benefits or "fringes" is after you've been accepted for the job and settled the salary.)

When you do go into the interview, do everything you can to defer the discussion of salary until it's clear that the company is very interested in hiring you; in other words, don't bring it up during the interview. The further you can go to make your case that you're the perfect employee, the more likely that you're going to be offered an attractive salary later on. And although salary is usually not raised as an issue by the interviewer during the interview, so this may never come up for you, it never really hurts to know what salary is typical for this job, and what you're looking for before you walk into the interview.

Once you're at a point to discuss salary, the negotiation would ideally go something like this: You come to the end of the interview and ask, in your own words, "Well, can I have the job?" and the interviewer replies, "You seem like a perfect fit. I don't see why not!"

You: "Fantastic! I can't wait to get started. I suppose, however, that we need to discuss the salary. Can you tell me how much the position pays?"

> You always want the employer to be the first to mention a salary figure. The prevalent theory on salary negotiation is that the first person to mention a figure in a negotiation usually loses. If you're forced into it because the employer asks you what salary you're looking for, some research can save your hide. Quoting a middle of the ground average rate for that position would be a wise idea. You may want to adjust it for your level of experience (or lack thereof), but going in too low will hurt you, and going in too high will throw them off. In any event, it's almost always in bad taste to ask, "Well, what can you afford?"

At this point, the employer has decided that you are the best candidate and that they want you. Knowing the pay range has minimum and maximum, the employer is likely to offer you a figure somewhere in the middle. If the offer is something like, "What would you say to $60,000?" you have an opening to counter-offer with something that's closer to what you figure the maximum is based on your research: "I was expecting more in the range of $64,000 to $70,000."

With any luck, the employer will up the "final" offer to somewhere closer to the maximum in the pay range.

Of course, it would be extremely optimistic to think that negotiations will be that simple or straightforward, with everything going your way. For example, the employer may reply, "The job pays $60,000; I'm sorry we can't offer more." This effectively closes the door on negotiation.

To a large extent, whether you have room to negotiate will depend on several factors:

• Whether the employer has a salary range that they're willing to pay

- Whether they *really* want you or you are perceived as a bargain candidate who can be persuaded to work cheap
- Whether you have done a great job impressing them with your skills, talent, and interview

If the interview goes well and your work is up to par with this company, then your leverage in a negotiation will be strong. If it's not such a great interview and your experience is lacking, you'll have less room to maneuver and may get offered considerably less than you hoped. At the very minimum, you should go into the negotiation knowing what your minimum salary should be. Everyone has a budget of some kind, and you need your paycheck to meet your needs. If you are going into a job at a financial loss, chances are you won't last very long at it, you won't be happy, and neither will your new boss.

However, if you are inexperienced, you should not expect a great salary. Your motivation should be to gain valuable experience and reel material rather than salary. Money comes with time, as Tim Johnson, Director of Human Resources and Recruiting with Black Ops Entertainment mentions:

Right off the bat, it's a combination of experience and work and what kind of money is somebody looking for. Is the salary requirement relevant to the experience that they've got? How flexible are they? You got a lot of people who say, "You know, I just want to get into the game industry," and the biggest thing there is, you have to be flexible. If that's really what you want to do and that's what your passion is, you've got to be able to take that first step and it may not pay you a ton of money right off the bat, but within a year or two, you should be able to make that up. —*TIM JOHNSON*

Freelance and Hourly Work

Most paid internships and short-term freelance work is paid on an hourly basis, and most companies to which you apply will ask you what your rate is. This is a killer question, and the less prepared you are to answer it, the worse off you'll be. You don't want to go in too low or too high, but how do you find the right number? That, boys and girls, is the $64,000 question.

With a little research, you can find out what the typical pay is for piecemeal, freelance work. Just as you would research a yearly salary by calling your colleagues and friends to find out what they make in similar jobs, you should contact freelancers and search the Web for clues. Hourly rates always depend on the work being done and the experience of the artist, so they are hard to nail down, which is why this is perhaps one of the most asked questions.

RESEARCHING SALARY RANGES

Finding out how much a job pays is about as easy as threading a needle in the middle of a tornado. The pace in the industry is ever changing, and so are the salaries animators earn, especially those just starting out. Geography, experience, market demand, skill level, and artistic style all contribute to the salary you can demand in this industry. Any salary survey information is speculative at best. You'll find scattered sources and opinions online, but they honestly won't give you anything more than a very basic idea. Asking your friends and people in the industry in your area for their opinions is your best bet. People are generally reluctant to answer surveys online, but they usually aren't as reluctant when speaking to a friend or colleague.

For television effects work, for example, hourly rates for a 3D generalist in Los Angeles, based on a 45- to 50-hour week, can range from as low as $17 to $20 for an entry-level freelancer (or even lower for some people fresh out of school) to $50 to $60 for very experienced 3D artists with solid reels. (These rates are lower than what experienced artists were commanding years ago when the CG business was new, booming, and hungry for talent.) Film work can be about the same on an hourly basis, perhaps a little higher, since films generally hire people with more experience, even for entry-level positions.

When figuring out your rate, use your prior experience, your skill set and the strength of your reel, the kind of work you'll be doing, and the market conditions in your area as factors. If there is a great demand for artists, your rate can be higher than when there is a rut in the market.

Fortunately, freelance work tends to be short term, and there will probably be more chances for different projects in the near future. For your first experiences, you should be willing to take a bit of a hit on your wages to be able to get some solid work under your belt. As the saying goes, "You're only as good as the last thing you did," so it's up to you to land good projects for the next gig, and that may involve taking lower pay at first.

Closing the Interview

Most interviews don't end with a job offer; they end with an opportunity to do more interviews. If you make it to the second interview, you've done pretty well and your chances of landing the job are getting pretty hot. All of the same rules apply for the second interview, but you should have much more information about the company and its expectations of you and the job you'll be doing.

Assuming this interview goes well and the person interviewing you is the person who will make the hiring decision, at the close of this interview it's time to get a feel for what they think of you. It's a bit off-putting to actually ask, "Can I have the job"; it's a very bold gesture, but finding out how you did is not a bad idea. You can put out a feeler like, "When will you be making a decision?" or "When can I expect to hear if I've been selected?" These questions show that you're eager to get to work and that you're sincere and will give them a chance to let you know how you did. It's also okay to ask if you can contact the interviewer after some time if you haven't heard back. Just keep in mind if they haven't called you back, it's probably because they're offering the job to someone else, so don't keep pushing the issue with them if they're just not getting back to you.

Finally, say thank you, offer a firm handshake, and leave.

Thank You Notes

When you get home from any interview, whether or not it's the last round, write a neat, concise letter thanking the interviewer for their time, possibly mentioning a few of the highlights of your qualifications and expressing your sincere interest in the position. Mail it no later than the morning after your interview. This vital step is overlooked by many candidates, but if performed is often mentioned by interviewers as one of the factors that closes the deal in a candidate's favor. ArtSource's Jo Ann Pacho says:

Always write a thank you note afterwards. I'm not talking about an e-mail, I'm talking about a hand-written thank you note, and mail it to that person. Make sure it's something cool looking if it's a gaming company.
—JO ANN PACHO

Some job hunting experts also recommend sending a thank you note to any employees in the company who helped you, including secretaries or anyone else you called to conduct your research. Getting in good and staying in good with people is always a worthwhile effort.

Summary

It's vital to know not only what questions the employer will ask about you, but also to know what questions you need to ask about the company. Treat the job interview as an opportunity to learn about the job, as well as an opportunity to convince the employer that you would be a unique asset to the company. Remember your manners, starting with eagerness and enthusiasm to work for a company that you admire and want to be a part of and ending with a handshake and a sincere thank you. It's amazing how such simple details can have life-changing consequences!

CHAPTER 10

Frequently Asked Questions— Insights from Reel People

In previous chapters, we quoted, paraphrased, and compiled the comments of many industry professionals we contacted for this book. A lot of the information we gathered didn't fit into the chapters, so we've gathered some of the most compelling insights from those out there doing the hiring. You will find, as we did, that the answer to the question often depends on the segment of the industry you're in or are aspiring to be in, so one size truly doesn't fit all.

In this chapter, we present responses to the questions we most often asked. These passages have been edited for clarity when the topic strayed far afield from jobs and 3D graphics; in addition, some names of companies or clients have been removed to protect confidentiality. The following people were interviewed and quoted in this chapter:

Amy Bendotti, Senior Technical Recruiter, Nintendo of America Amy Bendotti is senior technical recruiter at Nintendo of America in Seattle, Washington. She hires technical candidates in departments ranging from game development to engineering, testing, and localization. These jobs include art positions, programmers, level designers, designers, producers, and other game-related positions.

Carla Block, Director of Human Resources, Sammy Studios Carla Block is director of Human Resources at Sammy Studios, a startup game company on steroids that bought up several previously existing studios and games and is currently working on simultaneous development of four different games. Because of this, Carla had to hire a lot of people in a short time period. Sammy is located in Carlsbad, California.

Kevin Cureton, Technical Art Director, Electronic Arts Kevin Cureton is technical art director at Electronic Arts' Redwood Shores, California office. He is responsible for determining the interface between art and engineering, specifically working on game engines and art developing content for games.

Tina Dickey, Artist Representative, ArtSource Tina Dickey is an artist representative with ArtSource, which specializes in placing designers in everything from games and interactive media jobs to technical illustration and print design positions. ArtSource has offices in Palo Alto, California and Bellvue, Washington.

Jo Ann Pacho, Artist Representative, ArtSource Jo Ann Pacho is an artist representative with ArtSource, which specializes in placing designers in everything from games and interactive media jobs to technical illustration and print design positions. ArtSource has offices in Palo Alto, California and Bellvue, Washington.

Brian Freisinger, Modeling Supervisor, ESC Brian Freisinger is the lead 3D modeler at ESC Entertainment (Alameda, California). He worked on many of the sets, props, and characters for *The Matrix* sequels. Before that, he worked for NewTek and Alias.

Douglas Hare, Owner, The Collective Douglas Hare is one of the founding owners of The Collective in Newport Beach, California. He is in charge of hiring technical people, including producers and programmers, for the game company.

Tim Johnson, Director of Human Resources and Recruiting, Black Ops Entertainment Tim Johnson is director of Human Resources and Recruiting at Black Ops Entertainment in Santa Monica, California.

Craig Lyn, Visual Effects Supervisor, FrameStore Craig Lyn, is the CG supervisor for Frame-Store in London, where he won an Emmy for his work on *Dinotopia*. Before that, he worked at Industrial Light and Magic as a modeler in ILM's Rebel Mac Unit, the group (which has since disbanded) that did most of the CG work on the early *Star Wars* films, and as a matte painter and technical director in ILM's computer graphics group.

Marc Marrujo, Technical Recruiter, Microsoft Marc Marrujo is a technical recruiter in Microsoft's Home Entertainment Division, which encompasses the Xbox and all 14 of Microsoft's game studios, along with the software giant's other home and entertainment products. He's located in Redmond, Washington.

Ken Maruyama, Recruiter, Industrial Light and Magic Ken Maruyama is a recruiter for Industrial Light and Magic in San Rafael, California. He hires people for positions throughout the computer graphics departments, including artists, technical directors, and engineers.

Sean Miller, Lead Artist, Sammy Studios Sean Miller describes his lead artist position at Sammy Studios (in Carlsbad, California) as "part team manager, part art director." It's a dynamic role in a company that, a year after it started, was already working on four games and managing multiple acquisitions.

Randy Nelson, Dean of Pixar University, Pixar Randy Nelson is dean of Pixar University, Pixar's Emeryville, California training facility for in-house and up-and coming artists. He is also one of the original Flying Karamazov Brothers, was one of the animators of the animatronic robots in Chuck E. Cheese's Pizza Time Theater, and spent some time wearing the Chuck E. Cheese rat suit in his younger days.

Sangeeta Pashar, Recruiting Manager, Pixar Sangeeta Pashar is a recruiting manager at Pixar in Emeryville, California.

Andrew Pearce, Pipeline Supervisor, ESC Entertainment Andrew Pearce is the pipeline supervisor at ESC Entertainment in Alameda, California. Prior to ESC, he spent more than 15 years working for Alias as a software developer, and was ultimately the product manager for the first release of Maya for Mac OS X.

Evan Pontoriero, Lead Previz Artist, Industrial Light and Magic Evan Pontoriero is a lead previsualisation artist in the art department of Industrial Light and Magic in San Rafael, California. He has also received credits as a modeler, matte painter, and conceptual artist. His daily work includes anything from 3D animation and character animation to compositing, including compositing lo-res elements, to creating conceptual artwork and conceptual animation and 3D animatics. Prior to his work at ILM, he worked at a game startup called Hypergolic Studios.

Emmanuel Shiu, Background Artist, The Orphanage Emmanuel Shiu is a matte painter for The Orphanage. A few weeks after his interview for this book, he gave up a prime gig as art director at Sony Electronic Entertainment (PlayStation Games) and took a pay cut to follow his bliss and work as a matte painter and digital backgrounds artist at The Orphanage, a fast-growing effects studio in San Francisco. He also recently tutored his sister-in-law into a dream job at Industrial Light and Magic.

Mike Slisko, Freelance 2D and 3D Artist Mike Slisko is a freelance 2D and 3D computer animator based in San Francisco, California. He has worked as an art director, production artist, and animator for multiple game companies and has worked on numerous successful games, primarily character design.

Mitch Suskin, Visual Effects Supervisor, Paramount Pictures Mitch Suskin is a two-time Emmy-winning visual effects supervisor for Paramount Pictures in Hollywood, California. He currently directs the Visual Effects department on the hit television show *Star Trek: Enterprise*.

Matt White, Manager of Traditional Art, LucasArts Matt White is LucasArts' manager of traditional art, a job title whose irony isn't lost on the person who oversees the creation of art assets for futuristic games that primarily capitalize on the *Star Wars* franchise. LucasArts is located in San Rafael, California.

What Kinds of People Do You Look for When You're Hiring?

While you can't change who you are or the amount of experience you have when you apply for the job, you can probably project your best assets better, whether it's through your cover letter, resume, demo reel, or portfolio or during an interview. According to those doing the looking, you cannot overlook any single part of the package.

Carla Block, Sammy Studios In general, I know this is a cliché, but we're looking for really passionate people. I've worked in this industry for almost six years, and I've found that there are a lot of talented people out there, a lot. And just because they're talented at their core discipline doesn't necessarily mean they're passionate about what they do, so we're looking for that combination of talent, whether it be raw talent for a more junior-level position or seasoned talent or experience that somebody brings to the table along with that passion for creating a triple-A title or a topnotch, blockbuster game.

Amy Bendotti, Nintendo What we look for is experience, 100 percent. We hardly ever hire entry level just because we don't really have to. For artists, we don't really look at anybody that doesn't have at least two years experience and hasn't at least published one title. We look for education always. For programmers, they have to have a B.S. For art, they have to have some kind of art schooling. Education's really important. It's so dependent on the position. For art, we look for a really good demo reel. Good skills. A lot of our art positions, we look for really traditional art skills as well as 3D. If they can't draw and do all that kind of stuff, we don't typically look at them. So many 3D artists spend so much time doing this that they don't really keep up their traditional art skills, and it's really important for us that they have those and keep them up.

Matt White, LucasArts The ultimate candidate we look for, no matter which discipline we're hiring for, breaks down to some pretty similar criteria. We're really looking for people that have very, very strong foundation skills in the arts. Be that an animator, that they have some formal training with acting and animation. If it's for a model or texture artist, some fine arts background, be it sculpting or painting or what-not. But we do find that, and I think a lot of studios find that nothing beats those core art skills. You end up relying on them throughout your career. Beyond that, we look for people that have a deep appreciation for gaming. It is our business. We do hire from the film world sometimes, and we have made hires of people that perhaps haven't played a lot of games. But we have found over time that we have the most success with people that are fairly passionate about what it is we do.

It's nice to have them come in with a strong command of the tools. In this case, Maya. It's funny—that's become more relevant recently because I think a lot of studios and ourselves included were generally of the mind that, find the people with those core art skills and we can just train them in whatever technology we're using. But the marketplace is kind of starting to change that assumption. We can go out and find those people that do have those art skills and have the Maya skills. So obviously, those people that come with both have a leg up. That's just kind of a reality.

Marc Marrujo, Microsoft What I need are smart people that are in the industry, and that are hands on. That's the type of people I need. People that are in the industry that want to take it to the next level, that definitely work and strive to be the best they can be. Those are the types of people. I don't care if you have been developing games in Siberia or on the beach in Cabo San Lucas. Whatever. I'm just looking for solid people that are smart. From testing, I need solid people that have tested games extensively, white box and black box testing to the conceptual designer, to the architect, to managers, all walks of life.

But right now what we need are solid people that have both of those backgrounds and can come in and work well while being creative and really coming up with the look and feel. They partner with the designer, they partner with the producer, and they make sure from a 3D standpoint that the look and feel is up to par.

Douglas Hare, The Collective It depends on the position that we're trying to fill. Some people are coming in at an entry-level position. We're looking for something that's going to distinguish the applicant from everyone else. We get an enormous number of applicants for programming positions and we are looking for something that is going to stand out. If you're looking at someone who [has got no] game industry experience and potentially just coming out of university, for example, if someone has just a current university degree in computer science, we get about 50 applicants like that a week. So there's a great degree of competition if you're just looking at applicants with that one credential. However, if you have a person coming in with a degree and they also have work that they've done on their own time, maybe done some mods using existing game engines, or potentially just done their own demos and so on, then that's going to clearly elevate them, or push them beyond the rest of the pack.

We're looking for people who are going to have the right sort of personality perspective. We're looking for people who are going to be able to collaborate, work with groups of people from different disciplines, be open to criticism, be proactive, be able to follow direction, be able to understand that this is a very fast, evolving industry and there's always something to learn. You can't just learn something and then think that you're going to be able to sit with that knowledge for any length of time.

Ken Maruyama, Industrial Light and Magic Basically it all starts with the reel and portfolio. It doesn't matter what job you're applying for in the art area, whether it's in the art department or whether it's as an animator, you must show a reel or a portfolio or both. For example, for an animator, we look for those students who show evidence of knowledge in animation: how to make an object move and behave realistically, have an object that has weight. We've found that the schools that have a curriculum focused in traditional animation and also one in computer animation—the marriage of both of those disciplines—seems to turn out well-rounded students and people who can almost step right in and be productive. I think for animators, naturally we look at the work. We look at some of the exercises that they go through and we pay particular attention to how the person is moving the character, and we look at any of the performance that the character is going through. If it's a technical director, we generally look at the more experienced people. For animators, we have an entry-level position. Oftentimes when it's really busy, we will have an apprenticeship program where we have eight to ten of the top graduate animators come in, and we have an apprenticeship program through the summer. It's no guarantee of employment, but it does give us a chance to look at these people and then have them show us what they can do and get to learn some of our pipeline. The ones that excel will get positions.

Tim Johnson, Black Ops Entertainment Mainly, we look for a combination of things, kind of general 3D artists that would do anything from 3D modeling to environments, building levels, those kinds of things. We also look for animators. In our animation, we look for people who have experience with hand keying things as well as motion capture experience, implementing some of that. We use primarily 3ds max, so experience with that is usually mandatory. If somebody has done a lot of work with Maya, we will talk to them, but we want to see that they can do some work in max and at least know their way around as it kind of helps with the ramp-up time.

Kevin Cureton, Electronic Arts I think breadth of experience is a big one. Knowing, having experience on multiple programming languages, having actually done some serious development. Not necessarily CG, but pipeline development. When I was at PDI, I wrote a suite of asset management tools that they use. Just in general, when you're in an interview, they put scenarios before you. These are the kind of problems we're running into in production. How would you go about solving them? Being able to think and troubleshoot on-the-fly is very much a skill that's needed for this type of position, so you have to bring that to bear when you're interviewing and say, "Okay. Well, you're having these kinds of problems and it's taking this long to render stuff, maybe you can divide it up into things, and push it out to other machines," and just basically posit solutions to actual real-life problems. I think it's how you answer those questions—and not necessarily providing a flat-out, "this is how I would do it," but rather how you analyze that problem. You may never in the course of that interview come up with a solution, but how you approach that solution I think has a big impact.

Sean Miller, Sammy Studios For us here at Sammy Studios, we're very interested in artists. Artists first, more than technical people, although we do have some technical artists. It's very important to us that they have really strong art skills, that's one of the primary things. We are very interested in artists who have a traditional background, if not professionally, at least traditional skills that they can demonstrate on their reel or their portfolio. Most come from art schools: we have people from Savannah College of Art and Design, from Art Center of Pasadena, and from the Academy of Art in San Francisco. We put a high premium on artistic skills and artistic talent, because if you know good art, you're going to be able to create good art, regardless of what tool you use.

I'm more willing to train someone to use the tool than to train in art. It's much more difficult to train someone to be a good artist. There are exceptions to the rule, where you have guys who didn't need to go to art school who are phenomenal artists, but in general it's certainly helpful. If you don't have the art school you should be able to demonstrate the art skills, and the art background in your portfolio.

Evan Pontoriero, Industrial Light and Magic [For previz work] I think they have to be really good problem solvers, they have to be able to be kind of a—I don't want to say a loner, that's not the word I'm looking for. Someone who can work by themselves and yet be a part of a team as well, who can solve problems on their own but yet—like any place, the group is only as good as the people that are doing the work. It's important that people fit in. If you get someone who has a bad attitude, it can ruin the whole thing. It can really screw you up. So attitude is really important.

You have to be very resilient because you're going to be asked to do a lot of work in a very short amount of time. You're not doing three-week shots or two-month shots. We're asked to do probably at a minimum three shots a day. You need to be a pretty decent polygonal modeler or sub-d surface modeler. You have to be able to do pretty decent textures.

Craig Lyn, FrameStore In terms of skill sets coming in the door, it really depends on which side of the industry you're going into. I'm mostly looking for technical directors. Animation supervisors are looking for certain things, I'm looking for certain things. What we're all looking for is artistic background and a good eye. It's the same crap that everyone says that yeah, chances are that we're interviewing someone and they're not going to have a strong CG portfolio or reel, because if they do they're going to be outrageously expensive and coming in for a senior position. The kind of people I'm assuming are reading [this] book are coming in at the beginning. So we're looking for everything else in addition to a strong reel. Things like drawings, character drawing, painting, sculptures, everything in addition to that that shows you have some talent.

Some of the best people we've been hiring have been traditional illustrators, because they understand composition, they understand color, which is really good—you don't have to teach them that. We're looking for a really strong foundation in the arts.

On the other hand, I've been prowling the universities for people with good technical backgrounds that can actually script, that I can say, "Okay, I need a script to do this, this, and this, how do you do it?" And they'll be able to tell me. They'll be able to pick up something in Perl, C, BASH, Tickle, any of those.

Mitch Suskin, Paramount Pictures The real thing is, to me, what platform the people are on means nothing. As far as their skill set, and even whether they have a particular skill set for computers, doesn't really mean that much. To me, whether people have an artistic eye, whether they're painters or compositors or whatever, if they understand photography and editing, and film storytelling is more important to me than whether they can drive a particular platform.

Years ago, we weren't on resolution independent boxes. Actually when I started [*Star Trek: Enterprise*], this show was being composited on linear online editing systems. And it was a much more complicated process, but the real thing is that these guys were good at it not just because they could run the editing box, but because they had a really good artistic eye for how shots were supposed to go together and what they should look like and how they cut into the show.

It's also true in 3D animation. Whether you're doing motion control model shots or whether you're doing things in 3D, you've got to have people who understand filmmaking and photography and lighting first. I guess eventually anybody can learn to run one of these boxes if you're doing it eight or ten hours a day, but if you don't have the artistic eye to begin with, it doesn't matter how much you train someone, they'll never get it. And so there are a lot of guys who can run the computers really well and can turn out something looking like shots, but the guys who turn out the best shots are the guys who are less technical and more artists first.

What Do You Look for in Specialized Positions?

It's one of those questions where nearly all of our interviewees said, "It depends." Keep that in mind, and by all means, find out as much as you can about a particular position before you apply for the job.

Brian Freisinger, ESC Did you ever read Robert Heinlein? He has a quote: "Specialization is for ants." I don't believe in specialization. I've got strengths. I'm stronger in some areas. I'm not a good animator, but I like to animate, and I like to play with it. I would never try to get a job as a character animator, but I enjoy doing it on my own. I am a good rigger. If you translate that, I'm a great character modeler, because I'm a really good rigger, and I understand how animation works.

Some people will specialize so narrowly on something that they don't see the big picture. When you're in a house, you need to work in a team. What goes on in compositing, I don't need to know that, because it's so far removed from me. But within your immediate spheres of influence—definitely you need to know how texturing works if you're going to deal with UV maps. You don't need to be the best texturer in the world, but you should know. That would be something in the skill sets. Not being a complete blinded specialist, where you just model, and that's all you know. I know people like that, and I think they're limiting themselves.

Games

Amy Bendotti, Nintendo We look for 3ds max or Maya. We use max, but they're still flexible. Photoshop. The traditional art skills. 3D skills as well. We look for artists that can do everything. I mean, artists that specialize in one thing but can do model texturing, animation if they need to. They should have a specific focus, but both of our studios are so small that people are doing a lot of different things. Even if they're hired to be the animator, that's not exactly what they're going to be doing over a certain amount of time. At Nintendo, our games are so high quality and they're constantly changing, I think even more so than other companies out there, so they really, really, really need to be flexible. They can do something and think this is exactly what they're doing and finish it and it's like, scratch, that's over. You need to do this in 24 hours. I think that that's standard for the industry, but I think at Nintendo it's even more so. We were known for long development phases, taking longer because the games are so high quality, so they really need to be flexible and willing to adapt.

Matt White, LucasArts What the gaming environment offers for artists that is unique compared to, say, most film organizations I've worked for, is the ability for artists who are skilled and have interest in multiple art disciplines to put those to use. Our projects tend to have about 20 or so artists. That's everybody from concept down to animation. Because of those numbers, we rely on people being able to multitask. We can and do accommodate people who are specialists, but we need the other kind of artist as well, someone who can pick up a pen and give us a really great design while we're in the concept design phase and then over time, transition into a modeling texturing phase, or, maybe over time, someone who's modeling [will] transition into a lighting role in the company.

So, whereas I think feature film tends to be slightly more—or not even slightly, just more regimented out of design. The task to make a movie is so enormous, you need to come up with a fairly compartmentalized set of rules that everybody contributes to their specialty and then hands it to the next person who does their specialty just to keep the pipeline flowing.

In games, I think, we also depend and need to depend on people being able to do more than one thing, but their skill has to be there and their interest needs to be there. The one exception I'm finding over time is animation. Animation and modeling are two distinctly different art disciplines. We can find animators who, if they come from the 2D world, generally have a pretty highly developed sense of character design and posing and so we can put them to work sometimes doing that kind of work, character design. Or, sometimes layout is the other thing the animators tend to be strong at.

Sean Miller, Sammy Studios The jobs are fairly broad. Typically, someone is stronger at one than the other. If someone can only do one, they'd better be able to do that really well. I mean, so well that I don't care that they can't do the other. We look for in modelers and texturers, people who can visualize geometry in an economical way. Poly counts are getting higher, but they're still at a premium, and being able to get a piece of low-resolution geometry that looks higher than it is, is usually coupled with texturing ability. That's one of the tricks of the trade to be able to hide those polygons. So, we prefer that the people who do the modeling be able to do the texturing. But there are people who are just so much better at texturing than they are at modeling that we'll look at those people. And what I look for in those is, do I see the core ability to be able to train them in that other discipline that they're weak in?

In games you'll find that you do more of the other discipline. In some shops it's a modeler, texturer, animator. Our character people tend to model and set up as well as animate. But they rarely do much with props, unless they want to, then we give them the opportunity to do that. There's a different set of rules for the geometry, and what you're worried about and thinking about.

Modeling

Ken Maruyama, Industrial Light and Magic Well, a modeler, yes. Now that is a really strong skilled position. The creature modelers have to have a good knowledge of anatomy. We like people who have had formal education in the fine arts and in anatomy in particular. People who understand physiology and who have studied skeletal structure and muscular structure and how things move because it's important for a modeler to be able to model the human form accurately because oftentimes we're called on to model human characters. We call them digital doubles, but they have to be accurate in that respect, and they have to know the right perspective and proportions and that's important.

It's also important they understand the mechanics of how a human figure works because when they are doing creatures, the creatures have to exist in our space because of the work that we do. The nature of our work is that we are marrying our computer graphics objects and images and effects onto live action plates so that some of our characters have to be working and performing with the actors in the scene. The character has to look believable and they have to look like they belong in our atmosphere. That's why they need to know the mechanics of how things move, especially in creatures—the animators have to move them and so the support mechanisms, whether it's the legs or the feet or whatever, have to look like they carry weight. The muscles that support the weight have to look like they really are real and they can actually support that.

Emmanuel Shiu, The Orphanage The easiest thing is if you want to be a modeler, show your modeling. That's it. Turntables, nothing fancy. Good surfacing. Period. You've chosen an object that has complex surfaces and you show how you did it, basically by showing your wireframe and your turntables. Surfacing just means how the surface was put together, how it flows, whether it looks clean, whether it's achieving the curvature that you want. The biggest thing I can say for a modeling reel is to have reference. Have reference of real-world objects, because people will wonder whether you have a fantastical object, whether that's real, or whether you screwed up. In film models, the level of detail should be as high, or as much as there is in real life. Now you may think that they won't see this little thing, I'll texture map it. No. Model it. You won't break the hundred processors they have, but you might miss a chance for them to hire you in the little flaw that the thing isn't catching light. You need to put it all in there. If they don't need it later, they'll take it out, but it's always better to over-build than under-build a film model. Always.

Tim Johnson, Black Ops Entertainment It all comes down to modeling. Some people are stronger character modelers, so we may just have them do characters, but when we look at a 3D artist, pretty much modeling everything throughout an environment. One of the games that we have, we basically have one artist for each level. They're responsible for building that level, whether it be a police car that needs to go there or a building or a fence or whatever. They need to be able to texture that. They need to be able to create the model and make it look as realistic as possible.

Texture Artists

Emmanuel Shiu, The Orphanage In texture painters, they're really looking for your ability to paint. How do you see a surface? If it's concrete, how do you paint that, or how do you manipulate the photographs? Nowadays in film, I would say that 80 percent of what you see is a photograph, but it's also your eye for color, and how to make that photograph mapped on a surface look real, so you've got to put in a color channel, a diffuse channel, and a bump channel, and maybe a displacement and a specular map. All these things combined make the object look like the object, as opposed to just slapping on color and hoping that will pass. They need you to have an eye for that, and you show that by how you've surfaced some of your objects. They need it to look real. There's no ifs, ands, or buts about that.

What Do You Look for in a Demo Reel?

We covered this extensively in Chapter 5, but there are endless ways to put together a demo reel. Just make sure you tailor that reel for the job you're going for. Here's some more anecdotal information that may help:

Matt White, LucasArts We like to see some kind of demonstrated area of applicable specialties so if you are applying for a job as a modeler, I need a portfolio or reel that demonstrates your modeling strength. Within that reel, because we're a company that produces games of many different genres, whether they're sometimes very cartoony and sometimes they're hyper-realistic, it's nice to see not only a demonstrated strength perhaps in one genre, but also if you've got some broad talent so that we can be very, very flexible in how you end up getting placed.

Jo Ann Pacho, ArtSource For the online portfolios, specifically, I show them samples of the portfolios of other people who are more experienced. (I get permission from the other talent.) I show them samples, and I give them a list of the top three or four things my client is looking for; things they should clearly have showing on their resume or on their online portfolio. The tough part is when you're dealing with these clients, it's almost never the hiring manager that's looking at these portfolios. It's almost always the admin or somebody who has been given a laundry list of things to look for, and you have a very short amount of time to get noticed. We can help artists put their portfolios in a format that gets them noticed, or at least highlights the best of their capabilities so that they can be seen right away. I think the most important thing is the organization of the information so that you clearly define your categories: if you do 3D character animation and you also do level design, make sure those sections are clearly marked and separated so that if somebody is looking for character animation, they can go directly to that part of the portfolio and not waste time going through the entire body of work.

Amy Bendotti, Nintendo We look for the best of the best stuff. Not putting any of their mediocre work on there. Also, a specific outline of what exactly they've done on their demo reel. So many people put stuff on there that is done by a team or whatever so if they can outline exactly what they're responsible for in each shot, we look for that. For programmers, we have them send samples of their C++ coding. We don't do tests or anything like that. Just typically what most companies look for, but a lot of it, too, is the soft skills and the candidate. We really push them hard and find out how flexible they are.

Tim Johnson, Black Ops Entertainment We like to see a good, clean demo reel that has examples of different types of work. We don't want to just see buildings. We want to see that you can model and texture different types of items and just kind of how well-versed you are as far as that goes.

I think the first thing [we look at] is the resume and then at some of the work. Really, when we're looking at screening and whom we want to bring in, we're looking at the work, as it's relevant to what they'll be doing. Secondarily, once they get here, once they start talking to people, that's when they start investigating some of the traditional stuff and really want to look at a portfolio and see what else they've done. But right off the bat, it's a combination of experience and work and what kind of money is somebody looking for. Is the salary requirement relevant to the experience they've got? How flexible are they? You got a lot of people who say, "You know, I just want to get into the game industry," and the biggest thing there is, you have to be flexible. If that's really what you want to do and that's what your passion is, you've got to be able to take that first step, and it may not pay you a ton of money right off the bat, but within a year or two, you should be able to make that up. So that's some of the biggest things with people that don't have a lot of experience.

Randy Nelson, Pixar University The important thing to note is that there is an inverse relationship between successful candidates and coolness of [the packaging] presentation. That is inevitably what recruiting would tell us—we would all go, "Wow, how clever, that is so amazing, what a great thing!"—is that great reels come in, sort of, plain old beat up Sony six-hour tape cardboard packages with handwritten labels scrawled on them because film makers are too busy making films to have time for all that geek stuff. And so recruiting would tell us that the sad thing is that the enormous creativity that showed up in the packaging of the presentation was rarely reflected in the thing presented.

It became axiomatic, in fact, that one of these, like "I am so damn clever you can't believe how neat this thing is, this is the best box you have seen in a year," inevitably, that was all there was to see.

The really great folks just sent their work in and their work spoke for them. And folks whose work wasn't this great figured out some way of putting some creativity into it and, unfortunately, it should have just gone into the work on the reel instead of the package the reel came in.

Sangeeta Pashar, Pixar A comprehensive understanding of animation fundamentals—a good sense of weight, timing, movement, and acting ability should be reflected in the characters. Computer animation is helpful but not necessary. Your reel should also reflect a storytelling sense. It does not have to be long—three minutes is good enough!

Simple characters and a simple story—extra points if it's funny or brings out an emotion in the viewer. It should be short, and music is optional.

Sean Miller, Sammy Studios The HR department gets the reels, resumes, portfolios, and they go to our chief creative officer, who is in charge of hiring for all the teams. He is nice enough to cull through and pick out the ones that he feels have the most potential, and he passes that to the leads in the various disciplines for us to review. We take a look at it and look for the core ability. We're also looking for reels, resumes, and portfolios, and you tend to judge them not only by the strongest piece on the reel but also the weakest piece on the reel. Very often, the thing that gets you put into the No pile is going to be the weakest piece on your reel. If you've got something that's really great, and something that's really bad, we don't know which one we're going to get.

We expect people to be able to tell the difference between good and bad. If you put something on your reel that's bad, it becomes something we have to consider.

When you're trying to get an interview through your resume or your reel, one of the things that is important is you really only get one shot. The resume books, they'll tell you, you have like 20 seconds to make an impression with a resume. It needs to look professional, it needs to put your best foot forward. The same is with your reel and your portfolio. The moment you lose somebody's interest—when you're looking at 150 reels in an afternoon, and every one of those reels is anywhere from two to five minutes long, it's almost impossible to hold the art director's attention for five minutes on a reel. It should be the most amazing reel that anyone has ever seen if you're going to make someone sit through that for five minutes.

One of the key things I think to creating a reel and getting a job is editing. Being willing and able to say, you know what, I don't think that's good enough. I'd rather see a one-minute reel that makes me want to rewind and watch it again than a three-minute reel with one minute of really good stuff, and then some not so good stuff and a stinker. You have to judge that reel by the weakest piece on it. A lot of times, you've done an animation that's a cinematic sequence that's a minute and a half long, and there's really about 25 seconds of animation in there that are your best work. And the other stuff is not bad, but maybe it doesn't say your best stuff, it doesn't put your best foot forward.

One of the things you see is people just putting everything on their reel because they want to show they can do it. Don't do that. You can talk about that in your cover letter. You can talk about that in your phone interview. You can bring examples of that to the interview. Only put your best stuff. Whatever that is, that's what you put on there. In your cover letter, you discuss, "I also do modeling," but let's say you're a texture artist, you show your texture portfolio with your best textures on it and maybe some models they've been used on. In your cover letter, you say, "I also do some modeling. And I have experience doing a little bit of animation." You don't even have to say that's not your strong stuff. But if that's your skill level, and that's important, knowing your skill level, you don't put that forward, but you put it out there. Yes, I can do this stuff.

I want to see the best stuff, and if you only have that in a specialization, then do that. It's really distracting when you see something that isn't good. It colors the stuff that you see that is good. It makes it less than it really should be. When you lose someone's attention when they're watching a demo reel, you almost never get it back.

Evan Pontoriero, Industrial Light and Magic If you're applying for a modeling job, you want to see turntables, and you want to see wireframes. If you're applying for a character animation job, you don't need to have a fully blown-out character in 3D. It can be a block man. If you can get block man to emote, you've got him sold.

I mean, it's great if you can get someone who can cross over and do the modeling and do the texturing and do all of that stuff, that's great. I think every company is looking for that. But if that's not your strong suit, I wouldn't even try to do it because it can be distracting. It's better off if you focus on the animation, if you focus on the modeling. And don't try to waste your time on your reel making something that's a gorgeous matte painting background of the sky if you're not going for that job, you know. You want to focus—focus, focus, focus.

Or, sometimes people don't say what they've done. They just kind of put the shot on the reel and they don't describe what exactly they've done in that shot. Or, they've described something that they've done and it doesn't relate to what their job is, so they lose credibility that way, especially if you get another reel from somebody who's said they've done the exact same thing and their job is that. It's like, "I did the modeling and the texture mapping and the animation on this thing," and then you get a shot from another guy who's a modeler and he says, "Oh, I did the modeling on this." Well, you know, the guy who's said he's done all three things is going to look bad no matter what.

It's tough especially for people who are working at other companies and that's all that they can get. So I guess word to the wise is, make sure you describe exactly what you've done if you're using a final on your reel because we know that there aren't too many people who do everything in a shot. So describe it.

Brian Freisinger, ESC I've seen some of the most blitzing reels that have come in, that have some of the most fantastic structures and creatures and architecture, but you know, this guy sent in this thing, it was this really cool creature set, this really cool demon, but what the hell's a demon look like? You can do anything you want. It may look cool, and I can break it down structurally, would it really walk like that, would it look like that, but at the end of the day, I have hired people who had like, coffee pots and phone booths, and it looked real. But it was something that I could recognize: tanks, guns, you know, that's what we do. When creature work comes along, there's two or three creatures in the film. The majority of our work is nuts and bolts and pipes and lamps. You're doing stuff to help match—they move some objects in there, they need some debris, they need crashed cars. That's what you do.

My boss, Kim Labrary, says, "We don't try to re-create reality, we try to capture reality."

Often we're working off cyberscans, we're working off photographs, we're working off measurements. I'm not saying it's not a good thing to be creative, because creative means a lot of things, but if somebody sends me a reel full of fantasy, I look at it, aesthetically I'm interested in it, but generally, I shove it off to the side.

Obviously, if they're experienced people, if they've been working in the industry for awhile, it's different, but if they're new to the industry, students especially, sending me nothing but fantasy material. They should be sending their reel to Pixar or PDI, who are looking for that kind of thing often. I don't want to speak for Industrial Light and Magic, but the houses that do more visual effects and less character animation, we're looking for reality, because that's what we deal in.

Emmanuel Shiu, The Orphanage In film, they want to see a demo reel that whets their appetite. But what they want to see in the interview is your traditional artwork, your sculpting. My sister-in-law, who just got a job at ILM, didn't benefit from that, but they wanted to see that. It did cause a little bit of a kink for her getting hired there. She didn't have any sculpture experience, and she couldn't show any life drawing. That's very important for them, but never make that the bulk of your portfolio.

What they want to see is, can you do what we want you to do here? They want to see examples of what you can do, and they want to see examples of your training to back up what you can do. So you always want to show that in your portfolio.

In a games studio, they're looking for a little bit wider breadth of artist. Things are changing and getting closer to film nowadays, where they do want good quality artists. People can tell now what is what. They want to see your portfolio in an interview. It does matter now. A lot of places like EA, Sony, 3DO, they care about the fact that you can do it, but they still would like you to be more diverse.

There are places that are popping up, like EA, where they're hiring just character modelers, and you're just going to be a character modeler.

Fifteen seconds is basically how much I used to give on the tape. I'm a little bit more lenient now; I give about half a minute nowadays. At a pop, you've got 50 demo reels to view, and you've got your workload on top of that. It's because people don't have much time; that's why people are like that. It's not because they're trying to be mean. It's just that they are that busy. So in 15 seconds, I don't want to see a flying logo, I don't want to see any of that; I want to see something short and sweet. Get to your work soon, like within five seconds, and show your best piece first. You'd be surprised how many people show a lot of crap, and then at the end you see something that's like, "What was that? That was good."

But usually you don't get to that part because you already turned off the tape. So show your best things first, and go in order of that, and go no longer than two minutes.

Craig Lyn, FrameStore The things I always get suspicious of, especially in a small industry over here, when you see this shot, and you ask them what they did, and they say "Oh, I did all of it." Really? I just had someone in here three days ago who said the same thing about the same shot. It's okay to lie, but it's very important to be able to back it up. It's a small industry, and someone will call you on it.

Apart from that, there's really nothing bad. What is always a good thing though is if you're able to sit there and talk someone through your shot. This is what I did, this is how I did it, and this is what I was looking at, and this is what I was thinking when I did it. I had guys who said yeah, I just put it in there and I lit it.

…Everybody puts cheesy audio tracks on their reel. That's the very first thing. I'll turn the audio off.

What Do You Look for During the Interview?

You already know you need to put your A-game together to nail the interview. The people interviewing you were once on the other side of the hiring desk, but they now yield gatekeeper power to your employment destiny. Discover what woos them and what may prompt them to end the interview midsentence.

Matt White, LucasArts What we look for is the personality. I mean, it actually does figure in pretty high because this company compared to many I've worked for tends to keep a pretty civilized work environment, but we aren't immune from the crunch. I mean, we do find ourselves in positions where we just have to really work hard to get stuff out. And when we hit those times, there will be periods where people spend more time sometimes at work than they do with their friends and family. And you want to make sure that the people that you have aren't jerks. Really want to make sure that they can work well with a team, and our interview process is something you screen for as carefully as you can for just the kind of, the fit factor.

Amy Bendotti, Nintendo I recommend they dress professionally even in this industry. I would recommend that they bring extra copies of their resume, bring their portfolio. Most of the time we've looked at their demo reel already, but bring some traditional work. I would just tell job seekers in general—definitely research the company. Know the latest news and what the games are. If they're interviewing at Retro and they don't know that we do Metroid Prime, or they haven't played it, that's a huge strike against them. Be calm, and express their interest in the company and how excited they are about games. We really like people that are die-hard Nintendo people specifically. A lot of times they won't even hire if you're not. If you're like, "Oh, I just like games and I want to work in games." They want people that want to work for Nintendo. Be ready to answer some tough questions.

Ken Maruyama, Industrial Light and Magic We look for the personality of the individual. Since this is a real collaborative experience where you are working on a crew and you're having to rely on other people to help get your work done, we look for people who gravitate towards that team experience. Sometimes you'll find people who kind of want to be the star and they want to be the person who is singled out, who wants to be the guy that everybody points to, and those are the people we tend to shy away from. But it's the ones that have a real passion and a love for their work and who seem like they're the ones that really want to learn and they are truly interested in the type of work that we do here. Because oftentimes people, especially animators, will want to be on the digital animation feature and they want to work out at a Pixar or DreamWorks and right away we say that, "You know what? We don't do that kind of work. This is the kind of work we do." We are about visual effects and about just creating those pieces of the project, or the pieces of the film that the studios want us to do because we work for hire here. Unless you want to do that and you understand that process, and if you want to be on a digital feature and you want to work on the next *Shrek* or the next *Toy Story*, then this isn't the place for you.

Brian Freisinger, ESC Besides just having a decent reel, we look for eagerness, personality, interpersonal skills, and not just good communication skills. It's a tense industry; you're working late hours, you're working together. You might be spending every weekend together for the next six months. I think to myself often, can I spend every weekend for the next six months with this person without me wanting to kill him? It's hard to tell right away.

When I'm interviewing, I often ask little questions to feel them out, to see if they're going to jibe with the team. If people are really cocky, really arrogant, [it doesn't matter] how good their reel is. I mean I do not even care. I've worked with people like that before. It only takes you once to work with people like that and you know that person. They're all the same. You can kind of spot 'em a mile away. This whole prima donna, and they're usually really naturally talented and really good, but they have no interpersonal skills with people. They can't be really helpful or they're over-helpful, to the point of, "No, no, do it like this."

Craig Lyn, FrameStore I had some guys coming in to interview for render support, so it was the graveyard shift. Now this is an entry level, foot-in-the door position. I told them, "Now guys, this is a great opportunity. We're giving you free run of the farm. You can run your stuff at night. This is a great opportunity to self-train. This, that, and the other thing." The first people I interviewed were runners from our company, basically gophers, and the first line out of this guy's mouth was, "Well, how much more are we getting paid?" That's not what I'm looking for.

On the other, I had a guy who came in to interview for a junior TD position, and he wasn't ready. But he was willing to sell his soul to get in the door, and I said, "I can't give you a job as a TD, but how do you feel about render support? I gotta be honest with you, it's going to suck. It's going to be graveyard shift. It's thankless, and it's going to be high stress, but your opportunity of becoming a TD after a year is really good because all you have to do is impress me." And he said, "Yeah, I'll do it!" And I asked, "But don't you want to hear the rest?" and he said, "No, I'll do it." And you know, that's what you're looking for.

To go even further, I get so many e-mails from people saying, "I want a job in the industry." And the first thing they have to do is say, okay, what do you want to do? Do you want to be a TD, do you want to be a compositor, do you want to be a modeler, do you want to paint texture maps, do you want to paint matte paintings? They say, "I'd like to do all of them." Well, unless you're very good, no one's going to hire you to do all of those. Your reel has to be so focused on saying, "I'm going to be a modeler," because when you run a modeling reel, you want to see a wireframe, you want to see a render of it, but I really don't care about your texture mapping skills, because that's not why I'm hiring you. For the games company, or the games industry, absolutely, you're going to have to do all of those things. But here, it's so focused and so stratified that they really have to tie one thing down.

How Important Is Education?

"Education" means different things to different people. At its core, it's the foundation of knowledge you gain through going to a college, university, art school, or a certificate or training course. Additionally, employers are looking for what you've taught yourself on your own time. Oh, and don't forget hands-on experience.

Marc Marrujo, Microsoft We do look at special schools, however, they're not taken into consideration as much as hands-on experience and what you're doing right now. We think that smart people come from all walks of life. So they can have a high school diploma or [be] a Harvard graduate Ph.D., whatever. It doesn't matter. I mean, obviously, if we look at RISD [Rhode Island School of Design] or Carnegie Mellon School of Design, or art background from NYU or what have you, obviously, that reflects highly on someone. But if someone has something from Bellevue Community College right down the street or from Los Angeles School of the Arts in Pasadena, hopefully the person from Los Angeles School of the Arts is doing something a bit more than the person from Bellevue Community College, but it really doesn't matter.

Douglas Hare, The Collective If they're looking for a programming position, then a computer science degree is going to be a foundational element. However, there are other courses that you can do in certain universities or colleges that are quite a lot more geared towards game industries, or they have parts of their curricula that are actually geared towards it, although it's becoming more commonplace for people to apply with these mods. If someone came to us and didn't have any formal qualifications but gave a fantastic demonstration of their abilities, then that would actually count for more.

Ken Maruyama, Industrial Light and Magic It's hard to generalize, but if I were telling an animator, I'd say: "Look at previous work." That's the one thing that I tell a lot of students. I say, "You know, you have so many options available to you today, especially as far as resources go, things to look at, than I ever had when I was going through school." Anybody can go and get a DVD of a Disney film and you can single-frame the thing and study animation that way. I mean, right in your own home. There's hardware and tools available to students today that are just unbelievable. But it's about doing it. And it's about just striving to be the absolute best you can be. I know it's trite and it sounds really stupid, but it really is that. And for the people in the Art department, you just have to draw and you just have to excel and it's not any one thing.

Tim Johnson, Black Ops Entertainment It's important that they have some traditional art background just because it gives us an idea where they've come from and what kinds of things that they've done in the past. Or if it's not anything that they've done professionally, kind of where their vision's coming and how they picture things and that kind of stuff. So it's a little bit harder for me to look at that and evaluate it, but when we're talking with our art directors and those kinds of things, they're a lot more familiar with the different styles and how things work. So they like to see a lot of that stuff and just kind of see what you've done. It doesn't have to be anything fancy, but just what else is there other than games that you've worked on or commercials or whatever the case may be.

Sean Miller, Sammy Studios We do have a couple of people here who don't have art school in their background but are among the most talented. The art school is sort of a means to an end. The ones who don't go to art school have a harder time developing those art skills. That's where you get your mentorship and also get used to doing iterations. It's also a lot of times your first exposure to real art direction. You have to please the teacher who plays the role of art director for the class.

When I talk to students at colleges, one of the most important things is you're paying for your education. Use those teachers. Ask the questions. Don't wait for them to come to you. Go to the teacher. And never take "That's good" for an answer. Ask why it's good. Get that clarification. If someone says something is bad, make them tell you why they don't like it, because you'll never understand what impact your art is having on someone unless you ask those questions. And those people are being paid to answer those questions.

Mike Slisko, Freelance 2D and 3D Artist I think they definitely have to have a focus in fine art before anything. They have to know how to draw and paint, I think that is a really strong thing that 3D artists can have. It's not essential. I know 3D animators who don't know how to draw who are very good animators, but that's all they can do is move the wireframe around and develop the eye. But if you take someone who's accomplished in fine arts or a good 2D animator, and you teach them that, and if they have the mindset where they can sit down and work for eight hours a day at a computer, eventually when they feel comfortable with [the software], you'll end up having a stronger artist, a stronger 3D artist because he's already got this basis in art, and he's already got this developed eye, or developing eye. And he just ends up eventually, if not right away, making higher quality, better-looking work. Not that that's the way it has to be. There's some really good 3D animators that just don't know how to draw, don't know how to paint or kind of draw. But even if they kind of draw, it gives them a bit of an edge because they can sit there and thumbnail out their animation even if it's a rough, crude drawing with a stick figure. They can plan out their animation, whereas the guy who can't draw, well, he's got to think it out in his head and makes it maybe a little harder for him, or maybe he's got to think about it a different way.

Evan Pontoriero, Industrial Light and Magic Study film. Make sure that you're getting a firm grasp of cinema concepts, of filming concepts, of things they may not teach in an art academy or an art school. Go out and get the books, read up, and make sure you understand the concepts. That's kind of like the base foundation of understanding. Got to get some understanding of camera and lenses and why you shoot things certain ways and how to achieve different effects with different lenses because they're already going to be learning animation. If they're at Academy Art College in 3D, you're already going to be learning modeling and animation and most of that stuff would be fine, I think. Sort of grasping composition, I think, is the hardest thing to understand.

Brian Freisinger, ESC I come from a fine art background. I have some preference for people who maybe have some drawing skills. Not a lot of preference, but good design skills, a design base.

I hear people bitch when they go to art school, "I'm not going to take drawing classes; I'm going to be on the computer." But it's those core fundamentals, basic design skills—you know what, the software changes, the pipeline changes, everything changes, but your core skills, that's what you build off of. If you built your career on being an expert in this one software package and all its ins and outs, what happens if that software company goes out of business next year, and the next thing you know, you've got to start again. But not if you have this core of understanding things, you spread yourself out a little bit.

You don't have to be a programmer, but take a Perl class, or read a book. Take a drawing class, or read a book. Be broad-based in the fundamentals. When you understand the principle concepts of how something works—like on the core level, how design works, and composition works, and how things are put together —for modeling, that's the basis of it. And for software, if you just understand the basics of how the software works, you don't have to understand everything, not how to program it, just the basics, you can pick the other stuff up very quick because you know what you're looking for.

Emmanuel Shiu, The Orphanage For students, I would recommend for the first two years of school to be as diverse as possible. Do as many things as possible: photography, painting, sculpting, drawing. Anything and everything to find out what particular strengths they have. Anything in general. And then, after that, you've got another two years left, focus on one thing. Because what I haven't seen from most of the students is their ability to focus on one thing, say animation, modeling, lighting. What they do is they try to do everything, and they end up coming out without knowing any specific thing. They know a little bit of modeling, a little bit of lighting, a little bit of texturing, but it's not enough. It's not focused enough and they're not strong enough in their trade. Most places now, even game places, will say, well you're really good at modeling, let's put you in modeling for the next nine months. They're going to scrap everything else that you know and you're just going to be modeling. So you need to show focus. That's what schools don't do a lot of, because they want to get your feet wet in everything, but they don't realize there's only a certain amount of time for that before they have to focus you on a particular discipline so they can get you out in the real world.

Craig Lyn, FrameStore I'd highly recommend [fine art training]. I think it's absolutely important. There are things that catch me now. As you slowly move up, a Cinematics 101 course really helps, so you know when someone says camera track left, jib up, screen left, your basic aspect ratios: 1.33:1 and 2.35:1, and all that stuff, what it means. The difference between anamorphic and 35 mil, or what VistaVision really is, is really just picking up a book—that's really helpful—it's literally bedtime reading.

But the fine art side, absolutely, the more you know the better. At ILM, they offered things such as character drawing classes and sculpture classes that really helped a lot.

Mitch Suskin, Paramount Pictures I did go to film school. I was in the College of Fine Arts at UCLA. I started out in the College of Engineering and Applied Sciences, and I switched to the College of Fine Arts and I studied filmmaking. I did learn a lot about filmmaking there, but I think the on-the-job training is the more important thing. I learned a lot more in the first few months I was actually working in the film industry than I did at film school.

Part of it is having a good eye. I mean, a big part of it is just sort of artistic talent to begin with. Again, I think there's a problem, because all of our work is done on computers now, that there's this sometimes mistaken belief that all you have to do is know how to run a computer to be good at this, and you don't. Again, I can take artists who have worked in conventional media and train them to use the computer, but people who are just computer operators, I can't train to be an artist.

But having said that, I think that if you were going to study something, if you studied—particularly to do what I'm doing—if you study, photography and animation and lighting and editing would be the things that would be really valuable. Certainly understanding what things look like photographically and what depth of field means and what angle of view means. It makes it a lot easier for me to talk to artists when they understand how a camera works and a lot of what we're doing is simulating cameras. Even if it's all done in 3D, it's nice for people to understand if I say, "I want that to be shot on a long lens, or I want that to be shot on a wide lens," how that changes what happens when the objects move through it.

I'd say in this business, education is less important than experience. I started with an education because I didn't have any relatives in the business, I didn't know anybody in the business, and it was the only way to get experience. So the best thing about education is that it gives you some level of experience and even if it's student experience, it's experience.

What Advice Do You Have for Expanding Your Skills?

Whether you're still in school or have been in the industry for 20 years, your education never really stops. Obviously, it's mandatory that you keep learning if you want to move into other areas of CG, but it can also keep you employed if you learn a thing or two about the other departments in your company.

Matt White, LucasArts It starts with listening and understanding, what core skills they already bring to the table, and what skills they want to develop in the future. For instance, if I bring somebody into the group as an objects modeler and texture artist, but I know that because we've had discussions, they have a real interest in doing character modeling. They may have a portfolio that demonstrates some basic skill toward that, but now it's going to be a matter of making sure they're hooked up with the right mentor within the group to help direct their study and then look for opportunities where perhaps a secondary character modeler is looked for on a project. Knowing who the people are who have the skill and the interest in doing those jobs and making those jobs available to them. So in that way we kind of groom people over time to fill bigger and bigger roles within our art community.

Carla Block, Sammy Studios We do not have a formal training program; however, we have, within the 12 to 14 months, promoted a number of associate-level employees—we call them associate-level, they're more in layman's terms junior-level employees—to various new departments. We just recently promoted a product analyst, our game tester, into our design group. We do not have a formal training program established yet, but we are working with people to continue their career growth in order to provide them with some type of advance and opportunity on more of an informal basis, I guess.

Matt White, LucasArts There have been times where we have made changes to the job responsibilities that are going to affect a large group of our artists. In a situation like that, yes. We provide some very formalized training, sometimes from within the studio itself and sometimes using resources outside the studio to make sure that people get spun up on the stuff they need to know. For instance, two years ago we were embracing what seemed like every software platform on the planet. We were into Softimage, 3D Studio Max, Light Wave, Maya, to name four. We had a studio movement to choose one and embrace [it], and we ended up going with Maya as a studio solution. So we had vast numbers of our staff that were not savvy in the way with Maya. We selected people who were available and sent them for some offsite training and then had them bring that information back into the studio. And when people are either between projects or on downtime, we identify those people who need it and make sure they get spun up.

Ken Maruyama, Industrial Light and Magic We have what I think is an excellent, excellent training facility but it's geared to teaching our tools. We're not teaching Computer Graphics 101. We're teaching our tools and our software, and we have an excellent in-house training staff, and it's augmented by the experts on the line. Where, for example, if we're training animators into our tools and our network, we like to have animators work with animators. In other words, we get our senior guys working with the incoming animators just to show them the tricks of the trade and how to sort of navigate around the software.

How Do You Network?

Networking is so important [that] we dedicated all of Chapter 7 to the topic. Here's some more detailed information about the power of who you know and how to harness it.

Andrew Pearce, ESC I just talked to everyone I knew. I went to the job training for EDD (the California Employment Development Department). They had a class for harder-to-place individuals, which they made me attend because I was over a certain age and in management and they said, "Well, you fit the profile of someone who's going to have a hard time finding a job." So every Monday morning there was this group that would get together and they would discuss job prospects and if they had heard of anyone who was looking for employees in the area. Mainly these people were in aerospace, marketing, sales. But it was good in that they would have courses in how to go about finding a job.

And one of the ways was scouring the newspaper, sure, looking on Monster.com posts and checking companies they want to work for. But they also broke it down and said look in any kind of demographic statistics about the area. Who's the largest employer? Is there something there you could see yourself doing? Start learning about the companies where you want to apply. Make sure you understand where they're going with what they're trying to do—go and propose a job.

But the number one thing that helped me was just talking to every single person I know, especially those people who were employed. I contacted ESC really early on in that search and they had nothing, and there was really no good fit, but I talked to John Schlagg, who was one of the effects supes here and said, "Here's what I can do and I think I met you once a long time ago, and here's the kind of thing I'm looking for; here's my skill set. If you hear of anything, let me know. It doesn't have to be at ESC. Just let me know." We kind of left it. Well, it was great, because John knew about me at that point. He knew what I was capable of, what I wanted to do, and suddenly they developed this need ...and suddenly thought, "We should bring someone in who knows how to do this. Wait a minute, I know a tool developer who is looking for a job who would be perfect for this and who could expand the role if it became a bigger job than individual contributor," because that's what it was at first. They brought me in for the interview, I already knew John, so we had a good relationship. It's what everyone says: If you have that contact inside the company that can be your advocate, you're in such a better position than someone coming in with just a resume. The resume should be a backup to the conversation you have with someone. The resume should be just to remind them of what you talked about and what you sold your skills on.

Emmanuel Shiu, The Orphanage If you have a demo reel and you want to get it looked at, let's say you're in school. In any school, there are working professionals. That's your first avenue. To me, that's always your first avenue. Because you'll say to your teacher who's at, say, PDI, and he's coming here and teaching part-time. You'll say to him, "I have this demo reel. This is what I want to do. Tell me your honest opinion." If he thinks it's good, he'll tell you who to talk to. That's one way to do it. Because at any school, you're going to find working professional people, and you would hound those people. That's why they're there. But if you don't talk to them, then you're missing out on probably the biggest advantage of having them there. It's to teach, but it's also for the connections that they have. And it happens at the Academy all the time that Pixar teaches a class there, and they pick out the best students and bring them back.

Now, if you're a really great person, a lighter, let's say, and they want to bring back animators, but it just so happens they also need lighters, you give them a tape and, all right, you know what, this guy looks at it, he likes it, he's going to give it to the appropriate person. Versus, if you send it in, you'll probably never get anything. They get hundreds of reels a day. How are you going to compete with that? It could be anybody's bad day, it could be your tape was lost in the mail, you just never know.

[If you're not in school] then you are in a little bit of a harder spot, because you don't have that resource. In that case, all you can really do, if you don't really know anybody, is to find out what the company's working on. That's the time I feel like I would target most to the company, so when they first look at the tape, they're going to be interested. I would send in the tape and I would make sure it got there. You have to. Otherwise you never would know. And build a good rapport with the recruiter. Contrary to most people who say, "Don't call, don't call," I've called before, and the recruiters don't mind you calling; they just mind you calling 50 times a day. So you call them, and you get a good rapport, so they know you. They're much more likely to slip your reel in than if you didn't call at all.

It's a little bit of a shaky one when you have no one to go to, because I've called before, and I've called to the point where people say it's too much. And I gradually learned to do it just enough so they'll remember you and give you a little boost. And once you're in, you're in.

Referrals

Marc Marrujo, Microsoft Personal employer referrals are great. Also, competitive responses are great. This industry is a very tough industry and a lot of companies fold and go under and so we try to go in and find candidates from that, or we get little tips on what groups are laying off. We do a lot of conferences. GDC, E3.

Carla Block, Sammy Studios There is no normal way to find them. We've had tremendous, tremendous success [finding employees] with our internal networking. I can't say enough about that. Employees do not recommend people that they wouldn't want to work with. It's really that simple. Typically when we bring in new employees, that's one of the first things that we talk about. I'm like, I'm going to come back to you in a short period of time and I'm going to ask you, "Who can you recommend for any position?" I mean, they may be coming into a programming job, but I ask them, "Do you know any artists? Do you know any sales or marketing people?" And it's really been a tremendous help to us because we are a startup and we're starting from ground zero with zero employees, so it's been very, very helpful.

Matt White, LucasArts Some of the most successful hires we make are through people who work here who already know the environment, who know what's required and know somebody who fits that mold, so it can cut to the chase pretty quickly.

Tim Johnson, Black Ops Entertainment Probably 40 or 50 percent of the people we hire have been referred to us by somebody internally. That helps just because we've got a frame of reference to someone who worked with them before. So we have an idea of the game that they worked on because maybe if they worked with someone that we're already famil- iar with, they can say, "This guy did this, this, this, and this, " and they kind of vouch for them as far as that goes. It also helps when people are working with other people that they feel comfortable with and that they worked with in the past. It helps the morale of the teams and those kinds of things.

Andrew Pearce, ESC Has he got friends in the course? As soon as one of them gets a job and the people that hired him see what a good job he's doing and he says, "Oh, you know what, John's also pretty good and he's looking for a job right now," they're going to go, "hey, we like this guy and he's saying this other guy's good, let's get him in." At least for an interview and at least that gets them a positive feeling towards you even before you get in the door.

If you have equal candidates on the resume paper, but someone is saying, "I know this person and I can vouch for their good work habits," it gives you just that little edge, and that's enough to kind of push that way.

Mike Slisko, Freelance 2D and 3D Artist I'd say more than a few [jobs I've gotten through word-of-mouth]. LucasArts was through word of-mouth. There was a company called Atari. Someone told me about that, I got in touch with them. They flew me down for an interview. It went great, they wanted to hire me. They got a lawyer involved for the immi- gration stuff because I'm from Canada. They ended up finding out that it would have cost so much money and taken so long that they couldn't wait to fill the position there. From what I was told, they even had a cubicle set up for me and everything. It was actually kind of heartbreaking at the time. So, the senior animator from there was kind enough to pass my stuff on to a senior animator at LucasArts. He said, "We brought him down here, we wanted to hire him, maybe you guys can help him out, do something for him. He's a good artist," and so he took a look at my work and they gave me a phone interview and hired me over the phone. Got a lawyer that knew what he was doing, worked that out. Sent me a contract to sign, then they sent me the plane tickets and I ended up coming down and working for LucasArts, and that was a really good experience.

Emmanuel Shiu, The Orphanage If you know somebody, of course, you have a lot better chance to get into a company. Let's put it this way: one person knows somebody, the other doesn't. They have the same demo tape. Whose demo tape are you going to see first? My friend's of course. So I'm going to end up hiring him before I even see the other guy's demo tape. That's just the way it's going to go, and that's the way the field is. That's the way any field is.

So it's always going to be advantageous to network and know people, even if you think you'd never make use of this person, or this person would never be able to help you out, it's always good to have those there, so that they might know somebody. It's all about net-working really.

Go to a user's group—a very good thing. Anything that has anything to do with your soft-ware, your art, anything. You're much more likely to meet people there. Say you meet one person, and he's from Alias, and he'll say, "Wow, your stuff looks cool. Hey, I know this person at this place, and let me get that to that person," and it ends up, guess where, in that guy's hands. As opposed to you sending it somewhere. It's always good to network. And yes, it helps infinitely.

Freelance/Contract Work

Mitch Suskin, Paramount Pictures Whether you work on film or television, you find artists you like to work with and employ them over and over again. Whether they stay at the same facility or not is another issue. Our artists have moved, at least in the years we've been working on this show, from three different facilities already. Because I have a certain way of working and I have artists who have compatible styles and we've also learned to work together, I try to as much as possible use people I'm familiar with and know what their work is. You're always looking for new people, too, but I think it's true at just about any facility, with any film people. As a supervisor, if you find somebody who works for you, try to keep that person. We have one artist who used to work with one of our com-puter graphics companies; she's a 2D compositor and animator. She's up at ILM now, but we still use her on a freelance basis sometimes because she knows the types of shots we do and she's very efficient at getting them done.

Ken Maruyama, Industrial Light and Magic The project could be in here for two years, but the amount of time that the digital artist can actually work on it can be nine months to a year. That's sort of an average.

Tina Dickey, ArtSource A company might be willing to bring someone on for a couple of months, and then you might be able to get more exposure to different groups because you're not just in one group indefinitely. A lot of people actually plan for that so they know they're going to have three months off in a year. I would say the flexibility is the best one.

Recruiters

Tina Dickey, ArtSource We can offer gateways into a lot of the game development groups. A lot of times people will be applying for full-time positions but they might not have a headcount there, but they have a position for a temporary position, in which case we can get somebody introduced to the group that way. We tend to look for modelers, environmental artists, animators. Sometimes character artists, concept artists, UI designers, console UI designers. Those are typical ones. Texture art, texture mapping. Sometimes on its own, sometimes wrapped into modeling positions.

Jo Ann Pacho, ArtSource They come to us because maybe we have connections with a client they don't have. Maybe they want to work for a company that is shown on our site to be a client, and maybe we can help them get a foot in the door. Another reason some candidates come to us, especially right out of school, is for resources. They call us up and they ask us, "I have no experience, but I have this degree. How do I get experience if nobody wants to hire me because I don't have any experience?" So in tough times, we offer resources to our talent and it costs them nothing. Our revenue comes all from the client. We help people out of school build portfolios. That's one of the things we do. We also do a lot of outsourcing. We go out to schools and give lectures on what a portfolio should look like, what the elements are that most employers seek on a portfolio, how to put an effective resume together, how to draft a cover letter. Creative ways to get noticed when you're drowning in a sea of available talent. That's what we offer to our talent.

General Advice

Not all the information we gathered fits into a category. The people we interviewed were very generous with their time and willingly offered some general nuggets of wisdom from their years in the business.

Matt White, LucasArts One question that I am asked continually in the schools that I go to is, "What do you want to see in our portfolio?" And my answer is, generally speaking, if it were an easy question to answer, you'd probably already know. The bottom line is, especially for students coming out of school, it's really important for them to identify which marketplace and which discipline they are really most interested in going into after so that they can gear their portfolios accordingly. Which generally just means, I don't need to see everything you've done while you were in art school. What I would really like to see is the stuff that you feel is your best work that directly applies to what we do.

It seems simplistic, but I think if you have five different studios, what it is they want to see, how many drawings do you want to see, you're going to get five different answers, and I think the safest universal answer is to put only the work that you feel a hundred percent competent in, that speaks to the position that you're going after in your reel—I get countless demo reels or portfolios that contain everything that they've ever done. And there are maybe, you know, six really strong pieces of work in there, and there may be four fairly bad pieces of work in there that totally detract from the six good ones. And when we're looking at a portfolio with an art lead and we're trying to assess this person's strengths, I've seen it happen where they initially get in and say, "Wow, this person has got a lot of promise," then they get to the section of work that should never have been included, and it ends up killing the deal for them. And the advice is, don't put it in.

If you don't believe in it and you don't think it's your best work, don't include it. Other than that, take any opportunity that you have to start learning the technology component to the job you want to do on your own because you're going to be competing against people for the job that may be very strong artistically and have those skills. So don't ignore it. It doesn't do you any favors. And, play games. Play games and have strong opinions about the art in games, and be ready to talk about them.

Douglas Hare, The Collective The only thing I would say is that any time you're entering into an industry that's fiercely competitive, you have to be thinking that you have to do something that's going to stand out. It's a difficult industry to break into and we do get a lot of resumes from people who simply send their resume with their name and address on it, the university they attended, their GPA, and that's about it. That, to be brutally honest, is not going to stand out at all. You have to be going in with the mind that you're going to be attracting someone's attention.

Tim Johnson, Black Ops Entertainment I think that it's important—and I'm not sure why this happens, but it's important for someone to do some sort of research and try to figure out what kinds of tools a particular company uses. It doesn't really take a lot of research, but usually in a job description, you'll say, looking for someone with experience with 3ds max. If that is the case and someone sends you a resume and it's all Maya, this person has got to either tell you that they've done some max before, that they've done it on their own, they've got a copy at home—something that's going to let me know that they know that we use 3ds max and they know how to use it.

Brian Freisinger, ESC Get real jobs. Don't work for this industry. Go do something else. That was always my big threat. I should have become a dirigible pilot, or I should have become a mortician. People are always dying.

Kevin Cureton, Electronic Arts I think back to when I first started at PDI. I had a friend who I worked with at Rice and he was just gung ho to work for PDI. That had been his lifelong dream because he was really big into CG and had been dealing with it a lot since it first came about. So he basically went after the job of render assistant or render wrangler. Basically, they'd baby-sit the render farm, make sure that stuff that was—the frames that were getting rendered were running along and things were moving along. So, he went to work for them in that capacity. At some point, he called me up and talked to me about positions that they had open. I thought, "Okay. This can be kind of cool."

They basically ended up hiring me because I knew Perl. That was pretty much the only reason. I found that out a few months after the fact and thought that was really interesting that this skill that I had just by happenstance picked up when I worked at Rice ended up being what really got me in the door at PDI. So that's why I think the breadth of skill comes into play. And you don't necessarily know what skills are going to be useful. That's why I say when you're at a systems architectural level; you've got to know a lot of things. Not necessarily a huge amount of detail, but you should know the operating system that you're dealing with, you should know various computer languages somebody might be dealing with, you should have an understanding of what kind of tools are used. Then I think what really ended up making me successful at PDI was the ability to troubleshoot problems and provide solutions in a quick timeframe. I think that's not one that comes across in an interview really quickly, but I think once you get into a company by whatever means, that's the one skill that will make you stand out above everybody else. The nature of production is it's a constant battle to solve problems, to keep the project moving along, and so people that can actually troubleshoot problems quickly tend to be very highly valued.

Real Reels

Getting a job is all about nailing your demo reel. Employers only want to see the best work you're capable of, and being able to distinguish that and show it off will make or break your job search. If you're just starting out—whether in school, in training, or putting together your first reel—you'll want to look at the demo reels on the CD-ROM at the back of this book. On the following pages, we discuss these reels from four recent graduates of the Art Institute of California at Los Angeles to help you successfully create your own.

Learn by Viewing

One of the best ways to start or improve your demo reel is to view as many reels as you can. For that reason we are very thankful to host reels from Daniel Gutierrez, Robert Jauregui, Juan Gutierrez, and Daniel Militonian, on the book's CD. Watching these reels is a strong step in creating your own winning demo reel.

These reels are from art school graduates with majors in animation. Each reel has been selected as a good representation to show you *tailored* reels. The biggest setback to graduating students in the job market is a reel that doesn't quickly demonstrate their strengths and effectively communicate what kind of work they want to do. Having a reel that shows an employer right off the bat what you can do and what you want to do is crucial.

Animation Reel

Daniel Gutierrez is already working on TV commercials as a CG effects animator with a small studio after studying computer art and animation. He currently spends his days making dogs talk, generating endless clusters of leaves to blow in the wind, and blowing things up.

Daniel set up his reel like a 1920s silent film. "I wanted to relate the bits together somehow to create a common thread to make the demo flow better," explains Daniel. It is a clever design that is eye catching and genuine without being over the top. It's not necessary to tie everything on one's reel together or to try to tell a story, but it is refreshing to see someone take the extra effort in such a way.

Daniel wanted to show his experience with lip synch, pantomime, timing, and personality. By focusing his reel to simple animations, he wanted to clearly articulate his interest in animation. "It wasn't killer robots, it was simple, and I got good feedback about it from my pals. It was just to prove that I could animate, not to storyboard or design or model, just to animate."

By doing so he also shows the potential employer a little bit of his setup skills. In conjunction with his portfolio, this highlights his technical skills and makes it clear he has the chops to create these characters as well as animate them. His portfolio contains several examples of his programming and scripting abilities that would have otherwise been impossible to show on the reel.

Showing simple characters performing simple actions is a good way to show your capacity for animation. If you can show some personality and depth to a very simple character, you will be surprised at the reaction you'll get. Too many people try too hard to create complex characters and backgrounds to show off their animation, and more often than not, that brings down the overall quality of their reel if their modeling or setup skills are not up to par. Daniel kept everything simple and makes a straightforward presentation for animation work with his reel.

Texture Reel

Robert Jauregui studied animation, but when he discovered texturing he quickly came to realize that his calling would be in CG. He worked with several other students at school and developed a knack for texturing their models, so he decided to create his graduating demo reel specifically for texture artist positions in either games, film, or television.

Robert shied away from putting on too much to keep a keen focus for his reel and to get the kind of job he wants. By putting on a lot of design, modeling, or animation work, he would dilute his chances for getting texture work, and perhaps confuse the issue.

In Robert's reel, by showing a compound texture map for a human face, he shows the depth of complexity he's capable of, but also follows it up with a low poly environment to show off his potential for game textures. This will ultimately keep more options open for Robert, whether he goes for gaming or film/TV work. As he gains more experience, he'll be able to further focus his reel for either industry with textures for one or the other.

At the end of his reel, Robert includes a "Shots Breakdowns" section where he shows the exact maps he used to texture the models. He hopes this will go a long way to show an employer that he understands the layers of work involved in creating a successful scene texture. Furthermore, it proves his ability to take a low poly environment and transform it into a rich background using some fine mapping work, which is essential in games.

In addition, his landscape shot of mountains and flying birds shows his ability to paint backgrounds and layer them. This will also keep his options a bit open to scenic and matte painting work, commonly used in complex composites for film and TV work, as well as game cinematics.

Overall his reel is well targeted and focused, but not just on his strengths as an artist, but also on his intent in the workforce. It is clear Robert is shooting for texture work and his examples should take him a long way in that endeavor.

Modeling Reel

Watching movies like *T2* and *The Abyss* left Juan Gutierrez amazed about their stunning visual effects. But the first animation film that made him start thinking of getting into CG was Pixar's *Toy Story*. He couldn't fathom anything better than cartoons in 3D. So when it came time to go to college Juan sought art school to learn the craft.

During his time in school, Juan came to appreciate that any work in 3D, be it modeling, animation, visual effects, or lighting and texturing, is not an easy job; and definitely not for everyone. He finds himself lucky to enjoy the work immensely and has no regrets entering the field, despite the hard work and long hours required for success. "When you're enjoying yourself, your time flies by. I mean, I'm having fun doing this."

Juan deliberately tailored his demo reel toward modeling since he found it was something that came easier to him than animation, though he enjoys animating and is always trying to improve his skills. Animation is something Juan believes is a skill that gets better with time. But he realized that he enjoyed helping his fellow students with models, and handing them to his colleagues for texturing and in some cases animation. You'll notice models from Juan's reel featured as texture examples on Robert's reel.

In his reel, Juan clearly and quickly demonstrates his aptitude for modeling, with a preference for characters. By displaying his best models in turntable format and in interesting poses, he shows he can tackle simple and complex characters alike. By concentrating on poses rather than trying too hard to animate his models, Juan keeps himself from being judged as an animator, a fact that may lessen the impact of his reel overall.

Juan now enjoys a position with a small effects studio working on effects for television and commercials, where he's quickly gaining experience with animation as well as modeling.

Effects Reel

Daniel Militonian was born in Moscow, Russia and before coming to America, had no idea what CG was. After living in the U.S. a few years and watching American movies, Daniel became very interested in how they accomplished the things they did on the screen. After some research on the various jobs available, he got himself a copy of TrueSpace and a book, and started teaching himself the program. Years later, Daniel finds himself seeking a career where he can create those amazing effects that he always loved to watch when he was a little kid.

Daniel's reel is geared toward effects animation, as the bulk of his work revolves around integrating CG with live action plates, which commands a good level of lighting and compositing skill. Though he shows he can texture, model, and animate to some degree of proficiency, this reel clearly communicates with the potential employer that Daniel is interested most in effects work. His skills demonstrate that he would work well in a lighting or compositing position, which are both good jobs for a budding effects animator to get experience and build up his or her reel.

Daniel shows he has experience with rotoscoping, which applies to a lot of entry-level compositing positions in the industry. Also, Daniel's reel demonstrates his experience with photo-realistic lighting with several of his shots, perhaps most notably with the airplane landing and the car driving through the tunnel and past the camera. These shots also demonstrate his capacity for compositing, which is quickly becoming a necessary second-nature skill for effects animators. And since most effects animation needs to be integrated in with live action, it is a plus to show that experience on a reel geared for effects work.

Lastly, Daniel's decision to include an ending section showing the process of his creations is a good one; it is sometimes nice to see a shot put together, and it adds some personality to his reel. With that, Daniel hopes to show an employer that he understands the complexities of layering effects shots and that he would make a good start as a compositor as well, with later transition to a CG lighter perhaps—a tough job to get that demands experience.

Summary

It may be difficult for you to get to see a wide array of reels, so any time you have the opportunity to view someone else's work you should take advantage of it. You never know what you might see that could help you evolve your reel from a good presentation of your work to the reel that blows them away. And don't be afraid to seek the opinion of others. Viewers may make suggestions that sound harsh or may be critical of the way you put the reel together, but keep in mind your objective: to show your work and demonstrate your ability to do a job. With that in mind, we thank the artists for sharing their reels. Seeing them and how they were put together is a great step in creating your own reel. Good luck, and have fun!

Index

Note to the Reader: Throughout this index **boldfaced** page numbers indicate primary discussions of a topic. *Italicized* page numbers indicate illustrations.

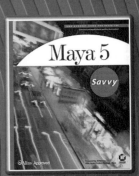

Soluti👁ns™ FROM **SYBEX**®

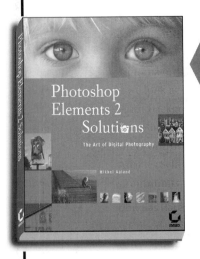

Photoshop® Elements 2 Solutions™
by Mikkel Aaland
ISBN: 0-7821-4140-4
US $40.00 🔘 full color throughout

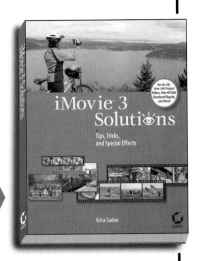

iMovie™ 3 Solutions™: Tips, Tricks, and Special Effects
by Erica Sadun
ISBN: 0-7821-4247-8
US $40.00 🔘 full color throughout

DVD Studio Pro® 2 Solutions
by Erica Sadun
ISBN 0-7821-4234-6
US $39.99 🔘 DVD

Acrobat® 6 and PDF Solutions
by Taz Tally
ISBN 0-7821-4273-7
US $34.99 🔘

SYBEX®
www.sybex.com

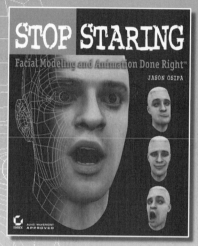